LECTURES

ON THE

ELECTRO-MAGNETIC TELEGRAPH,

WITH AN

HISTORICAL ACCOUNT OF ITS RISE AND PROGRESS,

CONTAINING A LIST OF THE NUMBER OF

TELEGRAPHIC LINES OF THE WORLD.

ILLUSTRATED BY

FIFTY-SIX WOOD CUTS AND TWO COPPER-PLATE ENGRAVINGS.

With an Appendix,

CONTAINING THE DECISIONS OF JUDGES WOODBURY AND KANE, IN THE CELEBRATED TELEGRAPHIC TRIALS.

BY LAURENCE TURNBULL, M. D.,

LECTURER ON TECHNICAL CHEMISTRY AT THE FRANKLIN INSTITUTE OF THE STATE OF PENNSYLVANIA.

PHILADELPHIA:
R. W. BARNARD, PRINTER.
1852.

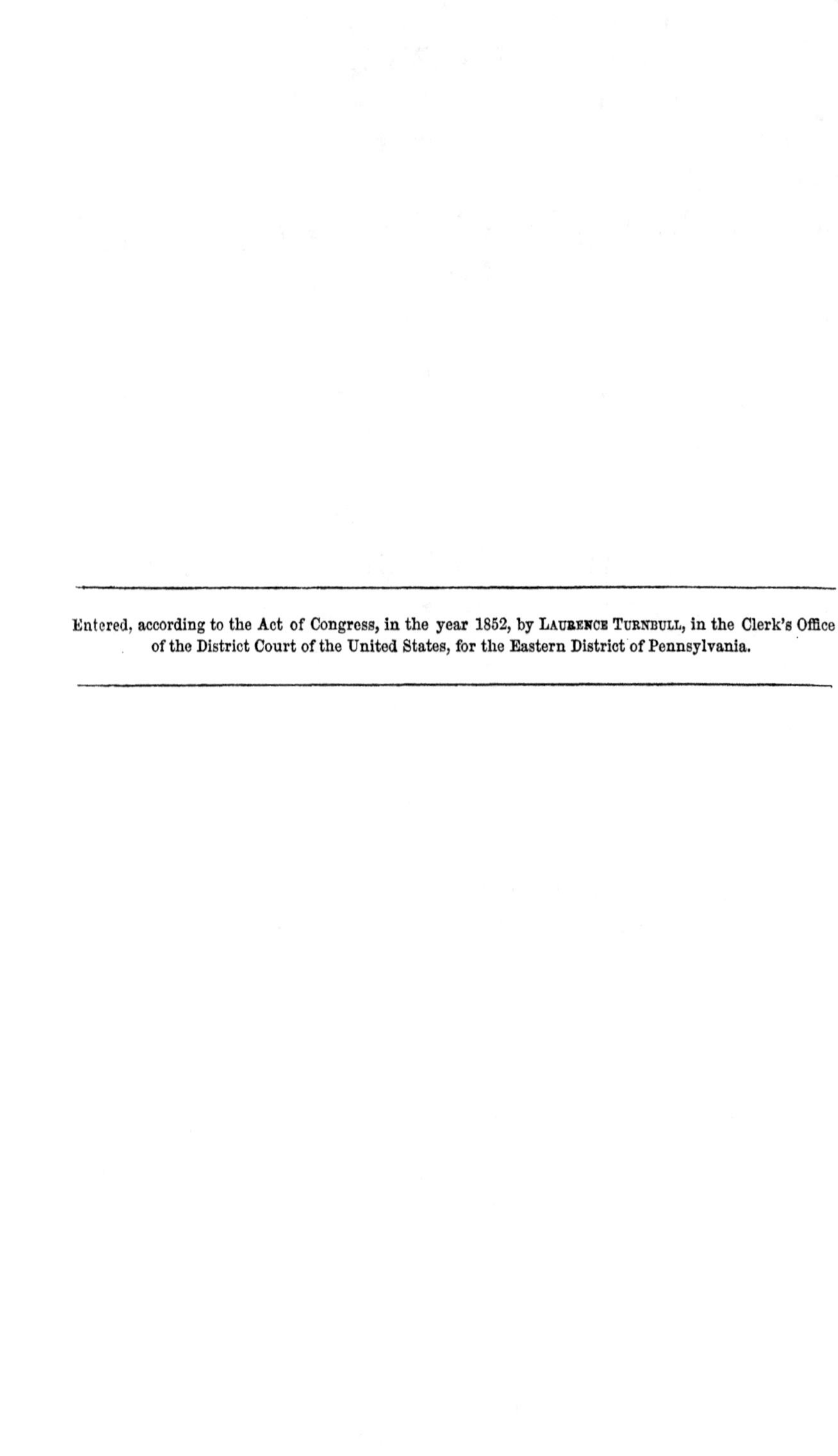

INTRODUCTION.

The Electric Telegraph is now, and has been, exciting a great deal of interest over all the enlightened parts not only of this country, but over the world; no one can view the extensive lines, and hear of and see its wonderful, nay, magical effects, without a strong desire to become better informed of its history and mode of operation. Like every other science, it has a history, a beginning, and a gradual advancing to its present perfect state. It has required a long series of years to develope and perfect it; it is not the invention of one man or any set of men, nor of one nation, but of many nations, each adding their mite to the noble structure. Its history is based upon two of the most interesting of the physical sciences, that of electricity and magnetism; had not these sciences been fully investigated, and thousands of laborers spent centuries upon them, we should never have seen an electric telegraph; had not such men as Œrsted, Ampere, Arago, Faraday, and our own Franklin, spent their days in experimenting, and nights in studying, we should have never reaped the rich reward of their labors.

In this country it becomes us to be proud of the electro-magnetic telegraph, having in operation a greater number of miles than all the known world; and yet many of our people are as little acquainted with it, as if they never knew of the name of the electro-magnetic telegraph, although its lines of iron wire pass before their very doors, and extend even into the most distant wilds of our country.

It was this knowledge, coupled with a strong love for its kindred branches of science, that induced me to select it as the subject of a course of lectures before the Franklin Institute of this city, for the Session of 1850 and 1851, and it received the approbation of the Committee of Instruction of that useful Institution.

The interest and attention with which the subject was there received, induced me, after the conclusion of my course, to continue the investigation of the subject, and finding there was no work at that time in the English language on the electro-magnetic telegraph, with the exception of Mr. Vail's, which is now out of print and not to be had in this city, I concluded either to translate the work of Dr. Schelling, published in September, 1850, from the German, or the work of Abbe Moigno, published in French; but as there had been many new and important matters scattered throughout the many Journals devoted to the physical sciences, and as in the United States, the subject has been brought to its most perfect state, I considered it better to edit a work, and not translate one.

I have received from the operators and proprietors of our telegraphic lines, every assistance, by the use of drawings, apparatus, and advice, and am, therefore, under many obligations to them; I have also the pleasure of being able to give a correct list of the number of telegraphic lines of the world, for which I am in part indebted to the work of Dr. Schelling; and the second edition of the work of Abbe Moigno, 1852, for telegraphic lines in Europe; and to E. Cornell, Esq., President of the Erie Telegraph Company, New York, for the principal information in regard to the extent of the telegraphic lines in the United States; I have also received valuable assistance in the materials of the work, from the interesting trials which have taken place between Messrs. Morse and House, and also between Messrs. Morse and Bain, which trials have caused the historical part of the electric telegraph to be very completely investigated, and every work upon the subject of electricity and magnetism, or that treated of telegraphing, has been obtained from the libraries of our own country, and many of the important works found in Europe.

The French works contain the original productions of Ampere, Arago, also those of the distinguished Germans, Schweigger, Ohm, Steinheil, Fechner, and of Gauss and Weber, with the masterly productions of the lamented Œrsted, of Copenhagen, the discoverer of the first link of that beautiful chain of the reciprocal action of electric and magnetic phenomena. Nor can I omit the great English physicists, Wheatstone, Cook, Daniel, Grove, Davy, and Faraday, whose writings and experiments have added much that is new and important to our knowledge of the subject of electricity and magnetism.

But it is to an American experimenter, Prof. Henry, that we are indebted for the corner stone by which the electro-magnetic telegraph received the most important and completing part, namely: the use of a long circuit of wire, the proper form of wire, battery, and magnet to be employed, and those masterly experiments of his which surprised the scientific world, and made his name known throughout Europe and his native land, as one worthy of being honored; it is to the joint labors of Prof. Henry, and Profs. Morse and Gale, that we are indebted for one of the best forms of telegraph the world has ever produced.

And still more recent is the most interesting of all the forms of telegraph, that of Mr. House, which, so far as I am aware, has never been described before so much in detail, which will add a new laurel to the brow of the American people, and which for beauty of design and utility, will strike at once even those uninitiated in the mysteries of electric telegraphing, by placing in their hands communications from their friends, thousands of miles off, in the course of a few minutes; a message printed in Roman letters, which requires no translation. This wonderful piece of mechanism is worthy of the study of those interested in the physical sciences, as it combines principles of mechanics, as well as the reciprocal action of electric and magnetic currents.

I have in the succeeding pages, arranged my subject under three heads, namely: Common, or statical electricity applied to telegraphing; second, Galvanic or chemical electricity; and, third, Electro-magnetism applied to telegraphing.

In an Appendix I have given an outline of the trial in the case of French *vs.* Rogers, with the decision of Judge Kane; also the decision of Judge Woodbury, in the case of Smith *vs.* Downing, tried at Boston, 1851.

In regard to rival claims of the first discovery of the electro-magnetic telegraph, I have endeavored to follow the rule of its first publication, as for instance, although Steinheil's telegraph is stated to have been in operation in the early part of the year 1837, still there was no published account of it until July, 1837, so that I have placed Prof. Morse's as the first electro-magnetic telegraph, his publication being in April, 1837. In 1851, during the publication of my articles in the Journal of the Franklin Institute, I received a work styled "Book of the Telegraph," a popular account of it, published by Mr. Daniel Davis, of Boston; but although in the English, it does not contain all the important points connected with electric telegraphing. I have also received the work of Brockman, published in Germany, and the original papers of Siemens, of Berlin, presented to the Academy of Science of Paris, from all of which I have culled whatever I thought would be useful in a work devoted to the subject of the telegraph. To show how much the telegraph is employed, I quote the folowing short article from one of our public Journals:

"Telegraphing, in this country, has reached that point, by its great stretch of wires and great facilities for transmission of communications, as to almost rival the mail in the quantity of matter sent over it. It has become indispensable to many business transactions, and an interruption of the communication between cities is severely felt by the business community. Nearly seven hundred messages, exclusive of those for the press, were sent in one day over the Morse Albany line. The Bain line at Boston, a few days after, sent and received five hundred communications, exclusive of reports for the press. These facts show how important an agent the magnetic telegraph has become in the transmission of business communications. It is every day coming more and more into use, and every day adding to its power to be useful."

September, 1852.

CONTENTS.

APPENDIX.

LECTURES

ON THE

ELECTRO-MAGNETIC TELEGRAPH.

FROM THE JOURNAL OF THE FRANKLIN INSTITUTE.

The term Telegraph is derived from the two Greek words Τελε (Tele) and Γραφω (Grapho), meaning "I write afar off." It is the name given to any mechanical contrivance for the rapid communication of intelligence by signals. Of late years the term semaphore (from Sema, (Σημα,) a sign, and Phero, (Φερω,) I bear,) has been introduced by the French, and frequently adopted by English writers.

Although the art of conveying intelligence by signals was practised in the earliest ages, and was known even to the rudest savages; and though its importance is not only obvious, but continually felt, wherever government is established, it has been allowed to remain in its original state of imperfection down almost to the present day. The first notice of any method of this kind of communication is to be found in the 6th chapter and 1st verse of the prophet Jeremiah. He says, "O, ye children of Benjamin, gather yourselves to flee out of the midst of Jerusalem; blow the trumpet in Tekoa, and set a *sign* of *fire* in Beth-heccerem.

The proposed object of the telegraphic art is to obtain a figurative language, the characters of which may be distinguished at a distance. Barbarous nations employed torches, fires on the tops of distant hills, hoisting of flags, carrier pigeons, drums, speaking trumpets, &c. More recently, since the invention of gunpowder, cannons and sky-rockets have been applied to the same use.

The first description of a telegraph universally applicable, was given by Dr. Hooke, in the *Philosophical Transactions* for 1684. The method which he proposed, (for it was not carried into effect,) consisted in preparing as many different shaped figures, formed of deal, as, for example, squares, triangles, circles, &c., as there are letters in the alphabet. He exhibited them successively, in the required order, from behind a screen, and proposed that torches or other lights, combined in different arrangements, should supply their place by night.

About twenty years later, Amontons, of Paris, exhibited some experiments before the royal family of France and the members of the Academy of Sciences, by which the practicability of the art was demonstrated. It was not until 1794 that these experiments were applied to any useful purpose, when the plan was adopted for conveying intelligence to the French armies.

The first telegraph actually used was the invention of Chappe. It consisted of a beam, which turned on a pivot in the top of an upright post, having a movable arm at each of its extremities; and each different position in which the beam and its two arms could be placed at angles of 45°, afforded a separate signal which might represent a letter of the alphabet, or have some other signification that might be agreed upon.

In the following year, 1795, several plans were submitted to the English Admiralty, of which, one proposed by Lord George Murray was adopted, and continued to be made use of down to the year 1816. It consisted of six shutters arranged in two frames, which being opened and shut according to all the different combinations which can be formed, afforded the means of giving sixty-three separate and distinct signals.

In 1803, the French erected semaphores along their whole line of coast, formed of upright posts, bearing two, or sometimes three, beams of wood, each turning on its own pivot, one above the other.

In 1807, Captain Pasley, of the Royal Engineers, published his Polygrammatic Telegraph, differing from the French semaphore by having beams turning on the same pivot; and, in order to obtain a sufficient number of different signals, he proposed to erect two or three posts at each station.

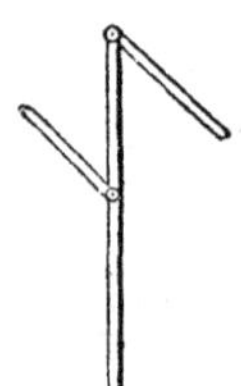

In 1816, Sir Home Popham considerably simplified this construction. His telegraph consists of merely two arms, movable on different pivots, on the same mast, as seen in the annexed figure.

Lastly, in 1822 General Pasley still farther simplified its construction, by placing the two arms on the same axis. For day signals, the telegraph consists of an upright post of sufficient height, with the two arms movable on the same pivot on the top of it, and a short arm called the indicator, on one side; as seen in the annexed figure. Each arm can exhibit the seven positions 1, 2, 3, 4, 5, 6, 7, besides the position called the *stop*, which points vertically downwards, and is hid by the post. The use of the indicator is to show the order or direction in which the signals are to be reckoned. In order to adapt the telegraph to the purpose of making night signals, a lantern, called the central light, is fixed to the pivot on which the arms move, and one is also attached to the extremity of each arm. A fourth lantern is also placed on the extremity of the indicator. Motion is communicated to these arms by means of an endless chain passing over two pullies; one fixed to the arm itself, and turning on the same pivot, and the other on a pivot fixed to the lower part of the post, within the reach of the signal-man. The required positions are pointed out by a dial plate, the index of which is moved by a lever attached to the lower pulley.

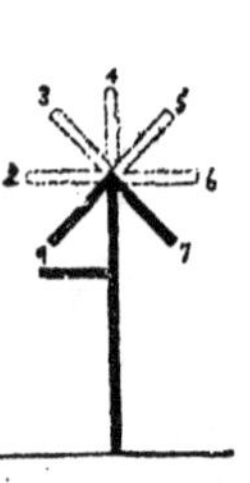

In the Report on Telegraphs for the United States, made at the request of the Hon. Levi Woodbury, Secretary of the Treasury, by the Committee on Science and the Arts of the Franklin Institute, the Committee say:—

"We are disposed to recommend a much more simple instrument, nearly similar to one lately introduced by M. Chateau, in a line of telegraphs which the Russian Government is erecting between Petersburgh and Warsaw, and which is described in a late number of the *Petersburgh Transactions*, by M. Parrot, together with a scheme of his own, almost identical with it, on which he had made successful experiments many years before.

"This proposed telegraph consists of a single arm, or *indicator*, which should be about nine feet long and one foot wide, with a cross piece at one end, about three feet long and one wide; the whole arm being movable about an axis at its centre. The arms are formed like Venitian shutters, and are painted a dead black; the apparatus and fixtures about it being white.

"The movements may be communicated with ease and certainty, either by an endless chain passing over a wheel on the axis, and a wheel in the building; or by bevel wheels on the axis, and on a vertical bar passing from the building; or by a cog wheel on the axis, and an endless screw on the vertical bar.

"For night signals, three lamps are used; one swinging beyond the end of the arm, the other two beyond the ends of the cross piece."

Every system of telegraphic signals, according to this plan, is of necessity accompanied with a telegraphic dictionary, containing the meaning of the different combinations of signs. They were defective, from inability to communicate all kinds of information, uncertainty in practice, a want of simplicity in operation, were too slow in conveying intelligence, and afforded no means for secresy in correspondence. The rapidity with which electricity traverses great lengths of conducting matter, coupled with the power which it possesses of deflecting electrometers, had at an early period led to the idea of employing it as a means of conveying signals from place to place; and this system has, within the last few years, been brought to such a degree of perfection, as to render it more than probable, that ere long it will supersede all other modes of conveying intelligence, not merely for telegraphic purposes, but also for many other similar and not less important uses. *Solley's Lec. on Tel.*) The peculiar properties of electricity upon which the action of the telegraph depends, are its passage along conducting bodies, the power to render iron a temporary magnet, its capability to decompose chemical combinations, and cause deflection of the galvanometer needle. An electric telegraph is an instrument or apparatus which, by means of conductors of iron, copper, soil, or water, conveys intelligence to any given distance with the velocity of lightning.

Previous to the publication of any inventions for this purpose, a number of experiments had been made as to the transmission of electricity through considerable length of iron wire, water, and even soil.

In 1729, Mr. Grey and Mr. Wheeler observed the instantaneous discharge or electricity through some hundreds of feet of wire.

In 1746, Winckler, at Leipsig, and Nollet Lemonnier, at Paris, made numerous experiments on the transmission of electricity through water, earth, &c.; in one case, wires of more than two miles in length were employed, (*Philosophical Transactions*, 1746.)

In July, 1747, Dr. Watson, Bishop of Llandaff, together with several other electricians, ascertained the passage of electricity through water, by sending shocks across the Thames; experiments which they subsequently repeated on a still larger scale through the New River, at Newington; and in August, 1747, they transmitted shocks through two miles of wire, and two miles of earth at shooter's Hill. The passage of electricity through water excited a great deal of interest, and these experiments were repeated in 1748, by Franklin, across the Schuylkill, at Philadelphia; and in 1749, by De Luc, across the Lake of Geneva.

Though electricity is the agent used in common by all telegraph operators, its mode of application has been as manifold as the number of laborers in this most interesting combination of science and art. Those now in use, and before described by historians, can be included in three divisions;—taking them in the order of discovery and application, we have first the electric, in which simple frictional electricity was alone used; next the galvanic, where voltaic electricity was employed; and last, the electro-magnetic, combining the agencies of electricity and magnetism. The first was used during the period from 1745 to 1800; the second from 1800 to 1825, the third from 1825 to the present time. From 1820 to 1850, there have been no less than sixty-three claimants for different varieties of telegraph.

The first electric telegraph appears to have been made about the year 1786; though long before that time the vague idea of a magical magnetic telegraph appears to have been entertained, for the Roman Jesuit Strada, who lived from 1572 to 1649, in a curious book, dated 1617, entitled *Prolusions*, describes a fabled contrivance of two magnetic needles, attached to dials, bearing a circle of letters, and which possessed the property of always indicating the same letter, so that when one needle was made to point to any particular letter, the other needle, however distant at the time, placed itself so as to point to the same letter. An account of this curious idea will be found in the *Spectator*, 241, and *Guardian*, 119.

The first real attempt which seems to have been made to render electricity available for the transmission of signals, is described by Moigno, in his *Traité de Telegraphie Electrique*. It is that of Lesage, a scientific Frenchman, who in 1774 established an electric telegraph at Geneva, composed of 24 metallic wires, separated from each other, and immersed in a non-conducting matter. Every wire corresponded with a particular electrometer, formed of a small ball of elder, suspended by a wire. By placing an electrical machine in communication with either of these wires, the ball of the electrometer which corresponded to it was repulsed, and the movement designated the letter of the alphabet, or whatever conventional signal it was wished to transmit.

In the 1st volume, page 42, of Arthur Young's *Travels in France* during the year 1757, will be found the following description of an electric telegraph:

"Mr. Lomond has made a remarkable discovery in electricity. You write two or three words upon paper; he takes them with him into a chamber, and turns a machine in a cylinder case, on the top of which is an electrometer, having a pretty little ball of pith of a quill suspended by a silk thread; a brass wire connects it to a similar cylinder and electrometer in a distant apartment, and his wife, on observing the movements of the corresponding ball, wrote the words which it indicated. From this it appears that he had made an alphabet of movements; and as the length of the brass wire made no difference, you could correspond at a great distance, as for example, with a besieged city, or for purposes of more importance."

Electricity was generated and retained by the common machine and a Leyden phial. Having but one movement, and using an apparatus extremely delicate, we must suppose this mode of communication to be limited and dilatory.

In *Voigt's Magazine* for 1794, Vol. IX., p. 183, there is a letter from Reusser, of Geneva, in which he describes an electric telegraph. In this contrivance, a number of strips of tin foil were fastened on a glass plate, each strip having a different letter marked on it, and connected by carefully insulated wires inclosed in glass tubes, with a corresponding glass plate at a distance. Thus there was a separate wire for each letter, and one return wire for the whole series. Signals were transmitted by sending electric shocks through the different wires, and noting down the letters attached to the strips of tin-foil, where the sparks were observed. The attention of the observer at a distant station was drawn by firing an inflammable air pistol attached to the apparatus, by means of an electric spark.

"A similar and yet more practical proposition was soon after made by Professor Boeckman. He proposed to choose as the signals the sparks passing at the distant station, using only two wires, by which first one and then, after certain intervals, more sparks being combinedly grouped," indicating the particular letter, so as to get rid of the large number of wires used by Reiszer, and also the twenty-six glass plates; in the same manner as the alarms of fire are indicated by our State House clock.—(*Dr. H. Schellen's Electro-Magnetic Telegraph*, *p.* 46, 1850.)

The *Madrid Gazette* of November 25th, 1796, states, that the Prince de la Paix, having heard that M. D. F. Salva had read to the Academy of Sciences, a memoir upon the application of electricity to telegraphing, and presented at the same time an electric telegraph of his own invention, desired to examine it; when, being delighted with the promptness and facility with which it worked, presented it before the king and court, operating it himself. After these experiments, the Infanta Don Antonio desired another more complete telegraph, and occupied himself in testing the quantity of electricity that would be required by the telegraph at different distances, whether on land or water.

Some useful trials were made and published in *Voigt's Magazine.* Two years after, the Infanta Don Antonio constructed a telegraph of great extent on a large scale, by which the young prince was informed at night of news in which he was much interested. He also invited and entertained Salva at court. According to Humboldt, a telegraph of this description was established in 1798, from Madrid to Aranjuez, a distance of 26 miles. Other writers affirm, that M. Betancourt established a line of telegraph between the same places in 1787, and worked it with frictional electricity.

M. Cavallo published some experiments which he had made on the transmission of signals in 1795. (4th edition, *Traité de Electricitie*, published 1798, vol. III., page 285.) The most important of these consisted in firing gunpowder, phosphorus, and hydrogen, by electric sparks, at a distance of a few hundred feet. He adds, that the same might be done at the distance of many miles.

The next electric telegraph in order of dates, was that of Mr. Francis Ronalds, who in 1816 constructed one, by means of which he was enabled to send signals with considerable facility and rapidity, through a distance of eight miles, using frictional electricity. He published a work in 1823, describing his telegraph, and illustrating it with plates; also, several other electrical instruments of his invention. This plan was very simple; at either end of the wires was a clock, carrying a light paper disk, on which were marked the letters of the alphabet, and certain words and numbers. By means of a perforated cover, only one letter and figure were visible at a time, and, as the clock continued to go, every letter in turn was presented at the aperture to the view. As the clocks kept accurate time, it is evident that the same letter would always be visible at both clocks, and therefore that if an electric discharge were sent from one station to another, when a particular letter was exhibited on the dial, the observer at the other station would readily know the signal intended. The wires were buried under ground, in dry and well insulated glass tubes. The attention of the observer was, at the outset, drawn to the instrument by an inflammable air gun fired by an electric spark, and the subsequent signals indicated by the divergence of two small pith balls suspended in front of the revolving disks, a distance of eight miles along a wire.

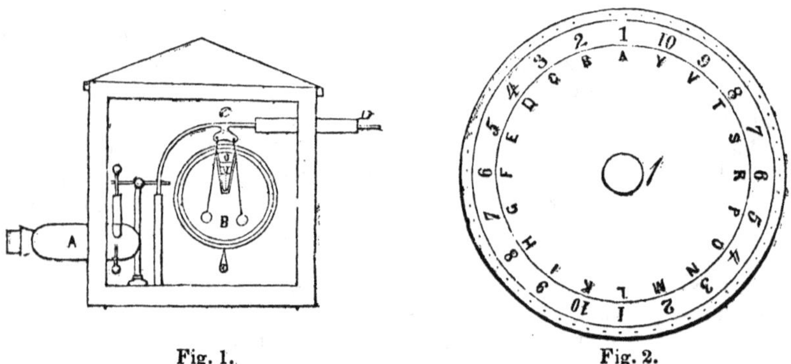

Fig. 1. Fig. 2.

Fig. 1 shows the form of the apparatus used at either end of the telegraph. A, the air pistol; B, the dial, exhibiting one letter only through a slit; C, pith ball electrometer; D, conducting wire. Fig. 2, the dial without the slit, showing the letters and numbers upon it.

Harrison Grey Dyer, an American, constructed a telegraph in 1827–8 at the race course on Long Island, and supported his wires by glass insulators fixed on trees and poles. By means of common electricity, acting upon litmus paper, he produced a red mark, and then passed the current through the ground as a return circuit. The difference of time between the sparks indicated different letters arranged in an arbitrary alphabet, and the paper was moved by the hand.—(*Bell's Evidence in House's Case.*)

Like many preceding it, this instrument appears to have been little more than a philosophical toy,—frictional electricity being too easily dissipated, rapid and incontinuous in action, confined with great difficulty to conductors, and devoid of that dense, energetic, yet almost imperceptible, force which renders galvanic electricity so available in this art. His instrument is far inferior to that of Sœmmering, invented twenty years before, and indicates a want of proper regard for, or information of, the discoveries of Galvani, Œrstead, Ampere, and a host of others.

Henry Haighton, of England, secured a patent in September, 1844, for certain improvements in electric telegraphs.

"The object of this invention being to adapt a system of telegraphing to common or frictional electricity, the inventor uses for this purpose a Leyden battery charged with Armstrong's hydro-electric, or other powerful electric machine. For the purpose of regulating the number of discharges sent, the nature of the charges as to positive and negative, and the times at which the discharges are transmitted, an instrument is employed which admits of various modifications according to circumstances. By this invention, it can be shown that, in ten discharges, any signal out of a number of sixteen thousand may be made; and by thirty discharges, any one of more than a thousand millions.

"The method of reading the signals at the terminal point is by means of two wires, one communicating with the point of transmission, and the other with the earth; they are placed at right angles to a sheet of paper which is moved along by machinery, so that each discharge may traverse the surface, and penetrate the substance of the paper close to the wire giving out the negative fluid. The paper is colored with chromate of lead, and moistened with sulphuric acid, to expedite the passage of the spark; and by this means the sparks leave upon the paper a register of the signals that have been made."—*Lond. Mech. Mag.*, *Vol.* XLII., *p.* 122.

Before considering the individual galvanic telegraphs, it will be proper to state the most important phenomena and laws of galvanism; also, the principal forms of voltaic apparatus.

The first instrument of importance, was the voltaic pile of Professor Volta, of Pavia, a description of which is published in the *Philosophical Transactions* of 1800; although the discovery of galvanism is due to Galvani, Professor of Anatomy at Bologna, who found that by forming a chain of conducting substances, between the outside of the muscles of the leg and the crural nerve of a frog, convulsions might be produced. Galvani previously entertained the idea, that the contractions of the muscles of animals were dependent on electricity.

The invention of the pile by Volta, was the result of profound thought on the development of electricity at the surface of contact of different metals.

The galvanic pile of Volta consisted of an equal number of silver coins and pieces of zinc of the same form, with circular disks of card soaked in salt water; of these he formed a pile or column by placing them alternately. If the uppermost disk of metal, either copper or silver, be touched with the finger, previously wetted, while a finger of the other hand is applied to the lowest disk, a distinct shock is felt, which is increased with the number of plates. Instead of the moist conductor, we now use liquids of various kinds, and electricians have devised various forms of batteries, but all based on the important principle discovered by Volta.

"By the voltaic pile, I mean such apparatus, or arrangement of metals, as contain water, brine, acid, or other aqueous solutions or decomposable substances between their plates; decomposition is an essential chemical part of every voltaic battery."—(*Faraday's Researches.*)

It was Volta who removed our doubtful knowledge. "Such knowledge is the early morning light of every advancing science, and is essential to its development; but the man who is engaged in dispelling that which is deceptive in it, and revealing more clearly that which is true, is as useful in his place, and as necessary to the general progress of science, as he who first broke through the intellectual darkness, and opened a path into knowledge before unknown."—(*Ibid.*)

According to Professor Faraday, the supply of electricity is due to chemical power in the voltaic pile, metallic contact not being necessary for the production of the voltaic current; and further, that electricity is only another mode of the exertion of pure unmixed chemical forces. It is proportional in its intensities to the intensities of the affinities concerned in its production, and its quantity to the quantity of matter which has been chemically active during its evolution. It is the union of oxygen of the water which determines the current; and though the acid is essential to the removal of the oxide so formed, in order that another portion of zinc may act on another portion of water, it does not by combination with that oxide produce any sensible portion of the circulating electrical current; for the quantity of electricity is dependent on the quantity of zinc oxidized, and is scarcely, if at all, affected by the use of either strong or weak acid. Galvanic differs from frictional electricity in its low degree of intensity, the larger amount set in motion, the greater constancy, more perpetual reproduction, less tendency to escape, and better conduction along metallic substances without being dissipated. The unequal character of all the batteries previous to the one introduced by the late Prof. Daniell, of King's College, London, was a serious obstacle to telegraphic operations; they are familiar to most persons who have taken any interest in this important matter, and I will therefore omit them.

Prof. Daniell was the first to invent a battery capable of constant and steady action, and thus overcame the defects of those previously in use. The defects which cause the electromotive action to subside rapidly, and soon to cease altogether, are: 1st, The sulphuric acid becomes saturated with the oxide of zinc. 2d, The hydrogen adheres to the surface of the metals, and thus prevents their perfect contact with the water. 3d, By the chemical action of the battery, the zinc, contained in the sulphate of zinc which is formed, is reduced to the metallic state at the surface of the copper, and deposited upon it in the form of a crust, where it acts locally and impairs the conducting power. 4th, Electricity is carried off and dissipated by the escaping hydrogen. 5th, Impurities on the surface of the zinc form small circuits, by which the electricity is conducted back into it, without going through the fluid to the copper, and then returning by metallic connexion.

The adhesion of hydrogen to the zinc plate, does not take place when that metal is pure or amalgamated with mercury. Prof. Daniell, therefore, employs a cylindrical rod of zinc, amalgamated with mercury, instead of a plate of the common and impure metal. The amalgamation has also the effect of preventing the small local electric circuits, by covering up the impurities which exist on its surface. This was first introduced by Sturgeon. But the peculiar and most vauable feature of this battery is the use of a porous partition, which may be formed of animal membrane, earthenware, plaster of Paris, paper, or any similar substance. This divides the vessels containing the metals into two cells, one of which, the zinc cell, is filled with dilute sulphuric acid, in the proportion of ten parts water to one of acid, and the other with an acid solution of sulphate of copper. The partition freely transmits the electrical current, but prevents the passage of the sulphate of zinc to the copper plate, and thus remedies the third of the above mentioned defects. The sulphate of copper is decomposed into sulphuric acid and protoxide of copper. The sulphuric acid passes through the partition into the zinc cell, there to act upon the oxide of zinc, while the oxide of copper is again decomposed into oxygen and metallic copper. The oxygen unites with the nascent hydrogen formed in the oxidation of the zinc to form water, and the metallic copper is deposited on the copper plate, keeping the plate constantly bright, and thus making it a better conductor. The hydrogen being consumed in the formation of water, it cannot interfere with the action of the conducting plate, nor convey away electricity. A little frame is fitted to the top of the cell, in which crystals of sulphate of copper are placed, in order that the strength of the solution may remain unimpaired.

Another form of battery, proposed by Prof. Grove, of London, is an improvement upon Prof. Daniell's, in respect to amount of force generated in a small space, and has been adopted in most of the telegraphic offices of this country. A platinum plate is substituted for the copper one of Prof. Daniell, and instead of sulphate of copper, strong nitric acid is used, which furnishes oxygen to unite with the hydrogen. The oxygen in nitric acid is held by very slight affinity, and many chemical substances reduce the nitric acid to hypo-nitrous and nitrous acid, which contains one and two equivalents less. The increase of power in Grove's battery over Daniell's battery, for the same amount of zinc dissolved, is equal to the difference of affinity between oxygen for nitrous acid and oxygen for zinc. The force of Grove's battery is, therefore, equal to the affinity of oxygen for zinc, minus the affinity of oxygen for nitrous acid. The energy of a galvanic arrangement depends to some extent upon the difference in the affinity for oxygen of the metals employed, which in the case of platinum and zinc, is at a maximum, zinc being most readily oxydized, and platinum least so. The zinc plate, as in Daniell's, is amalgamated and surrounded by sulphuric acid, diluted with eight parts of water, while the nitric acid is placed in the platinum cell. A Grove battery exposing a surface of zinc equal to twenty square inches, was found by its magnetizing power, to afford a current of greater quantity than a Daniell battery exposing 210 inches of zinc. The intensity of the current is also considered three times as great as Daniell's, and is remarkable for its constancy. The escape of nitrous acid, red fumes from this battery, render it disagreeable and unsafe to a careless experimenter. They are irrespirable, and injurious to nice apparatus which may be exposed to them. By placing a metallic covering (protected from the acid fumes) over the battery, and allowing the gases to escape through an orifice stuffed with cotton, wet with a little alcohol, these may be to some extent neutralized. The intensity of the current depends on the chemical affinities which are concerned, and on this account there is a gain in Grove's battery over Daniell's. Prof. Callan, of Maynooth College, Ireland, has invented a galvanic battery, cheap in its construction and use, yet powerful. He substitutes cast iron for the outer copper cell, and a flat piece of zinc for the inner one, with equal parts of nitric and sulphuric acids for the outer cell, and a mixture of two parts of nitric acid, five of sulphuric acid, and forty-five of water for the inner one.

The effect of the galvanic current on the nerves and muscles of animals, are essentially the same as those produced by frictional electricity, modified, however, in some degree, by the continuous action of it. They are also characterized by the presence of some chemical influence, which excites the organs of taste and sight in a remarkable manner. Very small batteries are adequate to excite the organs of taste and sight, but a large apparatus is needed to produce any perceptible influence on the sense of touch, so as to cause the muscles of the human body to contract, when it forms part of the circuit. Galvani, in his fundamental experiment, touched the nerves of a dead frog's spine and the muscles of one of his thighs with two different metals, and then forming a circuit by a wire between them, the leg became violently contracted. When the nerves of vision are made to form part of the voltaic connexion, peculiar luminous flashes will appear before the eyes. The excitement of the organ of hearing under similar circumstances is not less interesting, a roaring sound being heard as long as the wires are kept in place. On closely observing the effect of galvanic electricity upon the muscular and nervous system, three distinct stages in the process are readily seen. First, when the circuit is completed, an electric shock is experienced; next, the continued action of the current causes a series of contractions rapidly succeeding each other; and lastly, when the connexion is broken, a less violent shock than before is felt. The shock of the voltaic battery differs from common electricity, as the latter is felt far less deeply, affecting only the outer part of our organs, and being exhausted in a momont. The voltaic shock, on the contrary, penetrates farther into the system, passing along the entire course of the nerves. The influence of the galvanic current on the nervous system, has been successfully applied to the restoration of persons in whom animation was suspended. By means of it, Aldini set in motion the feet of a corpse, caused the eyes to open and shut, and distorted the mouth, cheeks, and the whole countenance. Ure, by completing the circuit through the body of a man recently hung, caused the muscles of the face to acquire a frightful activity, so that rage, despair, and anguish, with horrid smiles, were successively depicted on the countenance.—(*Peschell's Elements of Physics.*)

The chemical effects of galvanism are perhaps the most important of all that come uuder our observation. Prof. Faraday's investigations have recently added most materially to our knowledge on this subject, and it is to him that we are indebted for detecting most of its laws. To produce these affects, the electrical current must be conducted completely through the substance which is to be decomposed; as soon as the circuit is completed, the elements are set in operation, and so continue until the connexion is broken. The bedies to be resolved must be conductors of electricity, and also be in a liquid condition, that their particles may move freely among each other. The circuit may be completed through the fluid, by dipping into it the metallic wires which connect with the poles of the battery. These extremities of the wire are commonly termed *poles*, from an idea that they exert attractive and repulsive energies towards the elements of the decomposing liquid, just as the poles of a magnet act towards iron; and each is farther distinguished by the term positive, and negative, according as it affects an electrometer with positive or negative electricity. Now Prof. Faraday contends, and has proved by experiment, that these poles have not any attractive or repulsive energy, and act simply as a path, or door, to the current; he hence calls them electrodes, from *electron*, ελεκτρον, electricity, and *odos*, οδος, a way. The electrodes are the surfaces, whether of air, water, metal, or any other substance, which serve to convey an electric current into and from the liquid to be decomposed. The surfaces of this liquid which are in immediate contact with the electrodes, and where the elements make their appearance, are termed anode, and cathode, from *ana*, ανα, upwards, and *odos*, οδοσ, the way in which the sun rises, and *kata*, κατα, downwards, the way in which the sun sets. The anode is where the positive current is supposed to enter, and the cathode where it quits, the decomposing liquid; its direction, when the electrodes are placed east and west, corresponding with that of the positive current, which is thought to circulate on the surface of the earth. To electrolyze a compound is to decompose it by the direct action of galvanism, its name being formed from *electron*, ελεκτρον, and *luo*, λυο, to unloose or set free. An electrolyte is a compound which may be electrolyzed. The elements of an electrolyte are called ions from *ion*, ιον, going, neuter participle of the verb to go. Anions, are the ions, which appear at the anode, and are usually termed the electro-negative ingredients of a compound, such as oxygen, chlorine, and acids; while the electro-positive substances, as hydrogen, metals, alkalies, &c. which appear at the cathode, are cations. Whatever may be thought of the necessity of some of these terms, the words electrode, electrolyze, and electrolyte, are peculiarly appropriate.—(*Faraday's Experimental Researches.*)

Water, the first agent decomposed in this way, was electrolyzed by Messrs. Nicholson and Carlisle, soon after the discovery of the voltaic pile. From its low conducting power, water requires a powerful current for its decomposition, unless it be slightly acidulated. In 1803, Berzelius and Hisinger ascertained the power of the galvanic battery to resolve many other substances into their elements; that these elements observed regular laws in their resolution into more simple form, as oxygen and acids accumulated about the positive pole; while hydrogen, alkaline earths, and metals appeared at the negative one. Sir H. Davy communicated to the Royal Society, his celebrated Lecture on some chemical agencies of

Electricity in 1806; and in 1807, he announced the grand discovery of the decomposition of the fixed alkalies. Faraday's masterly productions on this subject were elicited in the period from 1831 to 1840, some of which important results have been mentioned.

It is an interesting matter to obtain a fixed rule or law, by which we can estimate the amount of projectile force needed by a galvanic current to pass over a certain length of telegraphic wire; though all such rules must be more or less inconclusive, from the number of contingent circumstances on which they depend; still, from experiment and observation, we can obtain those which may be useful in making what are termed rough calculations. To make such a computation, we must on one hand find all the sources which give motive power, and on the other seek those agencies which offer resistance to that power, obtain the sum of each, and then institute a comparison. The power is that electricity of intensity which a single galvanic cell is capable of generating. This multiplied by the number of cells gives us the whole amount of electrical power. The resistance is that obstruction the electricity meets in the conducting metal and the liquid of the cells. Find the amount of obstruction in a single cell; this multiplied by the number of cells affords the total sum of a battery. Then divide the whole sum of power by the total amount of resistance in the conducting wire and liquid of the battery cells, and the quotient will be the effective power of the battery.

The electromotive force of an electric current may be ascertained by the following important law of Ohm, which was discovered in the year 1827, being applicable under all circumstances, referring to all the causes which tend to impede the action of the battery. "It is, that the intensity of an electric current where a battery is in action, is directly as the whole electromotive force in operation, and inversely as the sum of all the impediments to conduction. It may therefore be expressed by a fraction whose numerator is the electromotive force, and its denominator the sum of the resistance of all its parts. Let I be the intensity of the current; E the effective electromotive force in the battery; R its constant retarding influence, and r the variable retarding influence in the connecting wires; then

$$I=\frac{E}{R+r}.$$

If, according to Ohm's formula, we put the intensity of the current in a simple voltaic arrangement whose excited surface is I,

$$1.\quad I=\frac{E}{R+r}.$$

Then the intensity of a current from a battery of n pairs of plates or cups will be,

$$2.\quad I'=\frac{n\,E}{n\,R+r},$$

and in a single voltaic arrangement whose surface is n times greater than I, the resistance to conduction being diminished inversely as the area of its transverse section, the intensity becomes

$$3.\quad I''=\frac{E}{\frac{R+r}{n}}=\frac{n\,E}{R+nr}."$$

The resistance to an electric current in a conducting wire is in proportion to the length of the wire, and inversely as its sectional area. That is, the longer the wire the greater the resistance, and the larger the wire the less the resistance. If the wire be many miles long, the resistance to the electrical current varies arithmetically as the wire increases in length geometrically. Arithmetical progression is constant addition, while geometrical progression is constant multiplication, and the ratio would stand thus:

Resistance, 1 : 3 : 5 : 7 : 9 : 11 : 13 : 15, &c.
Length, 1 : 2 : 4 : 8 : 16 : 32 : 64 : 128, &c.

The resistance of the liquid in the cells is in direct proportion to the amount and thickness of that fluid, and in the inverse proportion to its conductibility. Or the greater the thickness of the fluid, the more resistance it will oppose to the galvanic current; while, on the other hand, the greater the conducting power of the fluid, the less obstruction is presented.

Thus it will be seen that the data for such an estimate are numerous, and require much scrutinizing experiment to afford a system for practical deduction.

Professors Wheatstone, of London, Steinheil, of Munich, and Jacobi, of St. Petersburgh, appear to have been foremost among those who have endeavored to ascertain the velocity of the electrical current. Its rapidity previous to their labors was supposed incalculable; simple observation had impressed experimenters with the opinion that it was instantaneous; but, like the other imponderable agents, it has not only been shown to be progressive, but also, under peculiar circumstances, of much less celerity than light. It is greatly modified by the incidents connected with different trials. Not only the kind of electricity employed, but the nature and size of the conductor, temperature and electrical tension of the atmosphere, dissimilar means and instruments used by different operators for arriving at results, may perhaps account for the very discordant opinions of practical physicists on this topic. Prof. Wheatstone, making a current of frictional electricity pass along copper wire, and noting the intervals of reflected sparks from a revolving mirror, estimated the speed at 228,000 miles in a second. Our ingenious and distinguished townsman, Mr. Saxton, devised the instrument with which Prof. W. determined these facts. Some truly practical and indefatigable trials have been recently made under the direction of Prof. S. C. Walker, of the United States Coast Survey, which, like the rest, present a heterogeneous mass of probable velocity; taking the whole of them, he deduces the "resultant as 15,890 miles per second, as the most probable value."—(*Silliman's Journal, March*, 1851.)—He used galvanic electricity, and conductors of wire known in trade as No. 9.

Professor Mitchell, of the Cincinnati Observatory, experimented with a sidereal clock on the common telegraphic line, and inferred the velocity at 30,000 miles per second. And again, Messrs. Fizeau and Gounelle, in a paper published in the *Comptes Rendus* of April last, make their result as 111,886 miles per second in copper wire, and 62,159 in iron.—(*Jour. Frank. Ins., Vol.* xx. *p.* 62.)

Here are very many discrepancies, that may be perhaps ascribed to the variable contingencies attending the experiments. Matteucci, Baumgartner, Kirchoff, Ridolphi, and Smauren, are and have been prominent investigators of this subject.

Many trials were made at an early period, on the transmission of galvanism through water and soil. In 1803, experiments were made by F. H. Basse on the Weser, a distance of 4000 feet being included in the circuit, (*Gilbert's Annalen*, XIV. *p.* 26,) by Erman in the Havel, near Potsdam, (*Gilbert*, XIV. *p.* 385,) and by Aldini at Calais, across about 200 feet of sea water.

Prof. Steinheil, in 1837, first employed the earth as a return portion of the circuit between telegraphic stations, aud nearly all the telegraph lines are now arranged on this principle. Much speculation has arisen, as to the mode in which the electrical impulse is conveyed through the earth between the termini; though it is as much under our control as when transmitted through wire conductors, it is difficult to conceive the passage of the fluid in these cases as similar. In all our experiments we find the earth a vast receptacle and source of electricity, and from this fact modern physicists suppose no impulse communicated, but that electricity given to the earth at one end of the line increases the whole amount of it and the equilibrium is restored by the escape of the redundant fluid into the other extremity of the wire. Baumgartner inferred from experiment, that the geological structure of the intervening earth had some effect upon the time required for the appearance of the electrical impulse at the termini; this, if correct, is strong evidence in favor of conduction of electricity by the earth.

Application of Galvanism to Telegraphing.—"Mr. S. T. Sömmering, of Munich, first applied galvanism to telegraphing; in 1809, he constructed an apparatus, which by decomposing water enabled him to give signals. At the station where the news was to arrive, were arranged thirty-five small glass test tubes, filled with water, and reversed in a reservoir also containing that fluid. Into each one of these test tubes, projected through the bottom of the reservoir the gilt end of one of thirty-five wires, that came from the transmitting station. Each wire at the termini of the line was connected to its own distinct brass plate or cylinder. These plates were arranged in a row and perforated at one extremity; by introducing two conical metallic pins connected with the poles of a voltaic battery into these perforations, a circuit was established. Each glass tube was marked with one of the 25 letters of the German alphabet, and 10 numerals, and the plate connected to it by wire at the other station, was stamped with the same. The circuit being established, the water in two of the tubes was decomposed, the gaseous constituents of which rising gave two signs, whose succession was determined by considering the letter over the evolved hydrogen as first. Decomposition of water gives twice the volume of hydrogen that it does of oxygen, and thus no mistake could well be made in distinguishing them. The conducting wires, well insulated, after passing some distance from the apparatus, were wound into a rope to go on to their destination. Fig. 3 represents Sömmering's telegraph; A A water receiver. The points protruding into it are shown, the glass tubes are removed. B B the apparatus to close the circuit; C the voltaic battery; single wires coming from the wire rope D have connexion with the plates or cylinders. Into the perforations of these plates the metal pencils connected with the closing wires X y fit exactly; they are kept clean and free from oxidation in order that they may do so.

If the rod or pencil of the positive pole is put into the plate L, and that

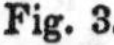
Fig. 3.

of the negative one into the plate S, the circuit is closed. Coming from X, the current goes into the wire in connexion with L, then to l, at the other station, through the receiver to S, thence into the conducting wire to S at the first station, through y, to the negative pole of the battery.

Oxygen rises from the positive pole in the glass *i*, and hydrogen from the negative one in the glass *s*, and thus a signal is given which reads *s l*.

The mode of completing the connexion is exhibited in the small fig. 4, by a lateral view of the instrument; B standard to support the frame of cylinders; C a single cylinder; *a* orifice in it where the rod P is introduced; *x* wire connecting with the positive pole of the battery; D wire leading to the opposite station.

Fig. 4.

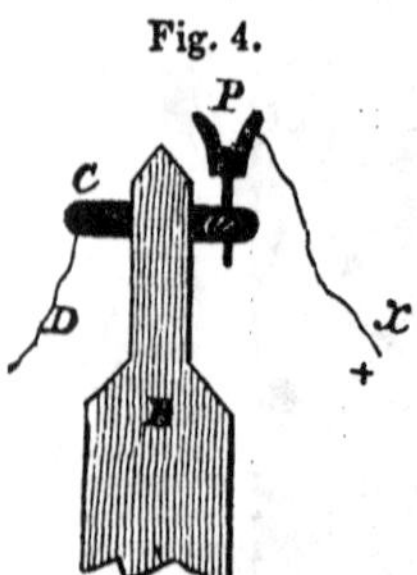

Especial signals are used to denominate the same letter used twice in succession, or to designate the end of a word. Sömmering connected with his instrument a curiously constructed alarm, to call the attention of the operator. It consisted of a two armed lever, the longer arm having the shape of a spoon, while the shorter supported a rolling brass ball. The arrangement was easily moved, and it was necessary to poise it after each telegraphic operation. The hollow end of the long arm stood over the end of one of the wire points, and at the commencement of an operation received the hydrogen that was evolved at this point. After one half a minute, sufficient gas was evolved to carry upward in its ascent the long arm of the lever, depress the shorter one, and by this depression permit the ball to fall through a tube on a lever connected to an alarm stop, set it loose, and thus put the alarm in active operation. Though very ingenious, the expense of so many wires, and their insulation, precluded the use of this instrument on a large scale; likewise, the necessity of constant attention on the part of the attendant to watch the evolution of gas in two of the thirty-five tubes, was a strong objection to it.

On the publication of this apparatus in his Journal, Schweigger proposed the use of two wires, which he considered sufficient, if two voltaic batteries, one strong and another weak, were used, and the time being taken into consideration partly during the evolution of the gas, and partly that which elapsed between the two evolutions following each other.—(*Schellen's Elec. Mag.*, *p.* 53.)

We find the following in Thompson's Annals for 1816, from the pen of Dr. J. R. Coxe, then Professor of Chemistry in the Univesity of Pennsylvania. This hoary headed veteran in the cause of knowledge, is still living in our midst. Though long since withdrawn from the active duties of teacher in the oldest medical school of this country, the mementoes of his labors remain emblazoned among the records of science. Speaking of galvanism, he says, "I have contemplated this important agent, as a probable means of establishing telegraphic communications with as much rapidity, and perhaps less expense, than any hitherto employed. I do not know how far experiment has determined galvanic action to be communicated by means of wires; but there is no reason to suppose it confined as to limits, certainly not as to time. Now, by means of apparatus fixed at certain distances, as telegraphic stations, by tubes for the decomposition of water, metallic salts, &c., regularly arranged, such a key might be adopted as would be requisite to communicate words, sentences or figures, from one station to another, and so on to the end of the line. As it takes up little room, and may be fixed in private, it might in many cases of besieged towns, &c., convey useful intelligence with scarcely a chance of detection by the enemy. However fanciful in speculation, I have no doubt, that sooner or later, it will be rendered useful in practice. I have thus, my dear sir, ventured to encroach on your time with some crude ideas that serve perhaps to elicit some useful experiments in the hands of others. When we consider what wonderful results have arisen from the first trifling experiments of the junction of a small piece of silver and zinc in so short a period, what may not be expected from the further extension of galvanic electricity! I have no doubt of its being the chief agent in the hands of nature in the mighty changes that occur around us."

Next in order of those depending on the galvanic principle solely, is the physiological telegraph of Vorzleman De Haer. He proposed the instrument on a small scale in 1839, basing it on the property of galvanism to produce physiological effects on the nerves and muscles, and making sensation the means of receiving the signals. He employed ten wires after Messrs. Steinheil and Morse had succeeded with only one, and experience has also taught us that many repeated shocks render the operator insensible; the workmen inthe gutta percha manufactory of Fonropert and Pruckner, at Berlin, engaged in proving insulated tubes, lose sensibi ity in their hands and forearms after a day's work. One constructed by a skilful organ builder, was exhibited in January, 1839, at a sitting of the Physical Society of Deventer. The keys have a similar arrangement to those of the piano forte, and connexion is established by depressing them into a cup of mercurial; no extensive use has been made this instrument.—(*Schellen's Elec. Mag.*, *page* 66.)

Mr. R. Smith, Lecturer on Chemistry, Blackford, Scotland, invented an Electro-Chemical Telegraph. A paper containing an account of which was read before the Royal Scottish Society of Arts, on the 27th of March, 1843, reported on by a committee, and approved the 12th June following. Since that time, many trials have been made, and various improvements in its construction have also been introduced by the inventor. The following is a description of it in its present improved form.

In the annexed wood-cut, A represents the indicating portion of the telegraphic apparatus, *a* is a leaden cylinder fixed upon a spindle, which is supported so as to revolve freely, by two standards attached to the bottom plate of the apparatus, *b b* is a piece of calico in the form of a riband coiled upon the roller *c*, placed in the trough *d*, its contrary extremity being attached to the second roller *e*, revolving loosely in standars attached to the opposite end of the bottom plate, B is the communicator, or that portion of the apparatus through which any given signal is communicated to the indicator A; *f* is a block of wood having a brass plate *g* attached to it, *h* is a slip of wood hinged to the block, and slightly raised above the surface of the brass plate *g* by means of a spring placed beneath it. The brass plate *g* is connected by the wire *k* with the positive end of the voltaic battery C, the negative end of which is connected with the wire *l*, which passes along to the indicator A, where it is attached to the leaden cylinder *a*. The other wire *m* is attached to the fingerboard *h*, through which it passes, projecting slightly on the lower surface, its contrary end being attached to the impress wire *n*, which is supported loosely by a cross-beam on the top of the centre-standards of the indicator, its lower end resting upon the calico riband on the leaden cylinder beneath.

To put this apparatus in action, the cells of the battery C are filled with water, and the trough *d* with a solution of ferro-cyanate of potass, to which have been added a few drops of nitric acid. The roller *e* to which the indicator cloth is attached is next put in motion by clock-work, and thus the cloth wet with the solution contained in trough *d* is caused to pass uniformly over the leaden cylinder *a* below the point of the impress wire.

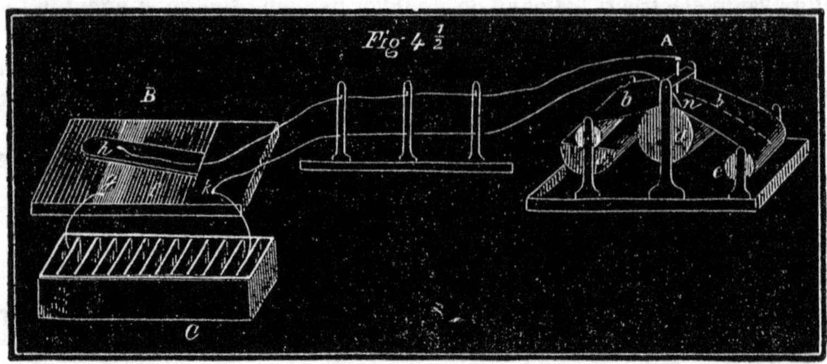

The apparatus is now ready for signaling, which is done by pressing down the finger board *h*, so as to bring the end of the wire *n* in contact with the brass plate *f*, thus completing the electric circuit. The impress wire *n* now becomes the positive electrode, and the cylinder *a* the negative one, and a blue mark is printed upon the cloth, by the electric fluid decomposing the ferro-cyanate of potass, thus forming cyanate of iron. If the circuit is formed and broken rapidly, a succession of dots will be printed upon the cloth; if formed and broken at long intervals, the result will be a series of marks. In this manner long and short spaces and corresponding lines will be formed according to the duration of the opening or closing of the circuit, and the speed with which the cloth is caused to pass beneath the metallic pen. An arrangement of these various marks thus forms the telegraphic alphabet, from which sentences may be composed, embracing any information which it may be necessary to transmit. For instance, a single dot may be taken as the index for A, two for B, three for C, and a dot and line for D, &c.

The species of battery which is the best adapted for producing the electro-chemical indications, consists of 40 repetitions of charcoal and zinc plates; the charcoal plates being composed of three parts pulverized charcoal, two of pulverized coke, and one of wheaten flour, mixed together with water; when formed, the plates are allowed to dry, and are then placed in an earthen crucible, in the lid of which is an aperture for the escape of the gases; in this they are heated to redness. This battery will keep up a uniform and energetic current for a considerable time, the cells being merely filled with water; the only attention which it requires subsequently, being to wash off any oxide which may be deposited upon the plates, and supply fresh water. The battery employed for making the electro-magnetic telegraph is a calorimoter or single circle, the electricity generated by this battery has a tendency to weaken in its progress, so that the defect must necessarily be provided for by placing batteries at different distances, according to the desired amount of power, this objection is completely removed in the voltaic apparatus. Experiment has proved that the electric energy from the intensity battery, in producing the electro chemical effects, *increases* instead of diminishing in regard to distance. Faraday ascertained that the quantity of electricity required to decompose a single drop of water, is equal to that of a powerful flash of lightning, while from the largest single circuit ever constructed, not the slighest chemical effect can be exhibited. On the other hand, a small single circle composed only of a few square inches of copper and zinc, will temporarily magnetize a large bar of iron, while a powerful voltaic trough will not magnetize a lady's sewing needle. Throughout the whole of the practical details of the electro-magnetic apparatus, a far greater amount of carefulness of workmanship is required than in those of the voltaic one. Thus, the whole of the joinings of the conducting wires, require to be in perfect metallic contact, and carefully isolated, whilst the electro-chemical communications may be transmitted through the medium of a wire fence. The inventor lately exhibited an experiment which proves the practicability of this application.

In this case the communicator and indicator were attached to the contrary extremities of an iron wire fence of a length of 1868 yards, when a number of signals were despatched with the greatest facility. This economical adaptation will doubtless render it worthy of the attention of railway proprietors, as a metallic fence may in this manner be rendered doubly useful.—(*Prac. Mech. and Eng. Mag., Glasgow, Vol.* I., *2d series, pp.* 36, 239.)

Succeeding this in our chronological series, comes the instrument of Alexander Bain, a native of the northern part of Scotland. Mr. Bain's instrument, dated December 12, 1846, in patent specifications, depends for its efficiency on electro-chemical action, and consists of a transmitting apparatus at one end of the line, with a recipient one at the other terminus. Figure 5 is an elevation, and fig. 6 is a plan of so much of a transmitting apparatus as is necessary to show its mode of action. A A is a thin roller of wood upon which is wound a long strip of paper, previously perforated with holes *a a a*, in the manner represented in fig. 7. Each group of holes as divided by cross lines, represent letters, numerals, words, or sentences, as may have before been fixed upon. From this roller A, the end of this slip of paper is passed between another roller B, and two metallic springs C^1 C^2. The roller B is composed of metal pieces a^1 a^2, mounted upon wood inside, so that their contiguous edges shall be some distance apart; and the roller is moved by clock work, whose velocity is regulated by a ball governor. The receiving apparatus at the other end of the line is the same as the transmitting one, except, that instead of the strip of perforated paper, there is wound on the roller A A, a strip of colored paper. This is first soaked in diluted sulphuric acid, and afterwards in a solution of prussiate of potassa; while wet it is wound on the first roller A, where it forms part of the galvanic circuit, and must be kept damp while the message is being sent. When the machines at both ends of the line are thus arranged, and connected together by wire, with the metallic springs C^1 C^2, attached to a galvanic battery, the operator at the transmitting end sets it in motion, like the lock which governs the striking of a clock; this lifts a detent in the receiving apparatus at the other end of the line, and puts that in operation. Thus, the two machines unroll their strips of paper at the same time, and as long as the contact between the springs C^1 C^2, and the second roller B, of the transmitting machine, is prevented by the paper which has no holes in it passing between them, the circuit is broken. As soon as the spring C^1, comes over one of the holes in the paper, the circuit is re-established, and the electric current flowing through these holes, passes along the connecting wire to the wet roll of paper at the receiving end of the line. The electricity passing through the wet paper destroys its color by chemical action in those parts which it enters, and thereby makes as many legible spots on the wet roll of paper, as there are holes in the dry roll at the other end of the wire. Thus, by alternately renewing and breaking contact by means of the holes in the transmitting roll, as many corresponding letters, numerals, &c., are made on the receiving roll.

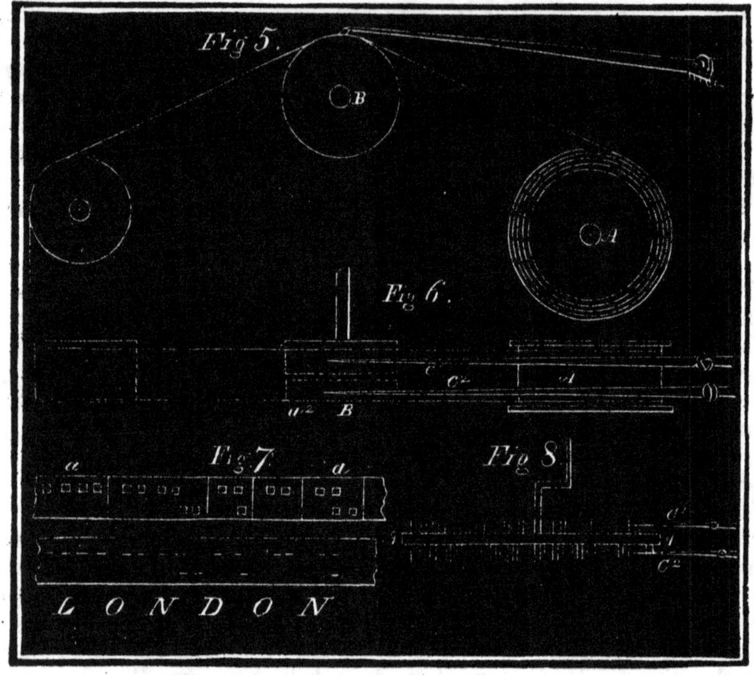

An exemplification of the alphabetical characters employed by Mr. Bain, is given in fig. 7, which represents at once the perforations which would be made in the transmitting paper, and the corresponding marks which would be made in the colored or recipient paper to express the word LONDON. When it is desired that the attendant at the receiving station should not know the contents of the message sent, the receiving roll is wet in diluted acid, passed through the machine, and afterwards immersed in the solution of prussiate of potassa, which makes the words plain. The holes are made in the paper by means of a separate machine worked by hand; the paper passes between two rollers, one of which is a small punch, which cuts the holes in the paper, and works by the slightest touch. After the holes are made in the paper, it then has to be wound on the transmitting roller. The rapidity of this mode of communication depends on the number of holes which a clever hand can punch in a given time, which is about 100 per minute; after the holes are made, the machine will transmit from 500 to 1000 impressions in a minute. Mr. Bain has lately remodeled this machine, by changing the rollers of the receiving apparatus into a revolving disk, in the periphery of which, there are a number of metallic rods or wires of equal length, which may be made to slide towards one side of the disk, or the other, at pleasure.

Fig. 8 is a plan of this modification. A is the edge of the disk; *b b* the wires; and C^1 C^2 springs, similar to those marked with the same letters in other figures. It will be obvious, that when the disk A is made to rotate, the springs C^1 C^2 will successively be brought in contact with the wires *b b*, on one side or on the other; and that as they are made the means of establishing the metallic connexion between the two ends of the line of communication, the effects produced upon the chemical substance will be the same as before described. In this case, the wires *b b* serve the purpose of the holes in the strip of paper, fig. 7.—(*London Mechanics' Magazine*, *Vol.* XLVI. *p.* 591.)

"In this form of telegraph," he remarks, "I have rejected magnetism altogether, and caused the pulsations of the electric current to be transmitted through groups of perforations, forming signs, which are recorded at the receiving station by pulsations of the electric current acting on chemically prepared paper, in the manner described and shown; so that the circuit is completed, and interrupted, by the operation of the composed communication itself, without the electric current having to produce any mechanical motion, and without any manipulation of the operator, in forming the intermittent pulsations of the electric current; thereby effecting the transmission of a communication to one or a plurality of distant receiving stations, with far greater rapidity than by any other mode."

This may be true in theory, but it will require more time than the simple passage of the current in practice. For in every case decomposition of the fluid will take place, and time is required for the operator to see the mark. If the paper should become dry, as it is known to do, the mark then becomes very indistinct from the want of proper conducting material; and as the wire is not of platinum, by becoming oxidized it prevents that proper metallic contact, so that it will require an intense and constant current, which cannot be produced and kept up in the form of battery described by Mr. Bain, namely, zinc and copper battery. There is also the inconvenience arising from the fumes from the chemicals employed in preparing the paper.

S. F. B. Morse's Electro-Chemical Telegraph, Patented in May, 1849. —"The nature of my invention consists: First: In the application of the decomposing effects of electricity produced from any known generator of electricity, to the marking of the signs for numerals, or letters, or words, or sentences, invented and arranged by me, and secured by patent, bearing date June 20th, 1840; re-issued January 15th, 1846, and again re-issued, June 13th, 1848, or their equivalents, through a single circuit of electrical conductors.

Second. In the mode of applying this decomposition, and the machinery for that purpose.

Third. In the application of the bleaching qualities of electricity to the printing of any desired characters.

In applying the decomposing effects of electricity upon any known salts that leave a mark, as the result of the said decomposition, I use,

Class A. A class of salts that produce a *colored mark* upon *cloth*, *paper*, *thread* or *other material*, under the action of electricity.

First. Iodide of tin in solution.

Second. Extract of nutgalls, and sulphate of iron in solution, making an ink which colors white cambric cloth a uniform grey.

Third. Acetate of lead, and nitrate of potash in solution.

Fourth. Iodide of potassium in solution.

Into either of these I dip a strip of cloth or thread, which is kept properly moistened. All these give a black mark upon the cloth, thread, or other material under the action of electricity.

Class B. A class of salts which color the cloth, paper, thread, or other material, and are *bleached* by the action of electricity.

First. Iodide of tin in solution.

Second. Iodine dissolved in alcohol.

Into either of these I dip a strip of cloth, paper, thread, or other material; and if in solution *second*, I also dip them into a solution of sulphate of soda, the cloth or other material, in these cases, becomes of a purple color more or less dark. The electricity in these cases, when a metallic point or type is pressed upon, or comes in contact with, the moist cloth or other material, *bleaches* it, and leaves the point or the type impressed in white characters upon the material.

Class C. A class of salts that produce a mark upon metal, through the intervening cloth or other material, and not upon the material, under the action of electricity.

First. Sulphate of copper in solution.

Second. Chloride of zinc diluted with water.

Third. Sulphate of iron in solution.

Into either of these solutions I dip the cloth, thread, or other material, and if into the third, I afterwards dip it into muriate of lime in solution. The electricity in these cases causes a dark mark upon a bright metal plate beneath the moistened material, but not on the material itself.

The mode of applying this decomposition by electricity, is by the use of so much of my machinery previously described in the schedule referred to in the Letters Patent, granted to me and bearing date June 13, 1848, being the re-issue of the original patent of April 12, 1846, as is employed in regulating the motion of the paper, substituting, however, for the common paper therein used, the cloth, thread, metal, or other material, chemically prepared.

Operation.—I consider the discoloring process better than the bleaching process, and for the discoloring process I consider the iodide of potassium in solution, as the best of the substances I have mentioned for the preparation of the cloth, paper, or other material. I wish it to be understood that

I do not confine myself to the use of the substances I have mentioned, but mean to comprehend the use of *any known substance already proved to be easily decomposed by the electric current.*

Claims. What I claim as my own invention and improvement, and desire to secure by letters patent, is, 1st, the use of the *single circuit* of conductors for the marking of my telegraphic signs already patented, for numerals, letters, words, or sentences, by means of the decomposing, coloring or bleaching effects of electricity, acting upon any known salts that leave a mark as the result of the said decomposition, upon paper, cloth, metals, or other convenient and known markable material.

2d, I also claim the combination of machinery as herein substantially described, by which any two metallic points or other known conducting substances, broken parts of an electric or galvanic circuit, having the chemically prepared material in contact with and between them, may be used for the purpose of marking my telegraphic characters already patented in Letters Patent, dated 20th of June, 1840; in the first issue, 25th January, 1846; and second re-issue, 13th June, 1848."

The marking instrument of Morse is a platina disk, and is described fully in the patent. As this apparatus has not been used practically, I have noticed it here more to keep up the chain of Galvanic Telegraphs, and I am surprised that Mr. Morse should have taken out a patent for a telegraph so far inferior to the one he has in operation since 1840, as there cannot be a doubt that the Chemical Telegraph, according to the opinion of the best operators, is far inferior to the Electro-Magnetic in regard to trouble, expense, and uncertainty in operation.

"The last patent of Mr. A. Bain, is one taken out in connexion with Robert Smith, Lecturer on Chemistry, Perthshire, Scotland, October, 1849.

"These improvements consist—

Firstly. In the peculiar mode of arranging the several parts herein described of our marking instruments of Electro-Chemical Telegraphs.

Secondly. In a mode of constructing a style or point holder, so as to afford a ready and convenient mode of regulating the pressure of the style or point on the surface of the chemically prepared paper or other suitable fabric.

Thirdly. In a mode of applying a weight for regulating the pressure of an upper on a lower revolving wheel, or roller, in motion, so as to grasp the strip of chemically prepared paper, or other suitable fabric, and ensure it being drawn continually forward.

Fourthly. In a mode of arranging the marking instruments, keys, wires, and batteries, in a single circuit, and in branch circuits, connected therewith, so that a copy of a message sent from any station may be marked upon the chemically prepared paper, or other fabric, at any desired number of stations in communication therewith, and also, if required, at the transmitting station.

We would here state, that the paper, linen, or other suitable fabric, may be prepared by being equally and thoroughly moistened by the following chemical compound, viz.: Ten parts, by measure, of a saturated solution of prussiate of potash, which will be best made in distilled water, and we prefer to use the yellow prussiate for this purpose; two parts by measure of nitric acid, of the strength of about 40° by Baumé's scale; two parts by measure of muriatic acid, of the strength of about 20° by Baumé's scale.

To keep the paper, or other fabric, in a sufficiently moist state, favorable for the action of an electric current, we add about one part by measure of chloride of lime; this mixture is to be kept stirred about with a glass rod until the chloride of lime is in complete solution. In connexion with this compound, it is proper to observe that we have found that prussiate of potash, combined with almost any acids, will give mark under the decomposing action of an electric current, but no other mixtures act so quickly, or give such permanent marks with feeble currents of electricity, as that herein described. The principal use of the chloride of lime is, that it absorbs moisture from the atmosphere, and thereby keeps the prepared fabric in a proper state to be acted upon by an electric current in all states of the weather."

"The system of correspondence made use of consists of *dots* and *lines*, the number, dimensions and relative positions of which form an intelligible code of signals, as is well understood.

We do not claim as our invention the train of wheels constituting the motive part of the marking instruments; neither do we claim or confine ourselves to any particular form of battery or other generator of electricity, which may be of any suitable form, several of which are well known and in common use.

We desire it to be understood that what we claim as new and of our invention, is—

Firstly. The modes of arranging the several parts of our marking instruments for Electro-Chemical Telegraphs, substantially as herein before described.

Secondly. We claim the mode of adjusting a style or point holder, as herein before described and shown, so as to afford a ready and convenient mode of regulating the pressure of the style or point upon the surface of chemically prepared fabric.

Thirdly. We claim the mode of applying the weight Q, for the purpose of regulating the pressure, as herein described and shown.

Fourthly. We claim the mode of arranging the marking and transmitting instruments, wires and batteries, in a single circuit, and in branch circuits connected therewith, so that a copy of a message sent from any one station may be marked upon chemically prepared paper, or other fabric, at one or any desired number of stations in communication therewith, and also, if required, at the transmitting station, without requiring the use of any secondary current."

On the 28th of May, 1850, Messrs. Westbrook and Rogers, the former of Washington, the latter of Baltimore, secured a patent for the "Electric Metallic Telegraph." In their specification they state that:—The nature of our invention consists in recording telegraphic signs on a metallic surface, connected with the earth by a wire conductor at one end, and to a galvanic battery and the earth at the other end of the circuit, by the use of the acidulated water or other fluid interposed between the point of the usual wire conductor leading from the operating apparatus, connected with the galvanic battery of the ordinary construction and the metallic surface, by which the use of paper is dispensed with; time also being saved in not having to moisten the chemically prepared paper, when it becomes too dry for use, and in having the telegraphic signs more clear and distinct on the metallic surface than on the paper; in avoiding the inconvenience arising from the fumes from the chemicals employed in preparing the paper, and evils arising from the corrosion of instruments, and annoyance to operators in preparing and using chemical paper, and other inconveniences.

The metallic recording surface, after being filled and transferred, is simply cleaned by the application of a sponge or other soft substance saturated with acidulated water. The wire conductor has the form of a tubular pen, of which the fluid flows by means of a barrel valve or sponge and porous substances, such as glass or ivory, open at both ends, through which the acidulated water or other fluid passes to the metallic surface, on which the telegraphic signs are to be made.

Before concluding the subject of electro-chemical telegraphs, I would bring before my readers a communication from the distinguished French philosopher, the Abbe Moigno, author of the "Traité de Telegraphie-Electrique," although not agreeing with the sentiments expressed in my former communication; but I have introduced it in justice to Mr. Bain, and from respect to the opinion of M. Moigno.

Communication on the Electric Telegraph.—The President of the Society for the Encouragement of National Industry, (Session, May 8th, 1850,) announced that Mr. Bain had arranged in the hall his ingenious systemof electric telegraphing, of which M. Sequier had during a previous session given a description, which greatly interested the members of the society.

The Abbe Moigno was invited to give an explanation of this apparatus, to which invitation he quickly responded.

In this consists the ingenious mechanism of this apparatus, to which, the author has given the name of electro-chemical telegraph, to distinguish it from the electro-magnetic telegraphs now in use, provided it be deprived of the magnet.

The message wished to be transmitted, is written on a piece of long narrow paper by cutting with the aid of a punch, the letters of a very simple alphabet composed of points and horizontal lines. This band is rolled on a wooden cylinder, and then unrolls itself with the aid of a crank, so as to pass on a second metallic cylinder, which supports four little springs which communicate with the conducting wire of the telegraphic line; the metallic cylinder is connected with the pole of a battery of small volume and very simple construction.

The band of paper presents in turn, a covered part and a vacant space; this last represents the letters of the alphabet, whilst the covered parts are of paper, that is to say, an insulating substance. When the small springs rest on the covered parts, the circuit is not formed and the current does not pass, but so soon as the springs touch an empty place, they are in contact with the cylinder; from that time the communication is established, the current circulating, and arriving instantaneously at the

3

station. There a small style is attached to the conducting wire of the line; below this style turns a metallic plate, which is covered with a disk of paper, chemically prepared by dipping it at first in a solution of sulphuric acid, and afterwards in a solution of prussiate of potash. The plate and the damp disk with which it is covered, communicate with one of the poles of the battery at the station of arrival. The current is afterwards completed through the earth.

The despatch is transmitted in the following manner: at a given signal the style is applied to the chemical paper; at every empty space on the band of paper, which is unrolled by the crank, the current passes, and under its influence the point of the style, by the chemical action which it exercises, traces a point or a little line of a very dark color, which is the faithful representation of the letter which must be reproduced at a distance.

The band on which an entire page is written unrolls itself with extreme rapidity, the plate, drawn by a clock-like movement, turns also with great quickness. After 45 seconds the 1200 letters composing this page appear very neatly drawn on the disks of the chemical paper, and were thus faithfully reproduced, and would have gone two or three hundred leagues further without any difficulty. The movement printed on the plate is a spiral one, so that the successive lines do not supersede each other, but remain entirely distinct.

These are the advantages which the author attributes to his system of electro-chemical telegraph: 1st, more economy and simplicity in the primitive construction: 2d, more rapidity in the transmission of the despatches; a single wire with a good insulator can transmit 1200 letters a minute, or 20 letters a second, that is, ten times more than is customary: 3d, an electric current more feeble than is ordinary, suffices to cause the apparatus to work, and is consequently less exposed to the chances of interruption by the imperfection of the insulation, which results sometimes from the vicissitudes of the weather and other circumstances: 4th, more simplicity and economy in the correspondence, and superintendence: 5th, fewer chances of error in the despatches sent.

Bain's telegraph is in operation in England, from London to Manchester, and from Manchester to Liverpool, over an extent of 300 kilometres, (186½ miles,) and in America on a line of 2000 kilometres, (1242⅛ miles.)

The President begs Mr. Bain to receive the congratulations of the society, on his system of electric telegraphing, and he renders to M. Abbe Moigno the thanks of the society for the complaisance with which he has given clear and precise explanations on the mechanism and play of this system.—*Bulletin de la Société d'Encouragement pour l'Industrie Nationale, May* 8, 1850, *p.* 236.

Before giving an account of the various forms of electro-magnetic telegraphs, it will be proper to give a brief account of the science which investigates the relations subsisting between the electric, galvanic and magnetic fluids, as all the forms of telegraph I am about to describe depends on the power of the electric current to deflect a magnetic needle, or the power of the current to impart temporary magnetism to iron, or to produce electric currents by magnetic induction.

Electro-Magnetism.—The power of lightning to destroy, and reverse the poles of a magnet, and to convey magnetic properties to iron, which did not previously possess them, was noticed at a very early period of electrical science, and led to the supposition, that common electricity and galvanism would produce the same effect. Attempts were made to prove this fact, but no important results were obtained, until the late Prof. Œrsted, of Copenhagen, published in *Thompson's Annals of Philosophy*, for October, 1820, the important discovery he had made in the winter of 1819, which laid the foundation of the science of electro-magnetism. He ascertained that when a wire conducting electricity is placed parallel to a magnetic needle properly suspended, the needle will deviate from its natural position, which is thus expressed in Ampère's brief and universal terms: "*that the north pole of a magnet is invariably deflected to the left of the current which passes between the needle and the observer, who is to have his face towards the needle, the electric current being supposed to enter near his feet, and to pass out near his head.*" Likewise, that this deviation follows a regular law, which can be stated in four general rules: 1st. If the needle is above the conducting *wire*, and the electricity passes from right to left, the north pole of the needle will be moved *from* the operator. 2nd. If the needle is below the wire, and the electricity passes as before, the north pole of the needle will be turned towards the observer. 3rd. If the needle is put in the same horizontal plane with the wire, and is between the observer and the wire, the north pole of it will be elevated. 4th. If the needle is in like manner placed on the opposite side, the north pole will be depressed. To exhibit this effect well, the needle must be very near the wire. Other new and important facts were soon after discovered by Ampère and Arago, in France; Davy and Faraday in England, and our own illustrious Prof. Henry, then of Albany, New York. Ampère satisfactorily referred all the observed phenomena to the laws which govern the mutual actions of electrical currents, by means of a very ingenious hypothesis—that magnetism consists in electrical currents, revolving around the minute particles of a magnet, in planes perpendicular to its axis. This branch of science is also named electro-dynamics, which simply means electricity in motion, while electricity at rest, is called statical electricity. The laws of electro-dynamical attraction and repulsion, experimentally established by M. Ampère, and which serve to explain all the known phenomena, may be plainly stated in a few general propositions.

Proposition 1st. Parallel currents, (Fig. 9) flowing in the same direction attract each other, where *a b c d* are the currents, whose directions are

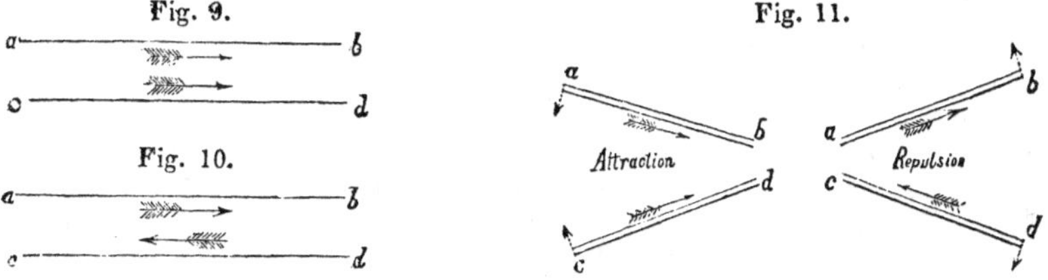

indicated by arrows. They mutually repel when their directions are opposite, as in Fig. 10, *a b c d*.

Proposition 2d. Two currents attract each other when they both flow towards or from a certain point, if they are not in the same plane, as in Fig. 11. And they repel each other, if one approaches and the other recedes from that point, as in Fig 11.

If two rectilinear currents, *a b* and *c d*, Fig. 12, cross each other, then by the preceding case they will attract each other between the vertical angles *x* and *y*, and repel between *z* and *w*. The result will be that both conductors will endeavor to take up a position in which the currents that flow through them may have a similar direction.

Proposition 3d. These attractive forces vary in their intensity in the inverse ratio of the square of the distance—or, as the distance increases, so their force diminishes

Fig. 12.

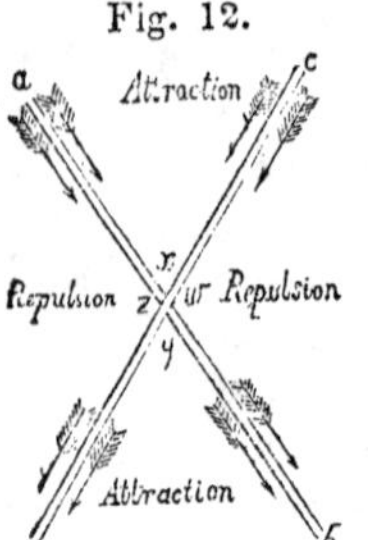

Fig. 13.

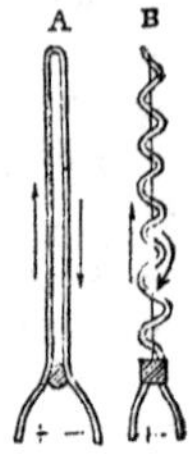

A B

Proposition 4. The attraction or repulsion exerted by a current passing through a tortuous conductor, no matter how numerous its windings may be, is exactly equal to that which is produced by the same current when it follows in a straight line between the points as in shown fig. 13.

A magnetic needle is a galvanascope, by which the existence and direction of an electric current may be detected. It was early employed with this intention, by Ampère, but, as the deflexion took place only when the opposite ends of the battery were in connexion, and ceased when the circuit was broken, he inferred that electricity passes uninterruptedly through the battery itself when the circuit is closed, and that there is no action in the interrupted circuit.

A magnetic needle will not only indicate the existence and direction of an electric current, but may serve by the degree of deflexion as an exact measure of its force. When used for this purpose it is called a galvanometer, the first example of which was invented by Professor Schweigger, of Halle, in 1820, soon after the discovery of electro-magnetism, and was called by him an electro-magnetic multiplier; an example of this form of instrument is seen in Fig. 14. Various forms have been given to this instrument, as it is the basis of all the needle telegraphs.

Fig. 14.

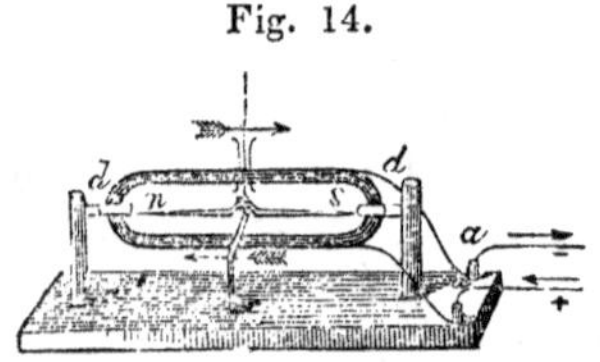

A current of galvanic electricity not only determines the position of a magnet, but renders steel permanently magnetic. This was observed nearly at the same time, by M. Arago and Sir H. Davy, who found, that when needles are placed at right angles to the conducting wire, permanent magnetism is communicated to them. Sir H. Davy succeeded in producing this effect, even with a shock of electricity from a Leyden jar. M. Arago, at the suggestion of M. Ampère, made a galvanic conductor in the form of a helix, or coil, into the axis of which he placed a needle, as seen in Fig. 15. This helix was simply a spiral coil of wire, the extremities of it being connected to the opposite poles of a battery,

Fig. 15.

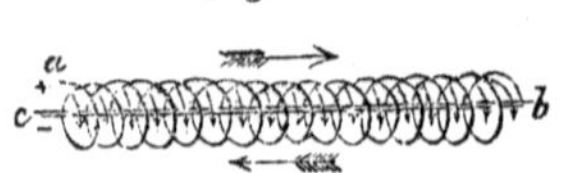

thus permitting an electrical circuit to pass through it. By this arrangement the current is almost at right angles to the needle, and as each coil adds its effect to that of the others, the entire action of the spiral helix is extremely powerful. In this way a needle can be completely magnetized in an instant, and this is the method now principally employed by artisans in the manufacture of compass needles.

When the conductors of a galvanic battery are brought near, or in contact with a quantity of iron filings, the filings will be attracted towards the conductors, and place themselves in the form of a ring around it. This action takes place while a current of galvanism is sent through the conductor, but as soon as that current is broken they fall off. By observation of this fact, M. Arago was led to the important discovery of what is termed magnetic induction by electrical currents. Namely, that a current of electricity passing through a conductor will induce, or make sensible, magnetic action in those bodies near it, which are capable of being magnetized. Arago was then the first to form a temporary magnet. That this property is magnetic, and not simply electrical, is shown by the fact, that the filings of other metals are not attracted in the same way. It likewise renders steel needles permanently magnetic when placed in the axis of the spiral helix or coil.

The word induction is here used to express that power which electricity has to make magnetic action apparent to our senses. That the effect of the galvanic current upon the iron filings and needles is one of magnetic induction, is proved by the reality, that they acquire this property without contact with, and even at a distance from, the conducting wire.

Some philosophers have ascribed the formation of iron filings into a circle around the conducting wire, to the influence of a magnetic current revolving about it perpendicular to its axis, and not to any action induced in the filings themselves. Dr. Bache, the eminent Professor of Chemistry, in the Jefferson Medical College of this city, many years ago publicly advocated the idea, that the filings were not inert agents in this movement. To prove it, he instanced the evidence that when their ring around the wire is broken, they immediately fall off, even when a current of galvanism is progresssing along the conducting wire; he maintained the opinion that they assumed the ring-like form, because of the magnetism induced in them, and the argument he has adduced in its favor is certainly quite conclusive.

Mr. Wm. Sturgeon, a native of London, about the year 1825, discovered that when wires of soft iron were placed within the coil of a conducting wire, they were rendered intensely magnetic. (*Annals of Philos. Vol.* XII, *page* 359.)

Our knowledge of this subject was afterwards greatly extended during the period from 1828 to 1831, by the researches of Professor Henry, Secretary of the Smithsonian Institute, at Washington.

Though soft iron does not retain magnetism, its magnetic properties, while under the influence of a galvanic current, are very surprising. A piece of soft iron, about a foot long and an inch in diameter, is bent in the form of a horse shoe; an insulated copper wire is twisted round the bar at right angles to the axis, and an armature or keeper of soft iron, to which a weight may be attached, is fitted to its extremities. As may be seen in this instrument, Fig. 16. On connecting the ends of the wire with a simple galvanic circle, the soft iron instantly becomes a powerful magnet, and will support a weight of 50, 60, or even 70 pounds. As soon as the galvanic circuit is broken, the iron immediately loses its magnetism, and the weight drops. When the number of coils is increased they give great additional power. The wire used for making the helix must be wound with waxed or silk thread, to insulate it, so as to prevent the current from skipping along the contiguous parts of the coil, and thus taking a shorter route for its circuit, instead of traversing around the bar.

Fig. 16.

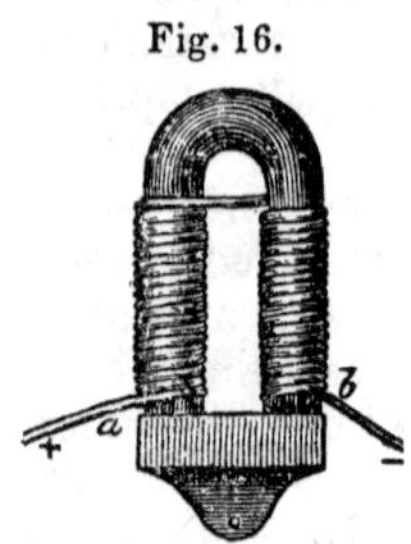

The instrument first used by Prof. Henry, in 1828, to illustrate electro-magnetic action, consisted of an iron bar, two inches square, twenty inches long, bent in a horse-shoe form, and weighing 21 pounds. The keeper weighed 7 pounds, and 540 feet of insulated copper wire, were wound in nine coils of 60 feet each around the horse-shoe shaped bar of soft iron. From the experiments which he made with it, he proved that a small battery is capable of producing great magnetic effects, if the spirals of the coil are numerous, and the resistance to the passage of electricity is not very great. He also showed the effect of varying the lengths of the conducting wires and the intensity of the current, and found that six short wires were more powerful than three of double the length. When the current was made to pass through all of the nine coils, the magnet raised 750 pounds.

After all his investigations, he concluded that we can use long or short wires as the case may require. Where we use long wires, the galvanic battery must have a number of plates, in order to give projectile force; on the contrary, a single pair of plates will answer for short wires.

"May it not also be a fact, that the galvanic fluid, in order to produce the greatest magnetic effects should move with a small velocity, and that in passing through one-fifth of a mile, its velocity is so retarded as to produce a greater magnetic action.

"But be this as it may, the fact that the magnetic action of a current from a trough is, at least, not sensibly diminished by passing through a long wire, is directly applicable to Wm. Barlow's project of forming an electro-magnetic telegraph, and also of material consequence in the construction of the galvanic coil. From these experiments it is evident, that in forming the coil we may either use one very long wire or several shorter ones, as the circumstances may require: in the first case, our galvanic combination must consist of a number of plates so as to give projectile force: in the second, it must be formed of a single pair.

"The wire used was 1060 feet (a little more than one-fifth of a mile) of copper wire, of the kind called bell wire, ·045 ($\frac{45}{1000}$) of an inch in diameter, were stretched several times across the large room of the Academy."—(*Silliman's Journal*, *Vol.* XIX. *January*, 1831.)

He afterwards endeavored to ascertain the best form of iron to receive magnetism, but did not succeed satisfactorily. However, he found that magnetic power resided wholly on the surface of iron bodies, though a certain thickness of metal is necessary for its complete development.—Hence the larger amount of iron surface we have, the more powerful will the magnet be, when all other things are alike. This is the reason that a bundle of wires will exhibit greater magnetic effects than a solid bar, containing much more iron. Bachhoffner of Germany, and Sturgeon of London, were the first who noticed this fact.

In 1830 Prof. Moll, of Utrecht, made some experiments of the same nature, and noticed particularly the sudden destruction and reproduction of magnetism when the current is reversed.—(*Bibliothéque Universelle*, 1830, *p.* 19.)

Subsequently, Prof. Henry constructed two of the largest and most powerful instruments of this kind at present known. One now in the cabinet of Yale College, weighing 59½ pounds, which sustained a weight of 2063 pounds; another, belonging to the cabinet of Princeton College, N. J., of 100 pounds weight, which could support 3500 pounds, or one and a half tons.

According to our present knowledge of the matter, the power of an electro-magnet depends on five important conditions, viz. 1st, The intensity and tension of the electric current. 2d, The number of coils around the magnet. 3d, The quantity of iron composing the magnet. 4th, The structure of the iron, the purest, softest, and most homogeneous receiving the most magnetism. 5th, The form of the magnet, as cylinders were found to support greater weights than solid bars, and bundles of wires more than cylinders.

Magneto-Electricity.—The power which electricity of tension possesses of causing an opposite electrical state in its vicinity, has been expressed by the general term induction, which, as it has been received into scientific language, may also, with propriety, be used in the same general sense to express the power which electrical currents may possess of inducing any particular state upon matter in their immediate neighborhood, otherwise indifferent; this is the meaning given to it by Professor Faraday, in his *Experimental Researches.* Previous to the experiments of this distinguished philosopher, certain results of importance had been obtained by Amperè, showing the induction of electrical currents by his experiment of bringing a copper disc near to a flat spiral; also his repetition of Arago's experiment, and the wonderful effects produced by Sturgeon Moll and Henry. Still, Faraday remarks, it appeared unlikely that these could be all the effects which induction by currents could produce.

These considerations, with their consequences, stimulated him to investigate experimentally, with the hope of obtaining electricity from ordinary magnetism.

Though baffled in his early attempts, he at last succeeded in laying open a new branch of electro-dynamics, which vies in interest and importance with the fundamental discovery of Œrsted. "A copper wire 203 feet long, was passed in the form of a helix, around a large block of wood, and an equal length of a similar wire was wound on the same block, and in the same direction, so that the coils of each helix should be interposed, but without m[illegible]ontact, between the coils of the other. The two ends of one of the helices, *a* and *b*, as in Fig. 17, were connected with a galvanometer, and those of the other, at *c* and *d*, with a strong galvanic battery, with a view of ascertaining whether the passage of an electric current through one helix, would create or induce a current in the adjoining helix. It was found that the galvanometer needle indicated a current to have been elicited in the under wire, at the moment of completing and breaking the circuit but that, in the interval, no deflexion took place. And likewise, the induced currents readily magnetized a sewing needle, while the electric current along the inducing coil was in the act of beginning or ceasing to flow, but at no other period. An electric current transmitted from a galvanic battery through a conducting coil, does not induce a current in an adjoining coil, except at the moment of making or breaking the circuit. When the circuit is closed, the direction of the induced current is opposite to that of the inducing one, but when it is broken, the direction of both is the same." To this phenomenon, Professor Faraday gave the name of volta electric induction. The power of magnetism, to induce or create an electric current in an adjoining body, is greater than that of electricity itself. One of the most convenient of Professor Faraday's arrangements to represent this action, consisted of a hollow cylinder of pasteboard, around which two compound coils were adjusted. On connecting one of these coils with a galvanic battery, the other coil moved the needle of the galvanometer, and magnetized steel needles, as in the experiment just described. But when a cylinder of soft iron was introduced into the pasteboard case, and a galvanic current transmitted as before, the effect on the galvanometer was much greater. This effect results from the induction of magnetism in the bar of iron, which magnetism causes the increased amount of electricity in the coil connected with the galvanometer. To the phenomena in the last experiment, Professor Faraday gave the name of magneto-electricity. With such an instrument, he caused convulsions in the leg of a frog, and when the ends of the induced wire were armed with charcoal points, sparks of electric-light were obtained at the moment the galvanic circuit was broken, and closed through the inducing wire. When a permanent magnet is placed in a coil of wire, a current of electricity is set up in the wire. While the magnet remains in the coil at rest, no action is perceptible; but on removing it, another current is perceived. The currents move in opposite directions. These singular phenomena, which establish such new and intimate relations between galvanic and magnetic action, and supply additional evidence in favor of Amperè's beautiful theory of magnetism, have led to an experiment, by which, at first view, an electric spark appeared to be derived from the magnet itself.—*Faraday's Researches, Nov.* 1831.

Fig. 17

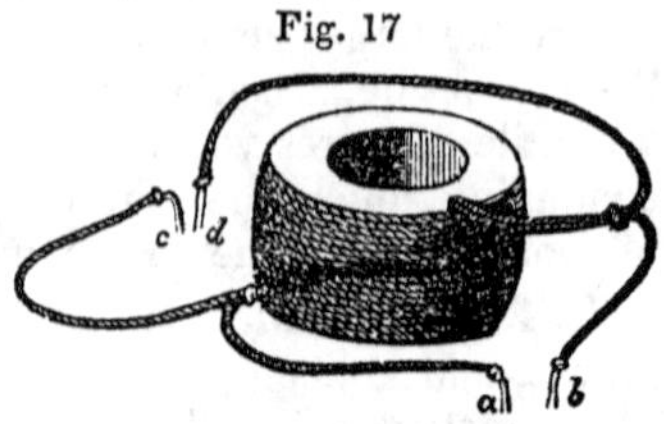

Amperè's theory was, that all magnetic properties of bodies can be referred to currents of electricity circulating around each particle of those bodies.

After Professor Faraday had announced his experiment of obtaining sparks from the induced wire, other attempts were made to effect the same object with a magnet, without the aid of galvanism. The first person who succeeded in Great Britain, was Professor Forbes, of Edinburgh, who operated with a loadstone, which had been presented to the University of Edinburgh by Dr. Hope. A helix of copper wire was formed around the middle of a cylinder of soft iron, which was of such length that its extremities reached from one pole of the loadstone to the other. On applying and withdrawing the soft iron cylinder to and from the poles of the loadstone, magnetism was alternately created and destroyed within it. At these periods of transition, electric currents were induced in the helix surrounding the soft iron: and when, at these instants, metallic contact between the conducting wires of the helix was broken, an electric spark was visible. The arrangement of the apparatus is shown in Fig. 18, A is the magnet, *a b* a cylindrical collector of soft iron passing through the axis of the helix *c*, and connecting the poles of

Fig. 18.

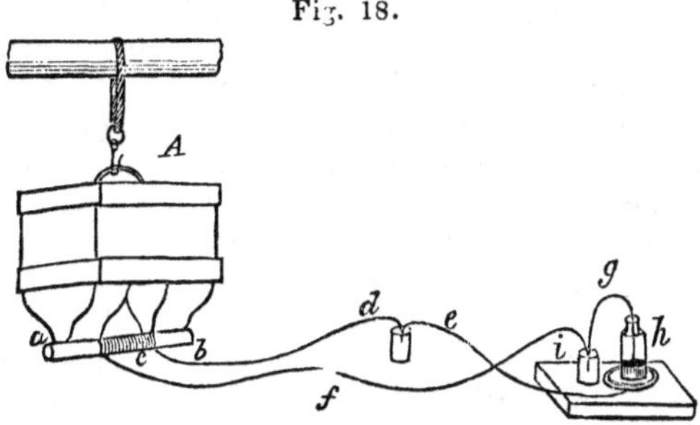

the magnet. The one termination *d e* of the wire passed into the bottom of a glass tube *h*, half filled with mercury, in which the wire terminated. The other extremity *f*, of the helical wire, communicated by means of the cup of mercury *i* with the iron wire *g*, the fine point of which may be brought by the hand into contact with the surface of the mercury in *h*, and separated from it at the instant when the contact of the connector *a b* with the poles of the magnet is effected. The spark is produced in the tube *h*.

In this experiment, therefore, the electricity was obtained from the helix, and was induced in it by the soft iron, while in the act of acquiring or losing magnetism. (*Phil. Trans. of Ed.*, 1832.) The same experiment was performed by Professor Faraday, with a loadstone belonging to Professor Daniel; and shortly before the experiment of Mr. Forbes, Nobili and Antinori succeeded with an ordinary steel magnet. M. Pixii, of Paris, performed this experiment in 1832, with great effect. He caused a strong horse-shoe magnet to revolve horizontally upon an axis, so that its poles should pass in rapid succession, in front of a soft iron armature or keeper of the same form. (*An. de Ch. et de Ph.*) Mr. Saxton, a native of Philadelphia, but at that time residing in London, made an important improvement upon the apparatus of Pixii.

At the meeting of the British Association, at Cambridge, in June, 1833, Mr. Saxton exhibited his improvement, which consists in making he keeper the lighter body revolve, while the magnets remain at rest; and, secondly, the interruptions, instead of being produced by the revolution of points, were made by bringing one of the ends of the wire over a cup of mercury, and depending on the jerks given to the instrument by its rotation for making and breaking the contact with the mercury. Fig. 19 represents the complete machine. A is a compound horse-shoe magnet, composed of six or more bars, and supported on the rests, *b*, *e*, which are screwed firmly on the board, B D, into the rest; *e* is screwed on the brass piller *c*, carrying the large wheel *f*, having a groove in its circumference, and a handle by which it can readily be revolved on its axis; a spindle passes from one end of the magnet to the other between the pole, and projects beyond them about three inches, where it terminates in a screw at *h*, to which the armatures, to be described immediately, are attached; at the further extremity is a small pulley, over which a catgut band passes, by means of which, and the multiplying wheel *f*, the armatures can be revolved with great velocity. The armatures as seen at F, are nothing more than electro-magnets; two pieces of round iron are attached to a cross piece, into the centre of which the spindle *h* screws; round each of these bars is wound in a continuous circuit a quantity of insulated copper wire, one end being soldered to the round disc, *i*, the other connected with the copper wire passing through, but insulated from it by an ivory ring. By means of the wheel and spindle, each pole of the armature is brought in rapid succession opposite each pole of the magnet, and that as near as possible, without absolutely touching. The two armatures differ from one another. The one termed the quantity-armature is constructed of stout iron, and covered with thick insulated wire. The other, the intensity-armature, is constructed of slighter iron, and covered with from 1000 to 2000 yards, according to the size of the instrument, of fine insulated wire.—(*Lond. & Ed. Phil. Mag. Vol.* IX, *page* 360.)

Fig. 19.

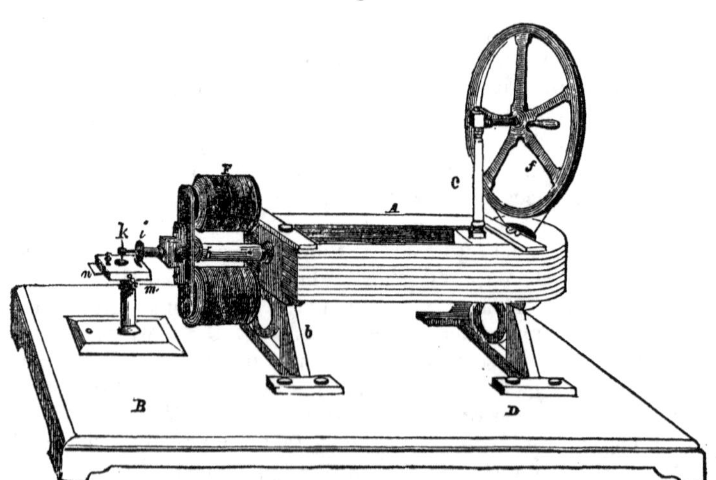

The quantity-armature is for exhibiting the magnetic spark, inducing magnetism in soft iron.

The intensity-armature, is employed for medical purposes, and for effecting chemical decomposition. This arrangement of armatures was an improvement by Wm. Clark of London, and was based upon the discoveries of Prof. Henry of this country, who found that an electrical current of quantity would induce a current of intensity, and on the other hand, that a current of intensity would make sensible a current of quantity.

According to Faraday, in the wire of the helix of magneto-electric machines, (as, for instance, in Mr. Saxton's beautiful arrangement,) an important influence of the principles of these actions of induced currents, is evidently shown. From the construction of the apparatus, the current is permitted to move in a complete metallic circuit of great length, during the first instants of its formation: it gradually rises in strength, and is then suddenly stopped by the breaking of the metallic circuit; and thus great intensity is given by induction to the electricity, which at that *moment* passes. This intensity is not only shown by the brilliancy of the spark and the strength of the shock, but also by the necessity which has been experienced of well insulating the convolutions of the helix, in which the current is formed; and it gives to the current a force at these moments very far above that which the apparatus could produce, if the principle of the inductive action of a current were not called into play.—(*Experimental Researches, Dec.* 8, 1834, *vol.* I, *page* 343.)

Another important improvement, or modification of the magneto-electrical machine, was made in 1838, by Prof. Page, of the U. S. Patent Office, According to Dr. Page's plan, two straight keepers, surrounded by coils of insulated copper wire, revolve between two powerful horse-shoe magnets, though much shorter keepers are used now than those he introduced. The steel magnets are fixed, with the south pole of one above the north pole of the other, at such a distance as just to allow the armatures to pass between them. The keepers are mounted on each side of a vertical shaft, in such a manner, that both keepers shall be passing between the opposite poles at the same time. They revolve in a horizontal direction around this shaft, while those before in use, revolved vertically around a horizontal axis. A little instrument, called a pole changer, was invented by Dr. Page, of Washington. It is composed of two semi-cylindrical pieces of silver, fixed on the axis upon which the keeper revolves, but insulated from that axis, and from each other. To each of the segments is soldered one end of the wire composing the coil. Two silver springs press upon these segments, and convey the electricity to the screw cups or point desired, by means of wires attached to them. The pole changer on the shaft, conveys the alternating currents in a constant direction to the screw cups, with which some metallic handles can be put in connexion for the purpose of giving shocks, &c. His improved form of the machine is represented in Fig. 20, made by Mr. D. Davis, Jr., of Boston, for Prof. Franklin Bache, of this city.

"Respecting the efficacy of this machine, the following is the substance of a statement in a letter from Dr. W. F. Channing, of Boston, to Prof. Hare, of this city. The unmitigated shocks from this machine are insupportable. When the wires which break the shocks are removed, the current becomes sufficiently uniform to be competent for electrolysis, or imparting magnetism to iron, included in a long helix of fine wire, comprised in the circuit of the helices of the machine. When sent through a circuit of a mile, the current from this machine was found abundantly competent to work the telegraph of Prof. Morse."—(*Hare on Electro-Magnetism*, p. 131.)

Fig. 20.

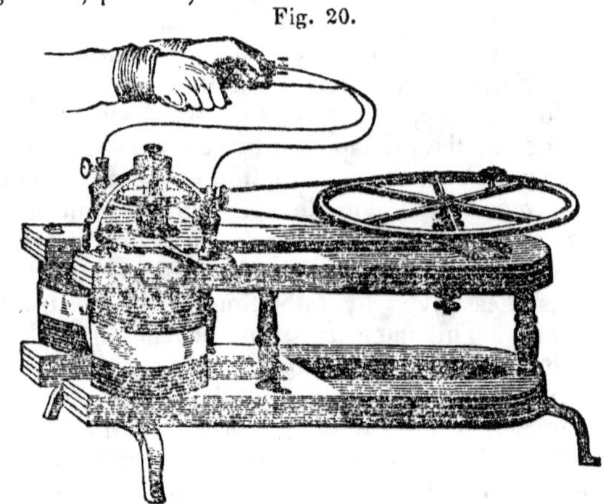

In Liebig's Annual report, (Vol. III, part 1, page 146,) it is stated that considerable improvements have recently been made in the magneto-electric machine.

Sinstedem, (Pogg. Ann, LXXVI, 29, 195, 524,) and Stöhrer, (Ibid, LXXVII, 467,) have published instructive suggestions for rendering them more perfect. Stöhrer has employed these machines, as it appears, with a satisfactory result, for the purposes of the electric telegraph. (Ibid, 485.) Dujardin, of France, has also used this instrument before the Committee on Electric Telegraphs, appointed by the legislative assembly: the circuit he employed being 140 leagues, by uniting two telegraphic wires at Paris and Lille, and employing a single magneto-electro machine, he caused his telegraphic machine to work with complete success, transmitting and printing under the eyes of the committee eighty-two letters a minute.

Many observers who have availed themselves of the magnetic-electro apparatus for the production of electric currents, have observed that the excitation of the current does not keep pace, as might have been supposed, with the velocity of rotation. In numerous cases, indeed, a maximum of the current-force has been observed to attend a certain velocity of rotation. This deportment has been explained by assuming that the production and disappearance of the magnetism in the iron cores requires a certain time. This explanation has, however, been proved by Lenz (*Petersb. Acad. Bull.* VII, 257.) to be sufficient for those cases only, in which the induction-currents set up are of a very low intensity, when, for instance, they have to pass through a great length of wire in addition to the coils in which they are developed. On the other hand, in the case of currents, which have only to surmount comparatively slight external resistances, their force increases, for equal velocity of rotation the more slowly, and, as this velocity increases, attains a maximum the sooner, the smaller the external resistance.

Lenz accounts for this phenomenon by the reaction of the induced currents upon the iron cores, by which magnetism is reproduced in the latter; the maximum of this magnetism coincides with the maximum of the current-force; not, however, for that very reason, coinciding with the maximum of the primary magnetism of the iron cores induced by the magnet, it consequently causes a deviation of those points of the rotation in which the induced current-force is at zero, or a maximum. The amount of deviation increases with the force of the current, and consequently with the velocity of rotation. It is therefore clear, why, in the commutators of the machine, which are empirically adjusted for the developement of the greatest current-force, (always in the same direction,) the change does not take place at the moment when the iron cores are opposite to the poles of the magnet; if the matter be only superficially examined; this is the instant at which the iron cores might be supposed to have attained the greatest possible degree of magnetism, and at which the induction in the copper wires would be at zero.

Electro-Magnetic Telegraphs.

When Œrsted's splendid discovery was announced, and it was seen that feeble electric currents would produce a variety of magnetic actions, electrical telegraphing received a new impulse, and numerous forms of telegraphic apparatus were proposed, of which I will now endeavor to give an account, describing each step in the progress of discovery, and commencing with

Amperè's Telegraph.

In 1820, Amperè, in consequence of a suggestion of La Place, was led to devise the first telegraph, employing the deflexion of the magnetic needle, by the agency of the galvanic fluid, which, however, it appears that he did not carry out practically. His plan was to have as many magnetic needles as there are letters of the alphabet, which might be put in action by the passage of currents through metallic conductors, made to communicate successively with the battery, by means of keys, which could be pressed down at pleasure, and might give place to a telegraphic correspondence that would surmount all distance, and be as prompt as writing speech to transmit thought.—*Ann. de Chem. et de Phys.* xv. 73.

The second telegraph was suggested by Peter Barlow, F. R. S., in 1825, that an instantaneous telegraph might be established by means of conducting wires and compasses.—*Edinburg Philos. Jour. Vol.* xii. *p.* 105.

In 1828, Victor Triboaillet de Saint Amand proposed to establish a telegraphic line from Paris to Brussels, by a metallic wire, about a line or a line and a half in diameter. He recommended to cover the wire with shellac, upon which was to be wound silk, very dry, which should be covered with a coating of resin. The whole was then to be put into glass tubes, carefully luted up with a resinous sustance, and secured by a last envelope, then varnished over and hermetically sealed; then, by means of a powerful galvanic battery, he would communicate the electricity to the conducting wire, which would transmit the current to the opposite station, to an electroscope, destined to render sensible the slightest influence, and left to each one to adopt at pleasure, the number of motions to express the words or letters which they might need.—*Report of Academy of Industry, Paris, from Vail's E. M. Telegraph, p.* 138.

Fechner's Telegraph.

Fechner, of Leipsic, in 1829, in his hand book of galvanism, remarks, that there is no doubt that if the insulated wires of twenty-four multipliers, corresponding to the several letters of the alphabet, and situated at Leipsic, were conducted under ground to Dresden, at which place the battery were situated, we could thus obtain a means, probably not very expensive, comparatively speaking, of transmitting intelligence from one place to the other, by means of signals properly agreed on before hand.

I confess it is a very seductive idea, to imagine that by future development of a system of such connexions at some time, a communication between the central point and the parts of a country can be established, which shall consume no time like communication between the central point of our organism and its members, by means of the nerves by what appears to me a very analogous arrangement.—*Lehrbuck des Galvanismus, p.* 269.

"Dr. Ritchie, in a lecture at the Royal Institution, London, in 1830, endeavored to illustrate the suggestion of Amperè, and exhibited a model of a telegraph constructed after his description; the arrangement was, however, very complex from the number of wires employed, &c., and Dr. Ritchie was not sanguine as to the ultimate practicability of the scheme."—*Journal of the Royal Institution, p.* 183.

Schilling's Telegraph.

In 1832 and 3, Baron Schilling, of Caunstadte, a Russian Counsellor of State, had occupied himself with an electro-magnetic telegraph. The Baron, who was attached to the Russian embassy, at Munich, at the time when Sömmering was engaged with his galvanic telegraph, already described, was much interested in the experiments of the latter, and shortly after Œrsted's discovery of the deflexion of the magnetic needle, Schilling was led to devise a needle telegraph, which consisted in a certain number of platinum wires, insulated, and united in a cord of silk, which put in action, by the aid of a species of key, 36 magnetic needles, each of which were placed vertically in the centre of a multiplier. Schilling was the first who adapted to this kind of apparatus, an ingenious mechanism, suitable for sounding an alarm, which when the needle turned at the beginning of the correspondence, was set in play by the fall of a little ball of lead. An improved form of his instrument was exhibited at the Bonn meeting of naturalists, by Dr. Munke, in 1835, (*Isis. Nog.* 1836,) and is described in detail, in Gehler's Physikalisches Wörterbuch, 1838, vol. IX, iii. In this improved instrument, light discs of card board, attached to magnetic needles enclosed in galvanometer coils, are moved by the galvanic or magneto-electric current. Five similarly prepared magnets, arranged so that the round disks of card-board were only seen edgeways, were connected by wires with the distant source of electricity; according to the direction in which the current was sent, the magnet was deflected to the right or left, in the one case showing to the observer, the one side, in the other case, the reverse of the card-board disc; thus ten separate signals were obtained, which by reference to a telegraphic dictionary, gave any required number of signals."

"Professor Henry, Secretary of the Smithsonian Institution, Washington, says, that in 1832, nothing remained to be discovered in order to reduce the proposition of the electro-magnetic telegraph to practice. I had shown that the attraction of an armature, could be produced at any distance, and had designed the kind of a battery and coil around the magnet to be used for this purpose. I had also pointed out the fact of the applicability of my experiments to the electro-magnetic telegraph. I make a distinction between the terms discovery and invention. The first relates to the development of new facts; the second to the application of these or other facts to practical purposes."—*House Case*, *p.* 93.

Gauss' and Weber Electro-Magnetic Needle Telegraph.

Counsellor Gauss and Professor Weber, two of the most illustrious philosophers of Germany, to whom the science of magnetism is deeply indebted, entered nobly into the list in establishing, by means of electricity, telegraphic communication between the Astronomical Observatory, Physical Cabinet, and Magnetic Observatory, at Gottingen, the first notice of which is found in Göt. Gel. Anz., 1834, 1273, and in 1836, Schumacher Jahrback, p. 38–39. It consisted of a double line of wire carried over the houses and steeples at Gottingen. It was constructed chiefly for the purpose of being able to make investigations respecting the laws of the force of galvanic currents on a large scale, under different circumstances. The circuit employed in 1833 was about nine thousand feet; and in 1834 or 1835, at least fifteen thousand, but part of this wire was reeled. The form of wire employed was mostly copper, of the size known in commerce as No. 3, of which a length of one metre weighs eight grammes; the wire of the multiplier in the Magnetic Observatory was of silvered copper, No. 14, of 2·6 metres to the gramme. They first employed galvanic electricity by employing small sized plates, and found that the action was much increased by adding to their number. They repeated and perfected their first form of telegraph, by applying the phenomenon of magnetic induction, discovered by Prof. Faraday. The divers movements or the slow oscillations of magnetic bars, caused by the passage of the currents, and observed by the aid of a glass, furnished to Gauss and Weber all the signals which they wished in corresponding, but the number of signals which could be transmitted was few, and the time occupied by each considerable.

The main apparatus was a magneto-electric machine, and to this, Counsellor Gauss adapted a peculiar arrangement, by which the direction of the current can be reversed by a single pressure of the finger.

Professor Weber had a delicate apparatus for setting off an alarm of a clock, placed at the side of the magnet in the physical cabinet, by means of the current conducted from the observatory.

The telegraphing apparatus consisted of the following parts:

1. The apparatus for generating the galvanic current.
2. The apparatus for observing the given signal.
3. The apparatus for the sudden reversing of the current, or the commutator (*pole changer*).

In the column A, fig. 20, are two or three strong magnet bars (each of 25 pounds) united in one strong magnet—their poles of the *same name* (like poles) are visible at B. Over these bars the reel E is placed (of course having a hole for the bars to pass through), and around its external surface a copper wire (insulated by silk winding) is wound.

Fig. 20.

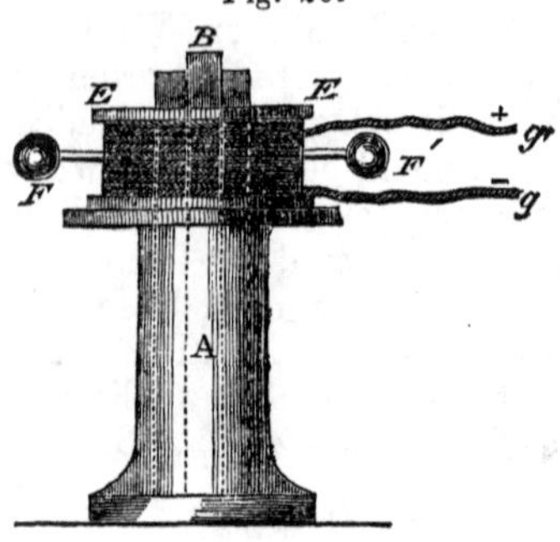

At the first arrangement, Gauss gave the reel 1050 coils; by a late arrangement, he increases the number of coils to 3537, with a length of wire of about 3600 feet; and still later, he used a reel with 7000 coils with a length of wire of more than 7000 feet.

The two ends, *g g'*, of this reel, E, (which on account of their inductive action are called *inductors*) are in connexion with a commutator (pole changer), and through that with the two principal conducting wires of the telegraph. If the inductor is taken by the two handles F F', and suddenly drawn off the magnet bars on which it rests, and immediately, without turning it round, replaced in its former resting place, there results two induction currents, one immediately after the other, in opposite directions, passing through the conducting wire; the duration of these currents is very short. Their intensity depends upon the strength of the united magnets in A, upon the number of coils in the inductor E, and upon the distance these coils are from the magnets.

Fig. 21 represents the *observing apparatus*.

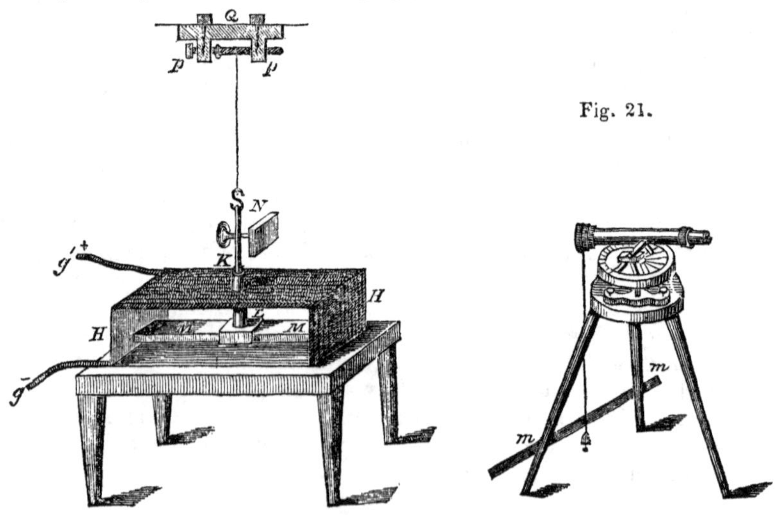

Fig. 21.

Whilst the inductor is set up at the station whence the signal is to be telegraphed, the observing apparatus is placed at the station where the communication is to be received.

It consists of a strong *multiplicator*, H H, that is to say, of a copper frame, around which an insulated wire is coiled. The two ends of the wire *g g* are connected with the two chief conducting wires coming from the other station, so that the multiplicator wire forms with the wire coiled on the inductor E, fig. 20, a single closed wire circuit.

At first, the multiplicator had 270 coils of wire, 2700 feet long; in later trials, it had 610 coils of wire, more than 6000 feet long.

In the coils of this multiplicator, there hangs for a magnetic needle a magnetic bar, M M, of at most 4 pounds in weight (later, 25lb. magnetic bars were used), which is suspended by a thread easily movable in the *little ship* L. This thread consists of 200 parallel cocoon threads, and is fastened to a wooden screw, P Q P, at the ceiling of the room, by which it can be raised or lowered.

On the brass rod K, which passes through the copper frame H H, there is a vertical mirror, N, which turns with the magnet, and is directed in such a manner towards the *cypher scale*, *m m*, fastened at the foot of the stand of the spy-glass, R, that the image of the parts of the scale can be seen in the mirror through the spy-glass.

3. The apparatus contrived by Gauss for the rapid change of the direction of the current was somewhat complicated—but any other simple *commutator* can be used for the same purpose.

The following is the mode of using this telegraph: At the station from which a communication is to be sent, the inductor E, fig. 20, is suddenly drawn off, and again, without turning it round, thrust down upon the magnet pole B, by which means two induction currents of opposite directions are passed through the conducting wire.

By means of the first current, the magnet in the observing apparatus, fig. 21, at the other station, through the action of the multiplicator's coils, is made to diverge in a determined direction, for example, to the right. By means of the second current in the opposite direction, it is immediately stopped, so that the magnet can make no further *excursions*, but only, in consequence of the two opposite currents, makes a little lively vibration to one side, and then immediately remains quite still.

These small motions of the magnet are observed through the spy-glass R, fig. 21, in the mirror N.

In a state of rest, the image of the null point of the scale, *m m*, is visible through the spy-glass; by the motion of the magnet, the mirror is also moved, and reflects to the spy-glass another part of the scale. In this manner, the smallest motion of the magnet is perceptible by the spy-glass.

Accordingly as the commutator (which is directly attached to the inductor) is fixed, the *first* induction current passes in one or the opposite direction through the conducting wire—and therefore, by a sudden drawing off and thrusting down of the reel E, fig. 21, a magnetic vibration to the right or left at the other station can be produced at pleasure.

By an ingenious combination of several magnetic motions, to form a signal, Gauss and Weber were able to make all requisite signs (letters and cyphers) with these two *motions* (*first blows*). 4*

The following are the alphabetical signs, as arranged:—

r = a	*r r r* = c k	*l r l* = m	*l r r r* = w	*l l r r* = 4
l = e	*r r l* = d	*r l l* = n	*r r l l* = z	*l l l r* = 5
r r = i	*r l r* = f v	*r r r r* = p	*r l r l* = 0	*l l r l* = 6
r l = o	*l r r* = g	*r r r l* = r	*r l l r* = 1	*l r l l* = 7
l r = u	*l l l* = h	*r r l r* = s	*l r r l* = 2	*r l l l* = 8
l l = b	*l l r* = l	*r l r r* = t	*l r l r* = 3	*l l l l* = 9

The variations of the magnetic needle signify a letter; *l* denotes a variation to the left, and *r* to the right, and by the combined deflexion of the needle, words and sentences may be transmitted.

Experiments of Messrs. Taquin and Ettieyhausen.

Messrs. Taquin and Ettieyhausen made experiments with a telegraphic line over two streets in Vienna, 1836. The wires passed through the air and under the ground of the Botanic Garden.—*Polytechnic Centra. Journal*, 1830, *Vail Electro-Magnetic Telegraph, p.* 189.

MORSE'S ELECTRO-MAGNETIC TELEGRAPH.

In the latter part of the year 1832, Samuel F. B. Morse, an ingenious American artist, while on a voyage homeward from Europe, conceived the idea of an electric or electro-chemical telegraph, and devised a system of signs for letters, to be marked by the breaking and closing of the electric or galvanic current.

Dr. C. T. Jackson, of Boston, a fellow passenger, well versed in the science of chemistry and electricity, and having witnessed numerous experiments during a recent visit to Paris, afforded him considerable assistance.

The following is a brief account of the methods proposed:—

1st. That electricity might be made visible in any part of the circuit, by dividing the wire, when a spark would be seen at the intersection.

2d. That it could be made to perforate paper if interposed between the disconnected wires.

3d. Saline compounds might be decomposed, so as to produce colors on paper.

The 2d and 3d projects were adopted for future trial, since they would furnish permanent records; the saline substances mentioned, were the acetate and carbonate of lead, which when decomposed by the galvanic current, left black marks on the prepared paper; again, tumeric paper, moistened in a solution of sulphate of soda, left brown marks on the passage of the current, produced by the disengaged alkalie. Platina points were also proposed to effect the changes in color.

Mr. Morse experimented for some time after arriving in New York, independent, however, of Dr. Jackson. While on board the Sully, Dr Jackson doubtless materially aided Mr. Morse in his conception of the electric telegraph, though they do not appear to have had any subsequent connexion, nor was the instrument they devised brought into practical use.

From a careful examination of all the evidence given by the passengers on board of the packet ship Sully, the telegraph devised by Morse and Jackson was not an electro-magnetic telegraph, but an electric or electro-chemical telegraph (see letters of Dr. Jackson to Mr. Morse, and Morse's pamphlet, and letters of J. Francis Fisher, Esq., of Philadelphia). Mr. Morse cast some type in 1833, but from limited circumstances, was compelled to desist from farther experiment, until his appointment to a professorship in the University of New York, in 1835, when he formed the annexed mechanical arrangement, which is interesting from the fact, that it is the basis on which a long series of improvements have been made to bring the instrument to its present unique construction. He exhibited it in January, 1846, to Mr. L. D. Gale, a colleague professor in the University, of high scientific attainment, who afterwards joined Mr. Morse in his enterprise, and made some useful suggestions for its improvement. But becoming satisfied that the electro-magnetic power was more available for telegraphic purposes, as exemplified by the experiments of Prof. Henry and his own trials, he directed his attention to that agent. Mr. Gale gives the following description of the instrument, in his evidence in the case of F. O. J. Smith *versus* Hugh Downing:—

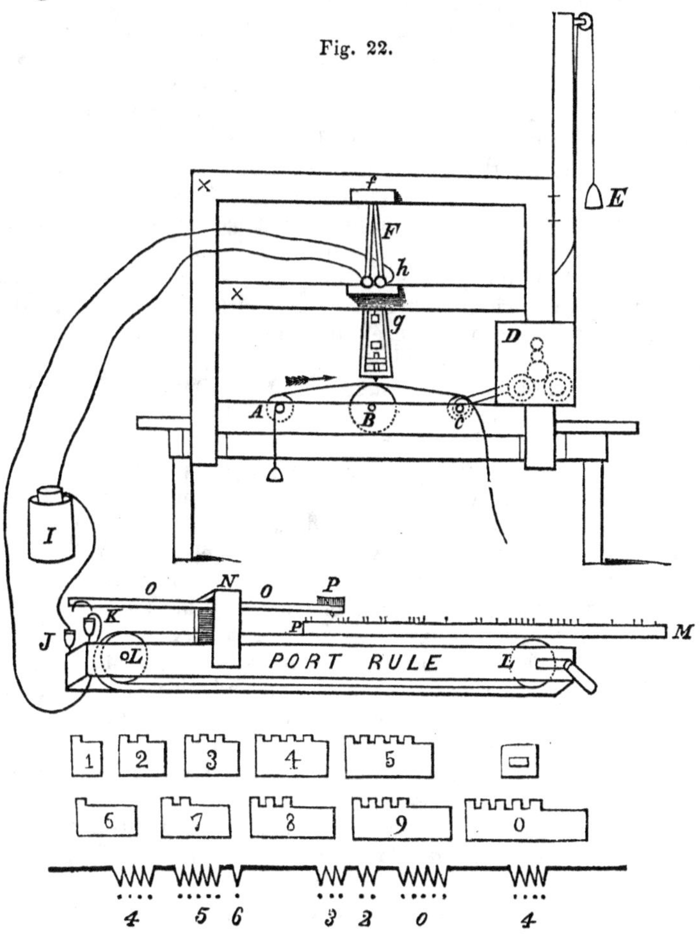

Fig. 22.

"A train of clock wheels were used to move a strip of paper, one half an inch in breadth. A, B, and C, are cylinders; the paper is unrolled from passing over the cylinder B to C, where it is connected to the clock work D, moved by the weight E. F is a wooden triangular shaped pendulum, suspended from the pivot *f*, over the centre of the cylinder B; its vibrations were across the paper, or at right angles to the motion of the latter. Through two cross-pieces in its lower part was fixed a pencil case, containing a pencil moving readily up and down, but kept in contact with the paper by a light weight, *g*.

An electro-magnet was fixed on the shelf *h*, which projected from the frame *XX*; this magnet attracted an armature affixed to the pendulum. One of the conductors of the magnet helix, passed to the single plate galvanic battery I, while the other joined the cup of mercury at the port rule K. The other pole of the battery was connected by a wire to the other cup of mercury J. The lower table represents a port rule; it consists of a rude frame containing two cylinders L L, two inches in diameter and two inches long, one turned by a crank, and that turning the other by a band one and half inch in width.

M, is a rule or composing stick, made of two small thin rules, two feet long, placed side by side, separated sufficiently far to form a trough for the type; the tops or cogs of the latter, are seen rising above the top of the rule M. A lever O O, is suspended from the united top of two standards that rise from the sides of the long frame of the post rule, on one end of which is a fork of copper wires that plunges when the lever is depressed into the two mercury cups K and J. A weight is attached to the other extremity to keep it down, and beneath this is a tooth, similar to the keys of a hand organ. There were eleven types one-eighth of an inch thick, having from one to five projections called cogs, save one that was used for a space. The first five numbers consisted from one to five cogs respectively, followed by a space, while the second five were the same, only having a long space double that of the first.

If, as an example, it was desired to send the number 456, the types 4, 5 and 6, with a space to separate them from the successive ones, were set up in the port rule M, which was placed on the bands of the port rule and sent forward by turning the crank; the cogs of the type operating the lever O O, broke and closed the circuit at the battery I; this being done, the magnet *h*, attracted the pendulum F, and moved the pencil *g*, about one-fourth of an inch; the pencil being in contact with the paper while it was moving, a continuous straight line was marked on it if the pendulum was stationary either at one or the other limit of its motion; but when attracted by the magnetic force, it marked a V shaped point as seen in the drawing; the points were marked on the moving paper as there shown by the successive breakings and closings of the circuits through the cogs of the type; the extremities of the V shaped marks were recognised for the figures by their number."

A dictionary was prepared, in which words were arranged in a manner that the numbers would represent them.

Mr. Morse found himself unable to make use of his instrument for great distances, from the resistance to, and dissipation of, the electrical current along the conductors. To overcome the difficulty, he adopted in the spring of 1837, a receiving magnet and a relay or repeating circuit. We do not know by whom this was suggested, but its principle is based on the discoveries made by Prof. Henry, relative to the intensity magnet. Prof. Gale, Dr. Fisher, and Mr. Chilton, had referred Prof. M. to these investigations of Prof. Henry. Prof. Wheatstone, of London, exhibited to Profs. Henry, of Washington, and Bache, of the U. S. Coast Survey, in February, 1837, a repeating circuit which was closed by the deflexion of a galvanometer needle.

Fig. 23.

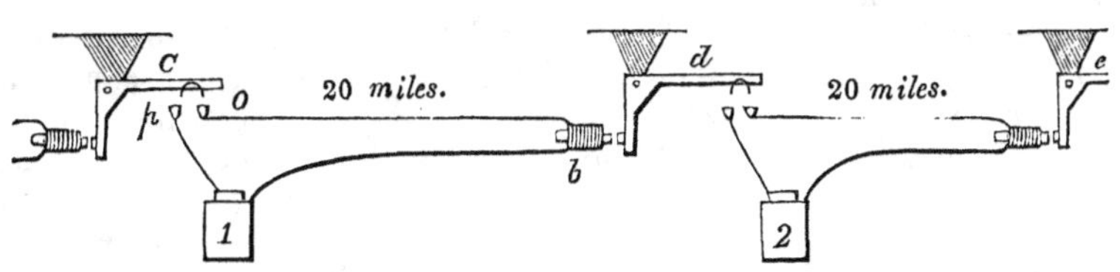

The one used by Mr. Morse is represented in the accompanying diagram. By means of the receiving magnet, the current of one battery was used to set off that of a second, the second a third, and so on, the last circuit being as strong as the first. 1 is a battery at one terminus of one line of conductors representing twenty miles in length; from one pole of which the conductor proceeds to the helix of an electro-magnet at the other terminus, (the helix forming part of the conductor;) from thence it returns to the battery and terminating in a mercury cup O. From the contiguous mercury cup, *p*, a wire proceeds to the other pole of the battery.

When the fork of the lever O, unites the two cups of mercury, the circuit is complete, and the magnet *f* is charged, and attracts the armature of the lever *d*, which connects the circuit of the battery 2 in the same manner, which again in turn operates the lever *e*, twenty miles further, and so on.

Publicity was given to it through the columns of the New York Observer, on the 15th of April, 1837, in consequence of an announcement that Messrs Gour and Servell had produced an instrument of miraculous capacity, to transmit information, which was, however, only an example of the visual telegraph; it was likewise noticed in the New York Journal of Commerce of April 27, 1837.

In September of the same year, an exhibition of the instrument working through 1700 feet of wire, was given at the New York University, to numerous visiters, among whom were some eminent scientific gentlemen. An account of this was given in the New York Journal of Commerce, of that date.

The ability of the instrument was so skilfully displayed, that Messrs. George and Alfred Vail were induced to "interest themselves in the invention, and furnish Prof. Morse with the means, material, and labor for an experiment on a larger scale;" at this time operations were commenced at the Speedwell Iron Works, near Morristown, New Jersey.

On the 10th of March, 1837, the Hon. Levi Woodbury, then Secretary of the Treasury, issued a circular, requesting information in regard to the propriety of establishing a system of Telegraphs for the United States. Prof. Morse sent three replies to this circular, containing an account of his invention, its proposed advantages, and probable expense, with a description of the kind of conductors required; two of these letters dated respectively, September 27th, 1837, and November 28th, 1837, were included in a report of the Secretary to the House of Representatives, on the 6th of December, 1837. In this report, Mr. Woodbury gave a favorable view to the subject of telegraphing.

Some extracts from Prof. Morse's letters, will show how far real progress has exceeded his expectations at that time, and the modifications that have since been made.

September 27th, 1837.—"The principal expense will be the first cost of the wire, or metallic conductors, (consisting of four lengths,) and the securing them against injury. The cost of single copper wire $\frac{1}{16}$ of an inch in diameter, (and it should not be of less dimensions) for 400 miles was recently estimated in Scotland, to be £1000 sterling, including the solderings of the wires together, that is, $6 per mile for one wire."

"Iron tubes enclosing the wires, and filled in with pitch and resin, would probably be the most eligible mode of securing the conductors from injury, while at the same time it would be the most costly." "Iron tubes of 1½ inch diameter, I learn, can be obtained at Baltimore, at 28 cents per foot. The trenching will not be more than three cents for two feet, or about $75 per mile." "If the circuit is laid through the air, the first cost will doubtless be much lessened." "Stout spars of some thirty feet in height, well planted in the ground, and placed about 350 feet apart, would in this case be required, along the tops of which the circuit might be stretched. Fifteen such spars would be wanted to a mile. This mode would be as cheap, probably, as any other, unless the laying of the circuit in the water should be found the most eligible." "I presume that five words can be transmitted in a minute; for, with the imperfect machine I now use, I have recorded at that rate, at the distance of half a mile."

November 28th, 1837.—"We have procured several miles of wire, and I am happy to announce to you that our success has, thus far, been complete. At the distance of five miles, with a common Cruikshank's battery of 87 plates, (4 by 3½ inches each plate,) the marking was as perfect on the register as in the first instance of half a mile. We have recently added *five miles more*, making in all *ten miles*, with the same result, and we have no doubt of its effecting a *similar result* at *any distance*."

The instrument was partially described in Prof. Silliman's Journal of October, 1837, which was afterwards copied in the November number of the Journal of the Franklin Institute of the same year, and the London Mechanics' Magazine of February, 1838.

A model enclosing a circuit of ten miles of insulated wire wound upon two reels, was finished in the latter part of the year 1837, and intended for an exhibition before Congress. This was soon after shown in the Hall of the Franklin Institute of this city, where it was subjected to the inspection of a committee appointed to examine it; its operation was eminently satisfactory to them, and they did it the honor to give the subjoined favorable report:

"The Committee on Science and the Arts constituted by the Franklin Institute of the State of Pennsylvania, for the promotion of the Mechanic

Arts, to whom was referred for an examination, an electro-magnetic telegraph, invented by Prof. F. B. Morse, of the city of New York, report—That this instrument was exhibited to them in the Hall of this Institute, and every opportunity given by Mr. Morse and his associate, Mr. Alfred Vail, to examine it carefully, and to judge of its operation. * * * *

"As exhibited to us, it was very satisfactory. The power given to the magnet at the register, through a length of wire of ten miles, was abundantly sufficient for the movements required to make the signals. The communication of this power was instantaneous. The time required to make the signals was as short at least as that necessary in the ordinary telegraphs. It appears to the committee, therefore, that the possibility of using telegraphs on this plan, in actual practice, is not to be doubted, though difficulties may be anticipated which could not be tested with the trial made with the model.

"One of these relates to the insulation and protection of the wires, which are to pass over many miles of distance, to form the circuits between the stations. Mr. Morse has proposed several plans; the last being to cover the wires with cotton thread, then varnish them thickly with gum elastic, and enclose the whole in leaden tubes. More practical and economical means will probably be devised; but the fact is not to be concealed, that any effectual plan must be very expensive. Doubts have been raised as to the distance to which the current of an ordinary battery can be made efficient; but the committee think no serious difficulty is to be anticipated on this point. * * * *

"An experiment is said to have been made on the Birmingham and Manchester railroad, through a circuit of thirty miles in length.

"It may be proper to state, that the idea of using electro-magnetism for telegraphic purposes has presented itself to several different individuals, and that it may be difficult to settle among them the question of originality.

"The celebrated Gauss has a telegraph of this kind in actual operation, for communicating signals between the University of Gottingen and his magnetic observatory in its vicinity. Mr. Wheatstone, of London, has been for some time also engaged in experiments on an electro-magnetic telegraph. But the plan of Prof. Morse is, so far as the committee are informed, entirely different from those devised by other individuals, all of which act by giving different *directions* to magnetic needles, and would therefore require several circuits of wires between all the stations.

"In conclusion, the committee beg to state their high appreciation of Prof. Morse's telegraph, and the hope that means may be given him to subject it to the test of an actual experiment made between stations at a considerable distance from each other. The advantages which this telegraph would present, if successful, over every kind heretofore used, make it worthy of the patronage of the government. These are, that the stations may be at a distance asunder far exceeding that to which other telegraphs are limited, and that the signals may be given at night, and in rains, snow, and fogs, when other telegraphs fail.

"By order of the Committee.

"William Hamilton, *Actuary.*

"*Philadelphia, February* 8, 1838."

It was subsequently taken to Washington, and kept in successful operation for several months in the room of the House Committee of Commerce, where it was visited by multitudes of people.

The examining committee were propitious to it, and in a warm and ardent report made on the 6th of April, 1838, urgently advised that it should be subjected to an adequate trial.

Prof. Morse sent in a caveat to secure his invention in October, 1837, filed his specifications, and made application for a patent in April, 1838, but withdrew them afterward, that he might be enabled to obtain patents in the European countries. Hon. F. O. J. Smith, a member of Congress, from Maine, was so interested in it, and sure of success, that he left his seat there, and joined Prof. Morse in a trip to Europe, in May, 1838. From the peculiar construction of the English patent laws (which require that the instrument should not have been published), he was unable to obtain a patent there, and though he secured one in France, it afforded him no profit, as his funds were too limited to bring it into operation within two years—the time specified in their patent regulations.

Though he failed at that time to remunerate himself as a momentary speculator, the instrument attracted the attention of scientific men in both countries, who accorded him much merit for the skilfulness of the invention.

It was put in operation at a meeting of the French Academy of Sciences, September 10th, 1838, and a description of it published in their weekly journal, the "*Comptes Rendus.*" On account of the disordered financial condition of the country, and his own restricted means, no farther advancement was made after his return, until June, 1840, when he secured his first patent, which was given on the specifications of April, 1838, for the rude instrument already described, including a second electro-magnet used to give an alarm, without the improvement up to the former date.

Unable to proceed further on a more extensive scale of experiment, he procured the support of prominent scientific men in a petition to Congress during the December Session of 1842. Prof. J. Henry, in a deposition made in March, 1850, states of Mr. Morse as follows:

"Shortly after my return from Europe, in the autumn of 1837, I learned that Mr. Morse was about to petition Congress for assistance in constructing the electro-magnetic telegraph; some of my friends in Princeton, knowing what I had done in developing the principles of the telegraph, urged me to make the representation to Congress, which I had expressed some thoughts of doing, namely, that the principles of the electro-magnetic telegraph belong to the science of the world, and that any appropriation which might be made by Congress, should be as a premium for the best plan, and the means of testing the same, which the ingenuity of the country might offer. Shortly after this, I visited New York, and there accidentally made the personal acquaintance of Mr. Morse. He appeared to be an unassuming and prepossessing gentleman, with very little knowledge of the general principles of electricity, magnetism, or electro-magnetism. He made no claims, in conversation with me, to any scientific discoveries, or to anything beyond his particular machine and process of applying known principles to telegraphic purposes. He explained to me his plan of a telegraph, with which he had recently made a successful experiment. I thought this plan better than any with which I had been made acquainted in Europe. I became interested in him, and instead of interfering with his application to Congress, I gave him a certificate in the form of a letter, stating my confidence in the practicability of the electro-magnetic telegraph, and my belief that the form proposed by himself was the best that had been published.

"Mr. Morse subsequently visited Princeton several times, to confer with me on the principles of electricity and magnetism, which might be applicable to the telegraph. I freely gave him any information which I possessed."

In respondence to his petition, Congress appropriated $30,000 for the purpose of testing its practical application. Thus enabled to prosecute his favorite theme with a freer element and more liberal spirit of investigation, he had the great gratification to exhibit to the American people his invention, working in an eminently successful manner, for a distance of forty miles, between the cities of Baltimore and Washington, in the month of June, 1844.

Prof. Morse has obtained for his instrument several distinct patents; the first was dated June 20, 1840; there were many important modifications introduced, such as a signal lever key substituted for the port rule, and a lever in the register in place of the pendulum, when it was exhibited before Congress, in 1838; this was re-issued January 15, 1846. A second patent was taken out on the 11th of April, 1846, containing the above alterations, with the addition of a local circuit and register, receiving magnet and adjuster, self-regulating break, the metal pen points, and grooved rollers for them to work in.

The device of the local circuit in the Morse Telegraph was founded in part upon the experiments of Prof. Henry, who had previous to this, "opened the circuit of a large quantity magnet at Princeton, when loaded with several hundred pounds, by attracting upwards a small piece of movable wire, by means of a small intensity magnet, connected with a long wire circuit and an intensity battery."

The re-issued patent of January 15th, 1846, and the patent of 11th of April, 1846, were both re-issued on the 13th of June 1848, and another patent containing improvements in the electric Telegraph was taken out on the 1st of May, 1849.

The line between Baltimore and Washington, is the only one constructed under governmental patronage, the remainder having been projected by private enterprise; the patentee being allowed one half the stock for the use of the patent, as his share of the investment; the capital invested in them up to January 1st, 1850, was nearly $400,000, exclusive of the patent right, upon which Prof. Morse up to that time had received some $30,000. The machine at present in use, consists of three main portions, the transmitting and receiving apparatuses with the connecting circuit.

The spring lever key as at present used in the Morse Office, was suggested by Mr. Thomas C. Avery, of New York, but has received various modifications; in Fig. 24, we have a view of its present improved form:

Fig. 24.

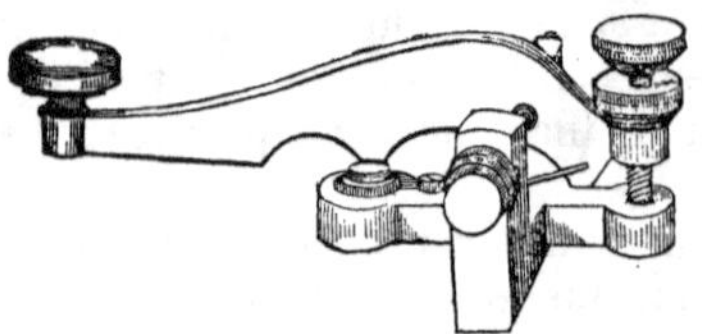

it consists of a nicely balanced lever, supported on standards raised from a small block of mahogany; thumb screws are fixed to each extremity of it, that on the longer arm being used for the operator to play upon, and the shorter one to adjust the distance of the connecting surfaces; on the short arm is attached a spring to keep those surfaces apart when not pressed together by the operator; the connecting surfaces called the hammer and the anvil, the former on the lower surface of the long arm of the lever, the latter on the mahogany support, are faced with platinum; they are respectively connected with the opposite poles of the galvanic circuit, and by their contact or separation, the circuit is united or broken.

If this key is at an intermediate station, by means of the screw on the short arm the surfaces are kept together; the circuit may be closed when not in use; this permits communications to be sent through the office between stations on each side of it, or rather it keeps the main circuit continuous; when operating, if they are merely touched, a point is made at the receiving station, if kept together any time a line is produced whose length is governed by the period of contact; the circuit connexions are beneath, one below the anvil, the other under the screw.

The receiving magnet is an intensity one, surrounded by a helix of

Fig. 25.

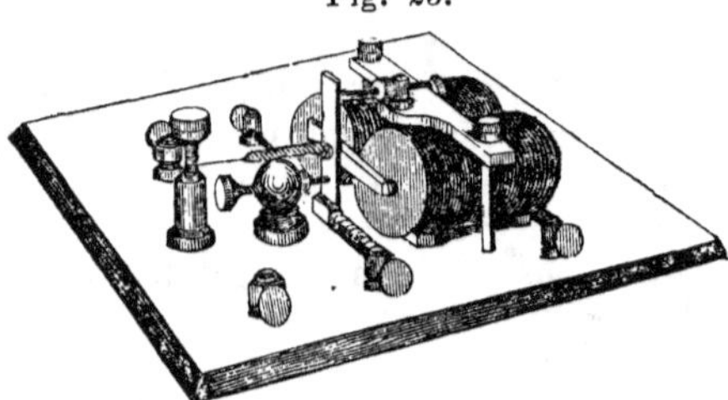

very fine wire, 3000 feet or more in length, having the horse shoe form, and fixed in a horizontal position. The main circuit passes through this helix unbroken to the next station; an armature is fixed to a vertical movable standard, opposite the poles of this magnet, in such a manner, that by means of a spring and adjusting screws, it cannot come in actual contact with the magnet, nor yet is it so far removed as to be beyond its influence; the object of this delicate suspension, is that the armature may be approached to or withdrawn from the magnet's influence according to the intensity of the current; much of the operator's skill depends on the management of this adjuster, as the varying electrical agencies of the atmosphere and generating forces of the batteries are constantly operating to increase or diminish its intensity.

The support of this armature forms part of the local circuit, the horizontal rod above another part, and that circuit is closed, by the attraction of this armature to the poles of the magnet, through the horizontal rod above, terminating in a platinum face, opposite another one fixed on the horizontal support above the magnet; the connexions of the local circuit are through screws seen on the right; when the current flows through the main circuit the receiving magnet attracts the armature, and thus closes the local circuit, the only place where it is open being above the horizontal bar over the helix: the local circuit is confined entirely to the office where it belongs, passing through the local battery and the helix of the register magnet, being distinct from the main; the registering apparatus has or should have, a quantity magnet of a horse shoe form, fixed vertically, the open extremity upward; the object being to indent impressions upon paper; force, rather than delicacy, is requisite. The figure from Davis' Manual of Magnetism, represents the mechanical

Fig. 26.

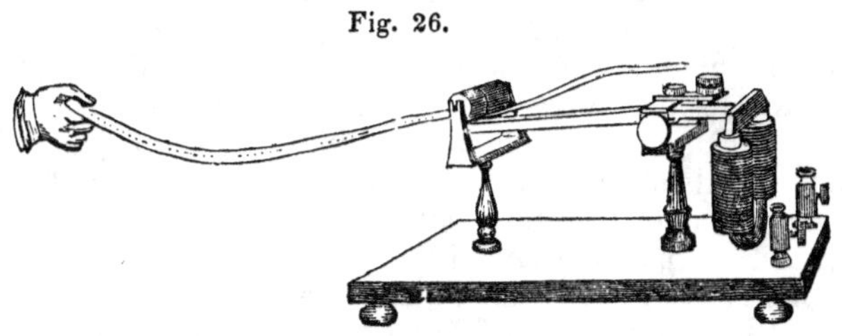

action of the instrument; above the poles of the magnet, is an armature attached to one end of a movable lever, which has on the upper surface of the other end, a metal point which fits into a groove of a roller above it; the passage of the galvanic current making the magnet attract and depress the armature, raises the points at the other extremity, and makes an impression on the paper in dots or lines, according to the duration of the current; a spring is used here to withdraw the armature from the magnet after the cessation of the current, which must be so arranged, as not to carry the armature too far from the magnet, or let the points too deep into the groove; a lead pencil was first used, afterwards a pen with an ink reservoir, which was laid aside for the hard steel points; the impressions on the paper resemble the raised printing for the blind; the connexion with the local battery is made through the screw caps on the right hand.

Fig. 27.

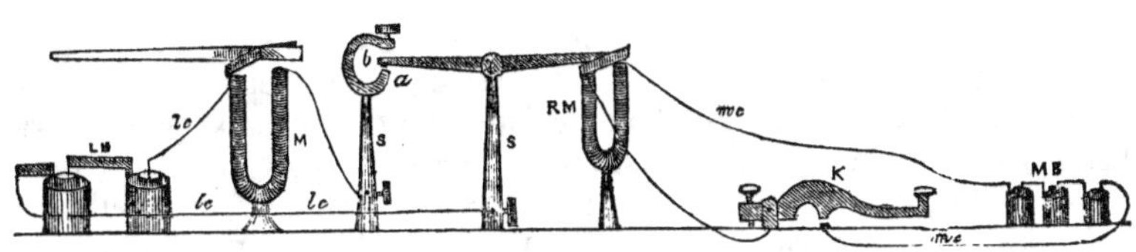

"Fig. 27 represents the arrangement and relations of the magnets, batteries, and circuits: R M representing the small magnet, *m c* the main circuit of indefinite extent, M B the distant battery, K the key which breaks and closes this extended circuit; *l c* and L B represent the local circuit and battery, M the helices of the register magnet included in the circuit, which, as the standards, S S, are metallic, is broken only at the points *a b*. Now, the least possible space between these points effectually interrupts the current, and as they are covered with platinum, a very slight contact is sufficient to establish the connexion. The little instrument is so delicately adjustable, that often, when the breath would stop the vibrations of the lever, the circuit is broken and closed with certainty and regularity; this is also shown on a larger scale in fig. 28."

Many forms of this instrument have been devised, some with the levers vertical; in others, the magnet was attached at one end, and the style at the other end of a shaft working through a horizontal tube.

The figure (28) slightly amended, from one in the *Phrenological Journal*, March, 1851, represents the whole combination of the registering apparatus and its connexions with the main and local circuits, together with the distant and local operating keys. The register occupies the centre of the picture, being supported on two standards: T is a spool carrying a roll of paper; this paper is prepared by manufacturers for this especial use, by winding it into large rolls, and dividing it into smaller rolls of one inch or more in width by a knife, while it is revolving in a lathe; from this spool the paper is drawn between the two rollers x and y, which are turned by means of the weight U, moving the clock work above it; D is the register magnet, E the lever, having the armature at L, and its axis or fulcrum to the left of it, also at the extreme left, the style playing in a groove of the lower surface of the wheel y; S on the right, is a screw to limit the motion of the style, a distance of one-eighth of an inch being usually allowed; it also contains a spiral spring below, to separate the armature and magnet; the paper is dealt off steadily from the spool, and a momentum is prevented by springs fixed on the axis of the spool between the latter and its standards; formerly a break was suspended from the lower surface of the lever upon some of the clock wheels below, to permit and arrest their motion, but this is now supplied by the small jack V setting into the cogs of the wheel W, the swiftest one in the train; this the operator pushes down immediately on the reception of a signal and the weight U sets the whole in motion, drawing the paper off the spool between the rollers x and y, the style impressing on it the required characters, and it rolls finally into the vessel on the left, ready to be read at the convenience of the receiver.

In the earlier forms an alarm was appended to call the attendant's attention, but this is thrown aside, as the click of the register answers the purpose; some experienced operators become so accustomed to this click that they can declare the message without referring to the character made by the style; thus it becomes phonetic, and operators conversing at vast distances, can make the little instrument by its varied action, slow, rapid, or impetuous, give expression to the different feelings of the mind; each office has its own peculiar signal, known to all the rest on the line, and an answer is expected as soon as it is given.

The machine is wound up by a key fixed to the axis of the largest wheel on the left; some guides are used to conduct the paper beneath the style with such regularity that several communications may be printed parallel to each other on the same strip.

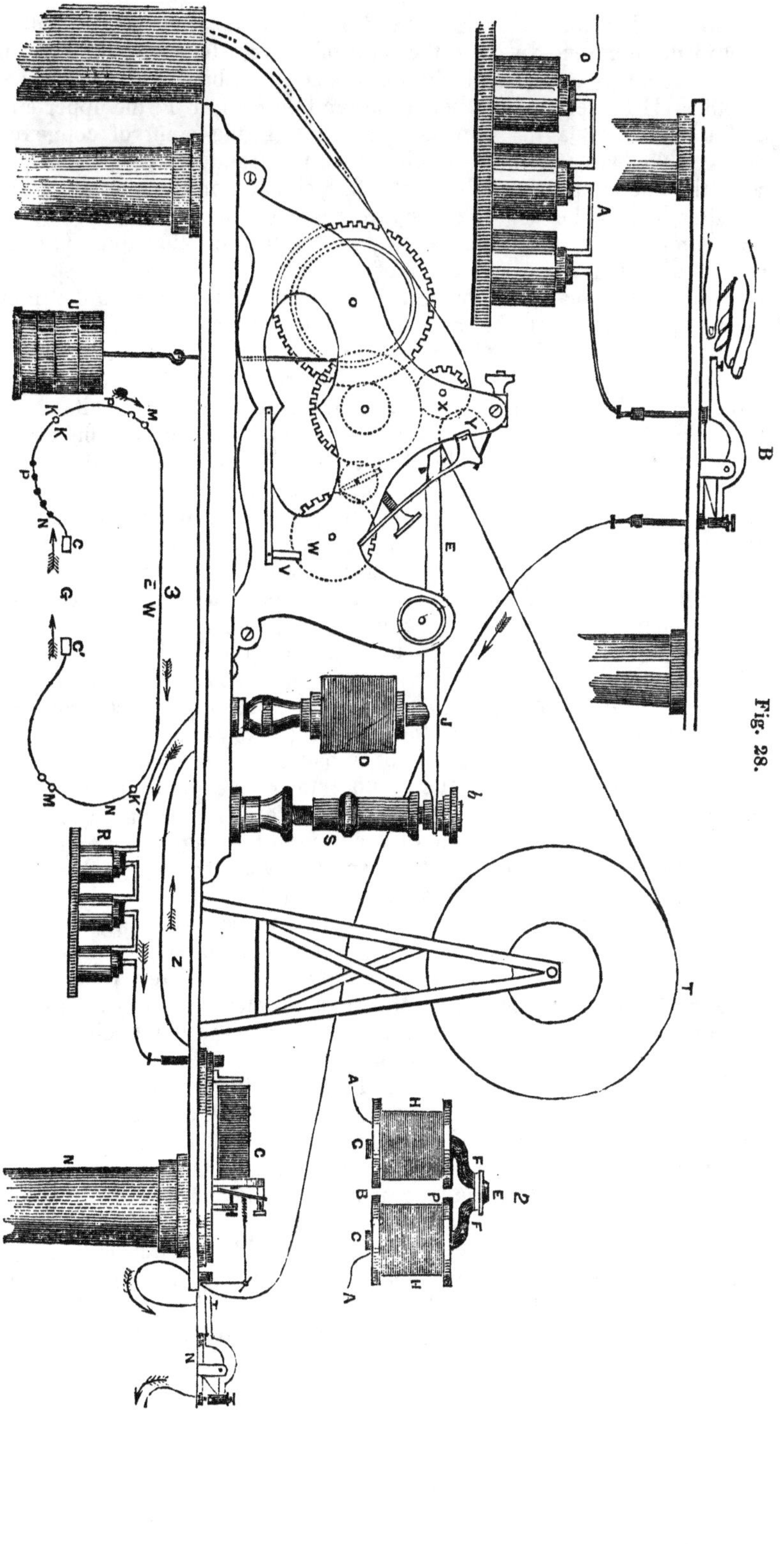

Fig. 28.

The peculiar form of magnet used in the registering department, is seen in the diagram No. 2, to the right of the register. A, A, the circuit connexions; C C, lower extremities of the soft iron bars, which are joined together; H H, reels of the helices around the iron; F F, the upper ends of the soft iron, having opposite polarities; P, the point of connexion between the wires of the two helices; E, the armature; B, above represents the operating key of a distant office, situated on the main line, with the attendant in the act of transmitting a communication; O, the main line coming from the distance; A, the battery on that line; Groves' battery is mostly in use, 30 cups of which are necessary in a space of 150 miles; they may be kept in one body, but it is better to distribute them at intervals along the line; they require cleansing and replenishing about once a fortnight. After passing through the key, the main circuit follows the course of the arrow to the receiving magnet C on the right, traverses the helix of that, and issues again from it, continuing its course to the right, to the next station, and so it might go on indefinitely, or around the world; N, is the local operating key through which the line passes in the same manner as at B; this is the entire relation of the main circuit to an office; it makes the receiving magnet close the local circuit, and it will do it not only at one station, but at all on the same line, and at the same time; so that an operator in Philadelphia, can transmit his message to St. Louis, and drop it at all the intermediate stations at one and the same moment; this has actually been performed.

Only one wire is now used on the main line, the earth affording the return circuit; No. 3, shows it very well; one end of the line may be supposed at Philadelphia, the other at New York; M M, receiving magnets of the two stations; K K, the operating keys respectively, P and N, the positive and negative poles of a battery on the line: C C, plates where the wires terminate in the ground: the connexion of the wires to a gas pipe, will answer every purpose; the arrows represent the direction of the current; G, that portion of the ground forming the circuit. By having two wires, one connected respectively to the keys and magnets of the different offices, communications may be sent both ways at the same time, but only one current can traverse the same line at once.

The local circuit Z is short, simple, and effective, being closed by the receiving magnet; C the current starts from the local battery R, consisting usually of from two to three cups, that must be cleansed every morning for efficient operation, runs through the helix D, back to the receiving magnet in the course of the arrow to the local battery; this causes the style to raise and make an impression on the paper; the whole operation then is very simple; the key depressed at a distant city or station, B causes the receiving magnet C, at Philadelphia, to close the local circuit: the iron of the helix D is made instantly magnetic, and the style goes against the paper, and stays there as long as the key is kept down at B. A simple contact makes a dot (·), a longer time a line (—). Considerable experience is requisite to make a good operator, either to transmit or read messages; some, however, become quite proficient after three months tuition; the interval between the times of contact, is regarded as well as the letter, for by its length, letters, words and sentences, are distinguished from each other; the adjoined table contains the Morse Telegraphic characters.

A	- —	J	— - — -	S	- - -	Numerals.		9	— - - —
B	— - - -	K	— - —	T	—	1	- — — -	0	———
C	- - -	L	——	U	- - —	2	- - — - -		
D	— - -	M	— —	V	- - - —	3	- - - — -		
E	-	N	— -	W	- ——	4	- - - - —		
F	- — -	O	- -	X	- — - -	5	— — —		
G	— — -	P	- - - - -	Y	- - — - -	6	- - - - - -		
H	- - - -	Q	- - — -	Z	- - - -	7	— — - -		
I	- -	R	- - -	&	- - - -	8	— - - - -		

If an operator at Philadelphia, wishes to send a communication to Baltimore, he first breaks the main circuit by opening the operating key at his station. All the receiving magnets in that circuit cease to attract their armatures, the spring draws them away from the magnets, and thus breaks all the short office circuits. The Philadelphia operator then makes the signal for Baltimore, by tapping on his key, the proper number of times; this produces a clicking of the registers, which is heard and understood in all the offices on the line, though none but the Baltimore operator pays any regard to it.

Then the Baltimore operator opens his transmitting or operating key, and breaks the main circuit in another place, so that the Philadelphia operator cannot operate his main circuit, which the latter discovers by the silence of his own receiving magnet when he operates his key; he then closes his key to permit the operator at Baltimore to return an answer.

The Baltimore operator closes his key, sets his clock work in motion, and returns word that his Philadelphia correspondent may send his communication, which the latter hears, and goes to work accordingly.

If the Philadelphia operator wishes to telegraph his message to several or all the stations on the line, he makes in succession, all the signals of those offices, and awaits their replies; after receiving them all, he commences to operate, and the communication is received by every one of them at the same moment.

The daily performance of this machine is to transmit from 8000 to 9000 letters per hour; there are a number of attendants needed about an office transacting much business, each one of whom has his respective department: they are divided into "copyists, book keepers, battery keepers, messengers, line inspectors and repairers"; the usual charge of transmission is 25 cts. for ten words sent one hundred miles; the messages vary in value from 10 cts. to $100; the amount of business which a well conducted office can perform, and the nett proceeds arising therefrom, may well excite our surprise; a single office in this country with two wires, one 500, the other 200 miles in length, after spending three hours in the transmission of public news, telegraphed in a single day, 450 private messages averaging 25 words each, besides the address, sixty of which were sent in rotation, without a word of repetition.

The public journals, however, often contain notices of errors committed by the operators on these lines, which, from their importance, have been the cause of considerable complaint among business and newsmen. This is variously attributed to careless attendants, disarrangement of the circuits, or the alphabetic combination, which renders the best receivers and copyists liable to mistake; this is not all, for instances can be cited where messages sent immediately, as the clerks promised to do, would have answered the desired end, but being delayed three hours, were utterly valueless.

Several important things are necessary to the successful operation of the instrument; skilful manipulators, good batteries and machines, and more than all, thorough insulation of the conductors; the latter can never be completely accomplished, as the best non-conductors will conduct in a slight degree. Copper wire first employed, has, on account of expense, been laid aside for iron, of which 300 lbs. are required to a mile: the method of insulation consists in winding them around glass knobs, passing them through caps of the same material, or enclosing them throughout with gutta percha.

"The figure shows the methods of attaching them to glass caps, by supporting the wire from their side (1,) or resting them in a groove on the top (2,) these caps fit over wooden or iron pins, which are fastened on the top of horizontal cross bars, or driven into the side of the post; two blocks of glass in the form of a parallelopiped, and dove-tailed together in such a manner, as to let a wire, without any other fastening, slide through a central opening; the glass being surrounded and protected by wood; the most recent method consists of glass blocks, fitted in cast iron caps and supported on the peg by a heavy glass tube (3.) The caps, of whatever form, are either upon cross-bars, or supported by iron staples driven into the post."

Fig. 28.

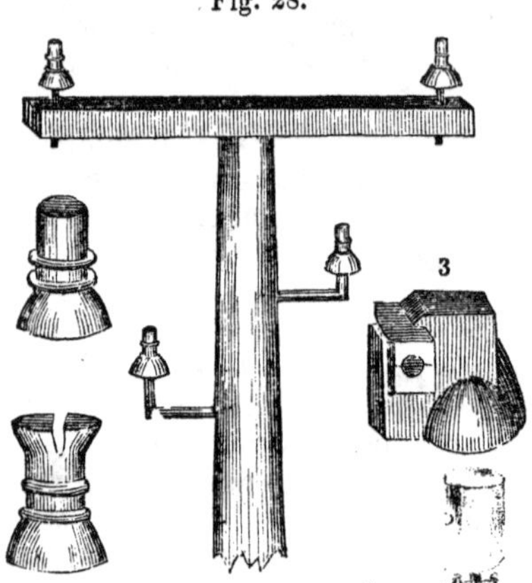

Notwithstanding these precautions, by the contact of wires blown about by winds, moisture, &c., connexions are made through the ground or otherwise, and a short circuit is formed, instead of going the entire route of the line, or part of the current of greatly diminished intensity, pursues the latter course.

The following method of ascertaining the existence of a break, or forming connexions with different offices at will, is well described by Mr. Chas. T. Chester of New York, in Silliman's Journal, Vol. v. 2d, series. It has been found that the intermediate offices on a main line are of great utility in determining the situation of the breech.

If the circuit is broken on one side, a current is at once obtained from the battery of the unbroken side, and the accident found is repaired. The diagram shows how to apply this test, and the method of dividing the long line into sections. The black dots, A B C D, in Fig. 31, represent brass terminations of conductors, sunk on a level with the surface of the operator's table; a metallic button, fig. 30, plays over their surface. This

Fig. 30.

button connects each brass stud with its opposite, and a change in its position changes the direction and channel of the current at pleasure. Thus, the intermediate operator wishes to break and close the "through circuit, (this is synonymous with main circuit,) he turns his button, bringing B in contact with D; the course of the current can be easily traced. But again, cutting off his left hand neighbor, he wishes to converse with his right, the button changed so as to connect A with C, the current passes directly to the ground through his instruments. Supposing a binding screw at S, the left or right hand wire may thus be brought in connexion with the ground. The buttons 1, 2, and 3, are simply used as convenient duplicate keys, or circuit closers, when the operator is receiving."

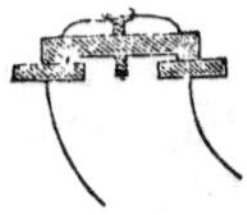

Fig. 31.

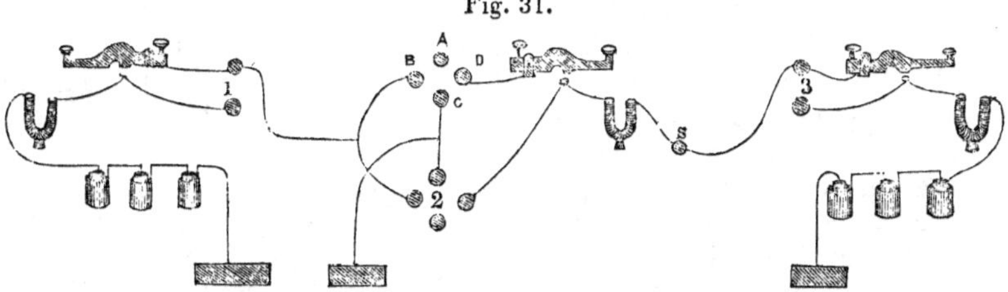

When the line is found deranged at an intermediate office, by the evidence of a current unnaturally strong or weak, the impression is that the wire is broken at one or both sides of the office. Supposing the wire continuous from one end of the line to the other, and a battery at each, the current passes through the intermediate magnet without interruption, and the circuit established is termed a "through circuit." When a derangement is perceived, the intermediate operator alters the through circuit, and by connecting with the ground, makes two short circuits.

Several methods have been devised to obviate the disastrous consequences that sometimes result from violent electrical action during thunder storms, such as the melting or breaking of wires, total destruction of long distances of the circuit, injury to office furniture or the operators connected with it; among the most important of which are those that combine the readiest communication with the ground to convey away the superabundant fluid; one is to have the circuit closer of a receiving magnet, employed for this sole purpose, pass into the earth; another is the metallic connexion with the surface of a brass ball, surrounded by a ring situated in and forming part of the circuit, from the inner circumference of which minute metallic points project towards, but do not quite touch the ball; both of these, however, are inefficient at times.

Professor Morse, has deservedly received the highest approbations of the American people for the invention that not only calls forth wonder at its accomplishments, but has proved itself an invaluable agent in political economy. Excepting efficient and economical batteries, most of the discoveries in this department of science had been made, which were essential to a proper foundation of his invention; some hand was necessary to elicit the remaining facts, combine and give them a mechanical arrangement and application, and then to thrust it before a distrustful public, to solicit the attention and patronage of the government for the proper attestation of its merits.

It was novel to the American people; no one had projected the thing here successfully, though many had thought of, and some tried it; through Professor Morse's indefatigable perseverance, the adjuvant resources of science were united in the form of utility; though dependant for most of his information upon others, he had the confidence in its final success, to master opposing obstacles, and bring to his aid, those who had labored honorably and prosperously in the progress of knowledge.

Wheatstone and Cooke's Needle Telegraph.

In 1834, Professor Wheatstone published a beautiful series of experiments on the velocity of electricity, which I noticed in the first of these lectures on the Telegraph. This seems to have had an influence in directing his attention to the subject of the Electric Telegraph. During the month of June, 1836, in a course of lectures delivered at King's College, London, he repeated his experiments on the velocity of electricity, but with an insulated circuit of copper wire, the length of which was now increased to nearly four miles; the thickness of the wire was $\frac{1}{16}$ of an inch.

When machine electricity was employed, an electrometer placed on any point of the circuit diverged, and wherever the continuity of the circuit was broken, very bright sparks were visible. With a voltaic battery, or with a magneto-electric machine, water was decomposed, and the needle of a galvanometer deflected in the middle of the circuit. Prof. Wheatstone gave a sketch of the means by which he proposed converting his apparatus into an electrical telegraph, so that, by the aid of a few finger stops, it would instantaneously and distinctly convey communications between the most distant points. The apparatus, as it is at present constructed, is capable of conveying thirty simple signals, which, combined in various manners, will be fully sufficient for the purposes of telegraphic communication.—*Mag. Pop. Sci.*, 1836.

This was Prof. Wheatstone's first telegraph, and having matured his plans, he took out a patent on the 12th of December, 1837, which was sealed on the previous 12th of June, 1837, in conjunction with Mr. W. F. Cook, who had devoted much of his time and attention to the practical application of the Electric Telegraph.

The principle on which this telegraph depended, was that of combining several peculiarly constructed galvanometer needles. It was an application of the famous discovery of Professor Œrsted of the deflecting influence of an electric current upon a magnetic needle, which I have already explained in a previous lecture.

"A signal board was employed, having five vertical galvanometers with double needles, the lower ends of each being slightly the heaviest, so as to ensure at all times a vertical position, except when deflected by the current. From the ends of these needles lines were drawn, both above and below, as in fig. 32, and at the points where these lines intersected, letters and numbers were placed. When an electric current was transmitted so as to deflect at the same time two of the needles, they indicate, by their convergence, one or other of the letters marked on the signal board. Thus, if the first and fifth needles converged above, they pointed to A, if below, to Y; or if the first and fourth converged above, they indicated B, and so on.

Fig. 32.

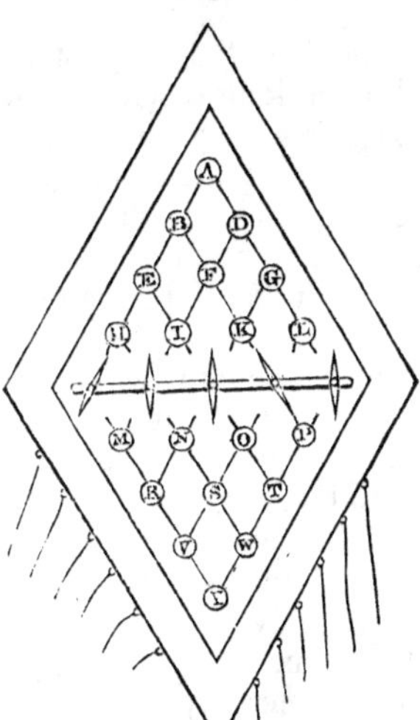

The signal boards were placed at either end of the line of telegraph, having a battery and keys so arranged as to render it easy to deflect at pleasure any of the five galvanometer needles at the distant station: the two sets of galvanometers being connected by six wires, one for each separate needle, and one as a return common to them all. The keys used to connect these wires with the battery were very simple, and at the same time perfectly efficient.

The arrangement consisted of five copper bars, thin enough to be elastic, fastened to a cross-piece of wood, as at A, fig. 33, and connected with the five wires of the telegraph, whilst their other ends pressed slightly, (but so as to be in good metallic contact,) against a cross-piece of copper, B. The terminal wires of the voltaic battery were attached to two small bars of metal, C D, and in the five longer bars, just where they crossed the battery bars, C D, there was a row of small metal pins, terminated with little ivory knobs. When it was desired to deflect any of the needles in the signal boards, all that was necessary was to press the ivory knobs above those bars, in connexion with the needles to be deflected; the slight pressure, by bending down the bars, insulated them for the time by breaking the contact at B; and the metal pins, by coming in contact with the cross bars C and D, became connected at once with the battery. By this simple arrangement the keys, though always ready for immediate use in sending a signal, were not any obstacle to receiving one, as the bar B, always completed the circuit of all the wires, except at the moment of using the telegraph, and then by the contrivance just described, it was thrown out of connexion. The wires of this first telegraph were insulated in tubes by means of a mixture of cotton and India rubber; then the prepared wires are all passed with certain precaution through iron pipes, which on some parts of the line were buried beneath the ground, and in others raised above it. It was afterwards elevated on wooden posts, as the moisture affected the wires, and destroyed the insulation. The battery employed by them was that of a vessel of copper, with plates of zinc, and acidulated water.

Fig. 33.

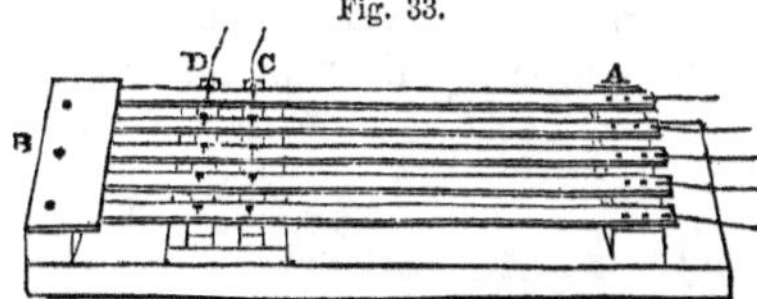

In order that the telegraph could be practically used, it was essential that some simple means should be employed to call the attention of the operator when a message was about to be sent, as the movement of the needles made no sound.

In order to overcome the difficulty presented by the very small amount of power which would be transmitted to a long distance, and which was not sufficient to make an electro-magnet of any power, and thus discharge an alarum, he placed a second battery at the distant station, having wires connected with a powerful electro-magnet attached to an alarum, or arranged so as to strike a bell as soon as the battery was brought into operation. But, as the circuit was broken, the battery, though charged with acid, and therefore ready to act, could not exert its magnetising power on the electro-magnet unless the circuit was completed. The current of electricity from the distant station from whence the intelligence was to be transmitted, though not powerful enough to make an electro-magnet, was abundantly powerful enough to complete the circuit of the second battery, thus waiting to be called into action. This was effected by a small piece of copper wire attached to a cross piece fastened to a delicately suspended vertical galvanometer; when the latter was deflected by even a feeble electric current, the copper wire, by having its ends plunged into two cups of mercury, completed the circuit of the secondary battery, causing the electro-magnet to attract its keeper, and thus let off the alarum to ring the bell. The general form of the arrangement is represented in Fig 34, which I have taken from a published lecture by Professor E. Solly of London, on the telegraph, which drawing proves correct on comparing it with the original in the patent.

Fig. 34.

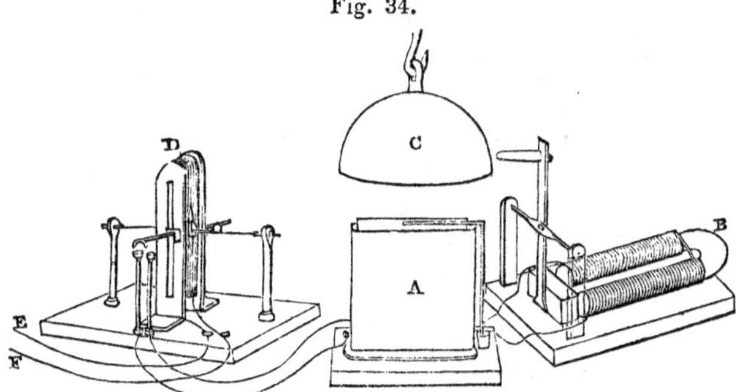

E F are the wires conveying the electric current from the distant station; D, the vertical galvanometer deflected by its influence; A, the secondary battery thus brought into action, and B, the electro-magnet which is made to act on the bell, C.

The line of telegraph upon the Great Western Railroad was finished in July, 1839, and had been in operation about seven or eight months. Thirty signals may be conveniently made in a minute. According to Professor Wheatstone, on his examination before a Parliamentary Committee on Railways in 1840, he states, "I have been confining the attention of the Committee to the telegraph now working on the Great Western Railway, but having lately occupied myself in carrying into effect numerous improvements which have suggested themselves to me,

I have, conjointly with Wm. Cooke, who has turned his attention greatly to the same subject, obtained a new patent for a telegraphic arrangement, which I think will present very great advantages over that which at present exists. This new apparatus requires only a single pair of wires to effect all which the present one does with five, so that three independent telegraphs may be immediately placed on the line of the Great Western; it presents in the same place all the letters of the alphabet according to any order of succession, and the apparatus is so extremely simple, that any person without any previous acquaintance with it can send a communication and read the answer."

Mr. Saunders, the secretary of the Great Western Railway, states the expenses of constructing the electrical telegraph on the line of that railway to have been from £250 to £300 a mile; whereas, the old form of telegraph in use between London and Portsmouth, independent of the original outlay, costs about £3300 a year; and the lines of telegraphic communication to Plymouth, to Yarmouth, and to Deal, were abandoned in the year 1816, on account of the expenditure for their maintenance.—*Civ. Eng. and Arch. Jour.*

According to the *Tyne Mercury*, the electric telegraph on the South Western Railway, from London to Gosport, cost about £24,000.

Professor Wheatstone specified a second patent for improvements, in the name of Mr. Cook, Oct. 18, 1838, still making use of the deflexion of needles as the signals employed, and using only two wires instead of five, and a combination of the two elementary instruments. It has two pointers, each worked by its distinct handle, and gave eight single signals, and a sufficient number of compound ones to admit of the twenty-six letters of the alphabet being used. By further conventional signs those letters are made to represent figures; and by blending both systems, a mixed sentence, consisting of passages from a code, spelling and figures, could be telegraphed together. The general form of the dial is shown in Fig. 35. Behind this dial a magnet is fixed on the same axis as the needle, so that both move together. A portion of the conducting wire is coiled many times longitudinally round a frame in which the magnet moves; by this contrivance, the magnet is subjected to the multiplied deflecting force of the voltaic current. The motion of this magnet is limited by fixed stops placed at both sides. The simple signals are given by the movement of the needles, either singly or combined.

Fig. 35.

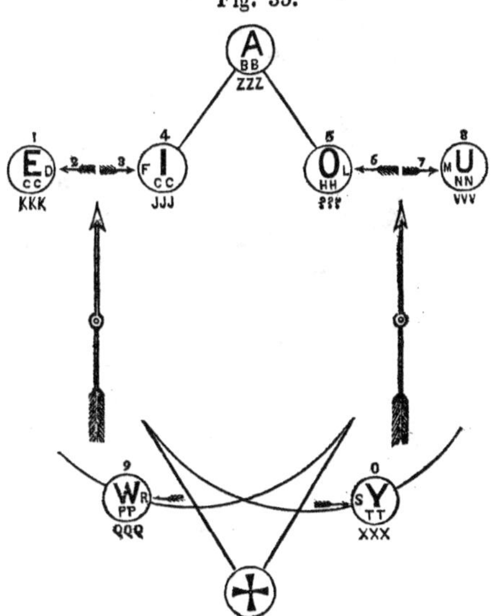

Thus the left hand needle moved to the left gives E, to the right I: the right hand needle moving to left gives O, and to right gives U. If both converge upward at the same time, their combined indication is A, and if they converge downwards it is +. If the pointers are made to rest parallel to each other in one direction, W is meant, and in the other direction they indicate Y. The consonants most in use are given by two movements of the needle, and those rarely required, such as J Q X Z, by three movements. C and U are generally used for K and V, but not necessarily.

Wheatstone's telegraph cost per mile £100. (*Mech. Mag.*, 1838.) This telegraph, which is the useful and scientific invention of Mr. Cook and Professor Wheatstone, has now been in operation for nearly twelve months; all the wires are enclosed in hollow tubes, not more than about an inch in diameter.—*London Mining Journal for* 1840.

The American patent for Electro-magnetic Telegraph, Charles Wheatstone and Wm. Fothergill Cook. Patent for fourteen years from 12th June, 1837, that being the date of the English patent.—*Franklin Inst. Jour., Third Series, Vol.* II. *p.* 120, *August*, 1840.

The American patent was of no benefit to the patentees, as it was never practically employed in the United States, Prof. Morse's instrument being the chief one in use from 1844 to 1846.

The defects in the practical working of his first and second telegraph led Prof. Wheatstone to devise a new form of telegraph, called by him an electro-magnetic telegraph, in January, 1840. The principles employed in this new instrument are well exhibited in Fig. 36 (*Daniells' Elements*). "It consisted essentially of an electro-magnet surrounded with a long and fine wire, A, and a keeper of soft iron, B, prevented from coming in complete contact with poles of the magnet, but so near as to be within reach of the attractive power of the magnet when the latter is under the influence of the current.

Fig. 36.

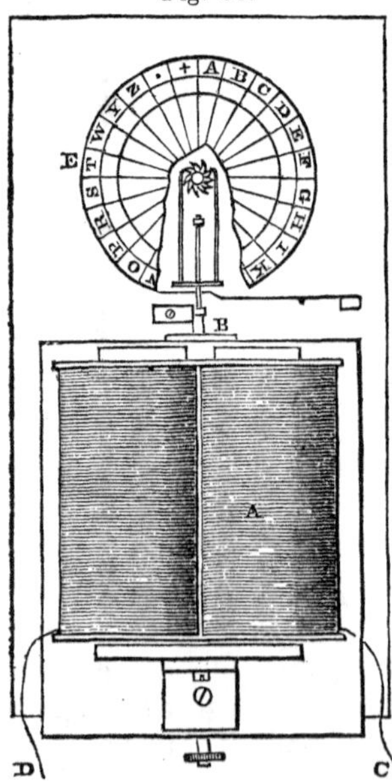

The motion of the keeper was made use of in various ways to communicate signals. In Fig. 36 it is represented as acting by a species of clock escapement on a small ratchet wheel, and thus causing the rotation of a light disk of paper or mica, E, on the circumference of which the letters of the alphabet, or other signals, are marked. In the diagram, part of this disk is represented, which resembles very much the signal dial of Mr. Ronalds, and is on the same plan. It is in part cut away to show the position of the ratchet wheel behind. The ratchet wheel resembles one invented by Burgengeiger, a German, to which he had attached an electric clock, as described in the *Morgan Blatter*, of September 23,

1815, and quoted by Mr. Ronalds in his work on electricity, published in 1825. Every time that an electric current is transmitted from a distance by the wires C D, and they may be made to succeed each other with great rapidity, the disk is advanced one tooth of the wheel, and consequently another letter; and when the electric current is interrupted, the keeper being no longer attracted, is drawn up again to its original position by a spring, and the disk advanced another letter. The whole instrument is inclosed in a case, having an aperture in front, which only permits one letter at a time to be seen. In using this telegraph, the instrument is always placed at the commencement with the sign of a cross only visible, which is before the letter A, on the round disk; if it is then wished to indicate the letter H, it is necessary to transmit four separate electric currents, in order to attract the keeper four times, and so cause the disk to move round eight divisions, the letter H will be exhibited. The transmission of the currents is managed by a little instrument represented in Fig. 37. It consists of a horizontal brass wheel, divided and marked on its upper surface like the disk of the telegraph, with which it perfectly corresponds; the circumference of this wheel is

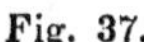

Fig. 37.

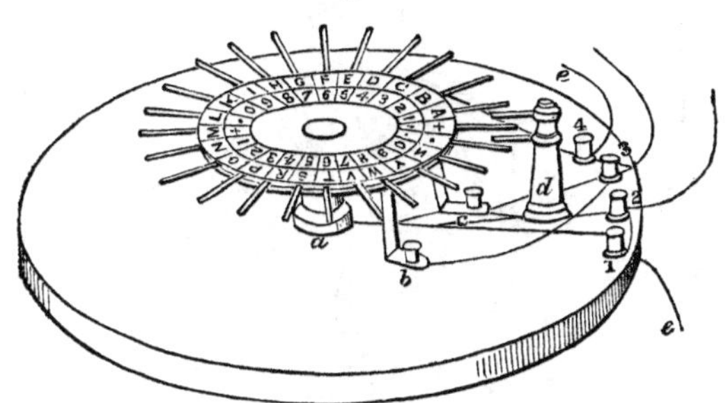

cut away in twelve places, and filled with small pieces of ivory. A metallic spring, *b*, pressing against the circumference of the wheel, is alternately in contact with the metal of the brass wheel and the ivory pieces when the wheel is turned round. When the instrument is not in use, the cross at the commencement of the alphabet is always placed opposite to the stop *d*, as in this position alone the metallic spring, *c*, by pressing on a small piece of metal connected with the stand *a*, cuts off the connexion with the battery, and therefore leaves the telegraph in a fit state to receive signals from the distant station. As soon as the wheel is moved from this position, the battery is brought into connexion, and as it is gradually turned round, the required number of interrupted currents is transmitted to the magnet. In the circumference of the brass wheel a number of iron pins are inserted, one corresponding to each letter, and, therefore, by taking hold of the pin corresponding to the letter we wish to indicate at the distant station, and rapidly turning the wheel till stopped by the cross piece at *d*, we cause the letter disk of the telegraph to revolve the required amount.

The preceding is one of the simplest forms of this telegraph, but the power is applied in many ways; thus, in place of moving the letter disk it may remain stationary, whilst a light hand or index only, is caused to revolve; or in place of an electro-magnet being used, the mere deflexion of a vertical galvanometer may be employed for the same purpose. But as it was found that a telegraph of this kind, though excellent for short distances, was not so suitable for long ones, a modification was adopted, in which the power required was greatly diminished, and the delicacy of the telegraph much increased. In this form a powerful clock movement, acted on by a strong spring, was employed to rotate the disk or index, the attraction of the keeper being only used to regulate the escapement, every current releasing a single tooth, and so allowing the clock movement to advance the disk one letter. He employed a magneto-electric machine instead of the battery, also doing away with the "communicator." Fig. 38 shows a vertical representation of one of the machines used for this purpose, consisting of a permanent magnet, A, an armature of soft iron, B, surrounded with coils of copper wire, and connected with the binding screws, E F. The armature can be made to revolve by the action of the larger wheel C, on the pinion D, which is thus caused to revolve just so many times by one revolution of the wheel C, as will give rise to the number of currents requisite to turn

Fig. 38.

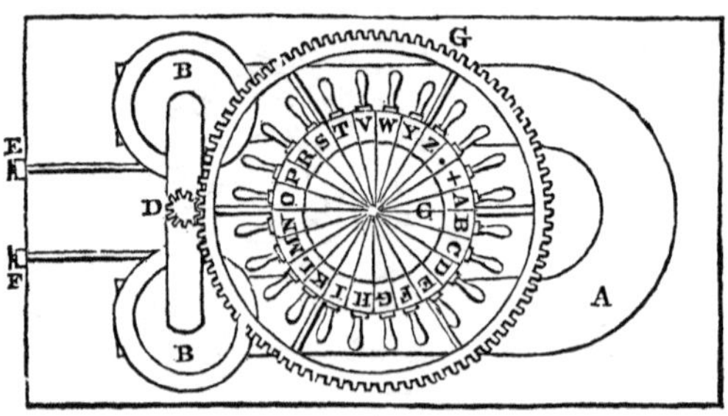

the telegraph disk once round. The whole of this instrument is inclosed in a box, and the axis of C, which rises through the top of the box, carries a solid brass wheel, G, having handles corresponding to the letters of the alphabet, and signals of the telegraph disk. I extract from the *London Artisan*, *Vol.* iii. *p.* 247, *for Nov.*, 1849, an account of the present condition of this telegraph in England, by Francis Whishaw, Esq.

The construction of the telegraphs, chiefly used in England, may be thus described:—Along the sides of the various railways (for by this system it is wise to have the telegraph wires protected, as far as possible, by a constant supervision) wooden vertical posts of fir timber are ranged at convenient distances. Each post is furnished with an insulator of earthenware, through which the wires are drawn, to prevent their connexion with the wooden posts. The wires are of stout galvanized iron, which are carried from one end of the railway to the other, except in passing through tunnels, or under bridges. In such cases, the insulators are attached to the brickwork; and thus the wires are prevented from being in contact with the brickwork. Each post is furnished with a lightning conductor, and is also capped with a wooden roof, with dripping eaves to throw the rain water from the wires. At each end of the telegraphs, the line wire is connected with an earth battery, consisting of a large plate of zinc or copper, buried in the earth—the object of which is to avoid the necessity of a return wire, which in the first telegraphs in England was made use of. At the various stations, one or more of Cooke and Wheatsone's needle instruments are set up, being connected with the line wires and batteries by wires of smaller size, generally covered with silk or cotton, which is easily destroyed by the alterations of weather, and, therefore, is objectionable. Each telegraph on this plan has two wires. The batteries used are of the most simple form, consisting of a trough, divided into any number of cells, according to the power required. Alternate plates of zinc and copper are connected throughout the pile, which dip into sand, saturated with dilute sulphuric acid—the use of the sand being to prevent waste of the acid in the battery, when required to be sent from one station to another ready charged. The signals are given by means of the needles, placed in front of a dial, on which are written or engraved, the letters of the alphabet, being moved either to the right or to the left. Each needle in *front* of the dial is placed on the same axis as a magnetic needle *behind* the dial, which latter is suspended freely in a space, surrounded by a coil of wire, through which coil, when the current is transmitted either in one direction or the other, the needle is deflected either to the right hand or to the left, as may be desired; so that, by a certain number of movements of each needle, and by the combination of the movements of both, every letter of the alphabet, or any numeral, is given. As many as thirty letters, under ordinary circumstances, are thus transmitted in a minute; but by expert manipulators many more. Although the requisite movements are easily learned, yet it requires many weeks for a telegraphist to work the needle instrument sufficiently well to be entrusted with a communication of any value, whether for railway or commercial purposes; moreover, it is requisite that the two persons communicating with each other should be equally advanced in the required manipulations. Some of the boys employed by the Electric Telegraph Company, have acquired wonderful rapidity in the transmission of messages; while I have known many persons give up the occupation altogether, although having no other employment to resort to. In case of a telegraphist attending the needle instrument being suddenly disabled by illness or otherwise, great inconvenience must be experienced, by reason of no one being at hand to take his place; whereas by other instruments, as that of Siemen's, &c., which can be worked by man, woman, or child, at five minutes' notice, this inconvenience is done away with. The exposure of the wires to atmospheric influence—to storms of snow, as lately experienced on the South Eastern Railway—to the destructive effects of trains running off the way, and to the destruction of the wires by malicious persons (rewards for whose apprehension have frequently been offered), are all fatal objections to the present English system ever becoming universal. Moreover, the expense to railway companies and others is a sad drawback to the further extension of this system in Great Britain and Ireland—for the railways of which alone an extension of at least 2000 miles is still required. The average charge for an electric telegraph, with two wires, as hitherto furnished to the various railway companies in England, may be stated at not less than 150*l.*

per mile; added to which an annual sum must be calculated on for keeping it in order, and reinstating, when necessary, the wooden posts, &c. The charge for transmission of communications by the Electric Telegraph Company's telegraphs in England, is at the rate of one penny per mile for the first fifty miles, and one farthing per mile for any distance beyond one hundred miles. The South Eastern Railway Company's charges for telegraphic communications are even much higher than those of the Electric Telegraph Company. Thus twenty words, transmitted eighty-eight miles, is charged the large sum of 11s.; whereas the same length of communication for the distance of 100 miles is only charged 6s. 3d. by the Electric Telegraph Company.

If we judge by the following remarks, some of the English journals appreciate the advantages of this form of telegraph.

"We have heard of things being done 'in less than no time,' and always looked on the phrase as a figure of speech signifying great despatch. The paradox seems, however, to have been actually realized in the invention of Wheatstone's Great Western Telegraph, a message having been sent in the year 1845, and received in the year 1844! It appears that directly after the clock had struck twelve, on the night of the 31st of Dec. last, the superintendent at Paddington, signalled to his brother at Slough, that he wished him a happy New Year; an answer was immediately returned, suggesting that the wish was premature, as the New Year had not yet arrived at Slough. Such, indeed, was the fact, for 'panting' Time was matched against the telegraph, and beaten by half a minute."

On the London and Portsmouth Electric Telegraph, (88 miles,) "Her Majesty's speech, on the opening of Parliament, was transmitted by the telegraph to Portsmouth, and published there almost as soon as in London. The speech contained 3600 letters, and was printed off as it arrived. It occupied about two hours in the transmission, being at the rate of about 300 letters per minute.—*Mech. Mag. Feb.* 1, 1845.

By the following decision of the Judicial Committee of the Privy Council, it will be seen that Messrs. Cook and Wheatstone were refused an extension of their patent, on the ground of their having been "sufficiently remunerated, and that the Electric Telegraph had not been so poor an investment as we have been led to believe by the English Press," as the share-holders have received a bonus of £15 per share, besides the usual dividend of 4 per cent. on £300,000.

"The Electric Telegraph Company sought to obtain the prolongation of letters patent which had been granted to William Fothergill Cooke and Charles Wheatstone on the 12th of June, 1837. The books of the petitioners were made up, it appeared, and balanced to the 31st December, 1850, and the subjoined statement will show the receipts and disbursements of the petitioners since the introduction of the electric telegraph:

Receipts from the railway companies for their use of the company's patents,	£122,285 13 2	
Receipts from maintenance and sundries,	7,301 13 1	
		£129,587 6 3
In addition to the foregoing, the company have received gross profits on the erection of telegraphs for railway companies amounting to		40,747 4 2
		£170,334 10 5

Carried over,		£170,334 10 5
Less charges, including part of the law and parliamentary expenses,		34,319 6 7
Making the total receipts,		£136,015 3 10
Total amount paid for patents,		£167,688 9 0
Showing that, after crediting the patent account with the above mentioned amount of £40,747 4s. 2d. received for erections, the total payments have exceeded the total receipts by		31,673 5 2
The Company have in their books charged the capital account of their commercial telegraph with £33,603 10s. 8d. as the estimated value of the patent employed therein. If this nominal charge be added to the amount of actual receipts, as above stated, the patent account will then show an apparent surplus for all patents of		1,930 5 6
The commercial telegraphs have yielded during the three years which have elapsed since the commencement of their working a total gross return of	£103,444 7 11	
At charges amounting to	83,265 6 11	
Showing a surplus of		20,179 1 0

Which surplus of 20,179*l.* 1s. is the total nett return upon a capital of 104,229*l.* 17s. 8d.—the actual cost, but much more than the present value of the patent—the amount actually expended in the erection of the commercial telegraphs; or upon a capital of 137,833*l.* 8s. 4d. if the patent account is to have the benefit of the above nominal charge of 33,603*l.* 10s. 8d.

The evidence which was adduced in support of the petitioners' case was chiefly directed to show the reasonable charges made by the company, and the accuracy of the accounts.

Their Lordships decided that, as the patentees themselves had been sufficiently rewarded, the company—who derived their right from them—had no *locus standi*, and therefore refused the application.

The following is an extract from "Newton's Patent Journal," giving the result of an interesting trial in connexion with the Telegraph above described. I understand from good authority that the Electric Telegraph Company have compromised and paid Brett & Little for their improvements, and intend employing them in addition to their Telegraph.

Opinion of Justice Cresswell, *in the Case of The Electric Telegraph Company vs. Brett and Little.*

Judgment delivered by Mr. Justice Cresswell as follows:—This was an action brought by the plaintiffs against the defendants for the infringement of a patent. The patent was granted in 1837 to Messrs. Cooke and Wheatstone, for "improvements in giving signals and sounding alarms in distant places, by means of electric currents transmitted through metallic circuits," and was afterwards assigned to the plaintiffs. The action was tried at the sittings after Hilary term, 1850, before Lord Chief Justice Wilde, and a verdict was then found for the plaintiffs; and in answer to certain questions put to the jury by the learned judge, certain special matters were found, on which the defendants had leave to move to enter the verdict for the defendants. A rule *nisi* was accordingly obtained, to which cause was shown; and in the argument the chief question raised was, what was the proper verdict to be entered in respect of the special matters found by the jury in answer to the questions of the Lord Chief Justice. To the third question, which was material, the jury found that the magnetic ring and indicator of the defendants was a different instrument from the needle claimed in the specification of the plaintiff's patent; and they also found, in answer to the fourth question, that "the sending of signals to the intermediate stations was new to the plaintiffs," by which expression was to be understood that it was a new invention of the patentees. The jury also found, in answer to the fifth question, "that the angular motions of the needles in vertical planes or horizontal axles, conjointly with the stops, was new to the plaintiffs," meaning that it was a new invention of the patentees. In answer to the sixth question, they found, "that as a whole the defendants' system of communicating with one wire and two needles was not the same as the plaintiffs'." It was insisted by the plaintiffs on showing cause, that on these findings they were entitled to retain the verdict in respect to the answers on the fourth and fifth questions. It appeared that the defendants, by means of duplicate coils and apparatus at the intermediate stations, had sent signals to all the intermediate stations, as well as between the terminal stations, and that they used an instrument moving in a vertical plane, called "a magnetic ring and indicator," producing nearly the same result as the needle described in the plaintiffs' specification. The jury, however, having found that the magnetic ring and indicator was a different instrument from the needle used by the plaintiffs, the defendants insisted that their use of it was no infringement of the plaintiffs' patent. The objection, however, mainly relied upon, was, that the plaintiffs' specification protected only the patentees' improvements as applied to metallic circuits, and that if the electric current was transmitted by improved machinery, not by a circuit wholly metallic, the improvements might be used without an infringement of the patent. The defendants using the earth to complete the circuit of the electric current, did not use a metallic circuit, and, therefore, they denied that the use of the plaintiffs' other improvements was an infringement of the patent. This was a grave objection, but the Court was of opinion, after full consideration, that it ought not to prevail. At the time of the grant of the patent the transmission of electric currents through metallic circuits was known, and also that the power of the current might be increased by coils in the wire. The discovery that the earth would complete the circuit of the current between the two ends of the wire struck into the ground, was made after the grant of the patent. The patentees did not, therefore, claim the invention of metallic circuits, but only improvements in the method of using electric currents—the currents being transmitted by a means open to the public. The circuit used by the defendants, so far as it operated in giving signals, and in all the parts to which the plaintiffs' improvements applied, was metallic: and it was not a necessary condition that the residue of the circuit should be metallic. The specification which claimed and described the invention was to be more strictly construed than the title of the patent, and the Court thought that the specification sufficiently comprehended all circuits that were metallic, as far as it was material to the improvements claimed that they should be so. And with regard to the use of the term, "metallic currents," in the title of the patent, the Court thought the title gave sufficient notice to any person acquainted with the discovery, or who had invented similar improvements to the patentees', to put him on his guard as to the nature of the plaintiffs' patent, and lead him to enquire how far any contemplated improvements would infringe it. The Court thought it but reasonable to hold that a claim for a patent for improvements in the mode of doing something by a known process, was sufficient to entitle the claimant to a patent for his improvements, when applied either to the process as known at the time of the claim, or to the same process altered and improved by subsequent discoveries. The next objection was, that the plaintiffs' patent was for a system of giving signals by means of several wires and converging needles pointed to certain letters, whereas the defendants used one wire, and made signals by counting the deflexions of the needle, which was found by the jury to be a different system. The Court thought this objection founded on a wrong discussion of the specification, which showed the patent to be not for a system of giving signals, but for certain distinct and specified improvements comprehending those now in question. The Court, therefore, thought the objections ought not to prevail to the grounds on which the plaintiffs claimed the verdict in respect to vertical needles and of the use of duplicates at intermediate stations. It might be doubtful whether the plaintiffs could claim the verdict with regard to the use of vertical needles by the defendants, considering the finding of the jury; but the Court thought that the use of duplicate apparatus at the intermediate stations, which the jury found to be a new invention, and which undoubtedly the defendants had used, entitled the plaintiffs in this respect to keep their verdict. If, however, the defendants' discovery enabled intermediate stations to send as well as receive signals, that was a very important improvement, for which the inventor might probably be entitled to a patent, though he might not be entitled to use it except by the license of the patentee of the less perfect invention on which the latter invention was grounded. For these reasons the Court thought the plaintiffs entitled to retain their verdict, and the rule must be discharged.—Rule discharged.

Steinheil's Electro-Magnetic Needle Printing Telegraph.

The next telegraph in order of date of publication is that of Professor Steinheil, the first published notice of which I find in a letter from Munich, dated December 23d, 1836, published in the third volume of the *Magazine of Popular Science.*

"Prof. Steinheil has fitted up a telegraph here according to the plan of Prof. Gauss, and similar in principle to that, which connects the Observatory and Cabinet of Natural Philosophy at Göttingen." This telegraph was in operation previous to July, 1837, but was not published and described until August, 1838. "His Memoir was communicated for the *Comptes Rendus*, July 19, and published in September, 1838. According to the authority of Prof. Morse, Steinheil's telegraph was adopted by the Bavarian Government, and was in actual operation during his visit to Europe in 1838. According to the same authority, in 1838, "Professor

Steinheil's telegraph was the only European telegraph that professed to write the intelligence. See Letter of Professor Morse to the Hon. C. G. Ferres, *Vail's Electro-Mag. Telegraph*, pp. 95, 97.

In the work of Dr. Schellen, published in Germany in 1850, it is stated that Steinheil's telegraph was in operation in 1837.

This is the first telegraph which I find on record, in which the earth was employed as half of the circuit—a most useful application of knowledge, gained at great labor, and not patented, but published freely to the world. His experiments are thus described by Dr. Schellen, in his work on the telegraph:

"Gauss had already conceived it possible to make conductors of the rails of a railroad, when Steinheil, in 1838, made the experiment, insulating the chairs of the rails by tarred felt; this was, however, imperfect insulation, as the circuit would not extend beyond thirty rails. To test the matter more thoroughly, he had some new rails constructed; but the points of contact were so numerous, and the establishment of a metallic connexion between the two rails by the wheels and axles of the cars passing over them so complete, that the current lost its force, and all idea of the measure was given up. This experiment demonstrating the conducting power of the earth, induced Steinheil to think of that as a means of return circuit, and thus dispense with one-half the wire. The fact by experiment he found verified, and immediately arranged his apparatus on this plan. This was a discovery of vast utility, and has contributed much to the extension of telegraphing. Steinheil says, you can make conductors of earth and water, as well as of wire, if you increase their size in proportion to the non-conductibility of the substance. Water was 100,000 times worse as a conductor than copper, and therefore the conducting surface should be made 100,000 times greater; in order to obtain this large conducting medium, it is necessary that the wires should terminate in submerged plates of the re-quired dimensions to include that medium between them. The same idea was afterwards brought forward by Dr. Cox, of this city, in regard to the use of railroads for telegraphic purposes, in September, 1845.

Steinhiel's alphabet is one of great beauty and simplicity, displaying the man of learning and refinement; as, for example, his musical bells, producing sounds which, striking upon a cultivated ear, conveyed a telegraphic language in imitation of the human voice. But he did not confine himself to the production of evanescent sound, he also employed the simple dot, so as to fix them permanently upon paper, that they could be recalled again. This form of telegraph is a combination of the successive fundamental discoveries of Professors Œrsted and Faraday, with the multiplicator of Schwigger.

I extract from the original paper of Steinheil, published in the *London Annals of Electricity*, March and April, 1839, an account of his telegraph, being the most complete which I can find on record:—

To Gauss and Weber* is due the merit of having in 1833, actually constructed the first simplified galvano-magnetic telegraph. It was Gauss who first employed the excitement of induction, and who demonstrated that the appropriate combination of a limited number of signs is all that is required for the transmission of communications. Weber's

*Gott. gel. Anz. 1834, p. 1273, and Schumacher's Jahrbuch, 1837, p. 38.

discovery that a copper wire 7460 feet long which he had led across the houses and steeples at Göttingen from the observatory to the cabinet of Natural Philosophy required no especial insulation was one of great importance. The principle was thereby at once established of bringing the galvanic telegraph to the most convenient form. All that was required was an appropriate method of inducing or exciting the current with the power of changing its direction without having recourse to any special contrivances for that purpose. In accordance with the principles we have laid down, all that was required in addition to this was to render the signals audible, a task that apparently presented no very particular difficulty, inasmuch as in the very scheme itself a mechanical motion, namely, the deflexion of a magnetic bar, was given. All that we had to do therefore was to contrive that this motion should be made available for striking bells or for making indelible dots. This falls within the province of mechanics, and there are therefore more ways than one of solving the problem. Hence the alterations that I have made in the telegraph of Gauss and by which it has assumed its present form may be said to be founded on my perception and improvement of its imperfections, in harmony with what I had previously laid down as necessary for perfect telegraphic communication. I by no means however look on the arrangement I have selected as complete; but as it answers the purpose I had in view, and it may be well to abide by it till some simpler arrangement is contrived.

As an inductor or exciter I employ a rotating apparatus whose construction, speaking in a general way, is similar to those of Clarke, of London. The multipliers of which my inductor is composed, consist of a vast number of turns of fine insulated copper wire; and this arrangement is necessary in order that the resistance offered by the thicker wire completing the circuit, even should it be many miles long, may be but little increased. Of the galvanic influence excited during the entire half-turn of the rotating double multiplier, only a small portion is employed, and that when it is at the maximum of its energy. By this means the duration of the current is but very short, an arrangement which therefore, in a manner, can cause merely a momentary deflexion of the little magnetic bars employed for giving the signals. In order to heighten the action of these indicators as much as possible, they are surrounded by powerful multipliers. Small detached magnets are so placed near these indicators, that they are thereby brought back to their original position immediately that the induced current ceases, or in other words, as soon as the deflexion has taken place: I thus am enabled to repeat signals in very rapid succession. The same indicator can be brought with ease to make five deflexions in a second, succeeding each other as fast as the sounds of a repeater when striking. Hence if bells are placed at the proper striking distance from these indicators, they will ring at every deflexion produced, and as it is quite immaterial at what part of the wire, completing the circuit, the multiplier containing the indicator is inserted, we have it in our power to produce the sign excited by induction at any part of the course the wire takes. Should it be desired that the indicator instead of producing sounds should write, it is merely required to adapt to one end of the little magnetic bar a small vessel filled with a black color, and terminating in a capillary tube. This tube, instead of striking on a bell, thus makes a black spot upon some flat surface held in front of it. If these spots are to compose writing, the surface upon which they are printed must keep moving on in front of the indicator with a uniform velocity, and this is easily brought about by means of an endless strip of paper which is rolled off one cylinder on to another by clockwork. This is in a general way the construction followed in the telegraph erected here, a fuller account of which now would be out of place, as it may be found on referring to the appendix. As far as the employment of this telegraph is concerned, it may be fairly said to perform all that can be reasonably required of it. The excitation of the current is produced by half a turn of the indicator, and is equally available at all times. The sounds of the bells close to the person making the signals, and which being produced at the other station too are also audible there, become, by practice, intelligible as a language. Should they, however, be overheard or misunderstood, the communication presents itself simultaneously written down. This can be done with closed doors, without any but the parties concerned being aware of it: the communications may be made at any distance, and either by day or night, without any appreciable loss of time. There is, therefore, every reason to be content with the performance of the instrument.

It is not, however, to be denied, that the establishment of certain conditions indispensable to its action is, nevertheless, a matter of some difficulty. We allude to the connecting wire joining the stations.

It has been stated above that Ampere required more than sixty such wires, whereas thirty or so were sufficient for Sömmering. Wheatstone and Cooke* reduced their number to five; Gauss, and, probably in imitation of him, Schilling, as likewise Morse† in New York, made use of but a single wire running to the distant station and back. One might imagine that this part of the arrangement could not be further simplified, such, however, is by no means the case. I have found that even the half of this length of wire may be dispensed with, and that with certain precautions its place is supplied by the ground itself. We know in theory that the conducting powers of the ground and of water are very small, compared with that of the metals, especially copper. It seems however to have been previously overlooked, that we have it within our reach to make a perfectly good conductor out of water or any other of the so called semi-conductors. All that is required is, that the surface that its section presents should be as much greater than that of the metal as its conducting power is less. In that case the resistance offered by the semi-conductor will equal that of the perfect conductor; and as we can make conductors of the ground of any size we please, simply by adapting to the ends of the wires, plates presenting a sufficient surface of contact, it is evident that we can diminish the resistance offered by the ground or by water to any extent we like. We can, indeed, so reduce this resistance as to make it quite insensible when compared to that offered by the metallic circuit, so that not only is half the wire spared,

* La France Industrielle, 1838, April 5, p. 3.

† Mechanics' Magazine, No. 757, p. 332. Silliman's Journal for October, 1837. Annals of Electricity, &c., Vol. II. p. 116.

but even the resistance that such a circuit would present is diminished by one-half. This fact, the importance of which in the erection of galvanic telegraphs speaks for itself, furnishes us with another additional feature in which galvanism resembles electricity. The experiments of Winckler, at Leipsig, had already shown us that with frictional electricity the ground may replace a portion of the discharging wire. The same is now known to hold good with respect to galvanic currents.

The inquiry into the laws of dispersion, according to which the ground, whose mass is unlimited, is acted upon by the passage of the galvanic current, appeared to be a subject replete with interest. The galvanic excitation cannot be confined to the portions of earth situated between the two ends of the wire; on the contrary, it cannot but extend itself indefinitely, and it became, therefore, now only dependant on the law that obtained the excitation of the ground and the distance of the exciting terminations of the wire, whether it was necessary or not to have any metallic communication at all for carrying on telegraphic intercourse.

I can here only state in a general way that I have succeeded in deducing this law experimentally from the phenomena it presents: and that the result of the investigation is, that the excitation diminishes rapidly as the distance between the terminal wires increases.

An apparatus can, it is true, be constructed in which the inductor, having no metallic connexion whatever with the multiplier, by nothing more than the excitation transmitted through the ground, will produce galvanic currents in that multiplier sufficient to cause a visible deflexion of the bar. This is a hitherto unobserved fact, and may be classed among the most extraordinary phenomena that science has revealed to us. It only holds good, however, for small distances. It must be left to the future to decide whether we shall ever succeed in telegraphing at great distances without any metallic communication at all. My experiments prove that such a thing is possible up to distances of 50 feet. For distant stations we can only conceive it feasible by augmenting the power of the galvanic induction, or by appropriate multipliers constructed for the purpose, or, in conclusion, by increasing the surface of contact presented by the ends of the multiplier. At all events the phenomenon merits our best attention, and its influence will not perhaps be altogether overlooked in the theoretic views we may form with regard to galvanism itself.

To sum up in a few words what are the results of what we have here brought forward respecting telegraphic communications, we see that, with the present arrangement of the apparatus, no principle can be brought into competition with the galvanic telegraph, but that the establishing the metallic connexion indispensable to its action, although now materially simplified, still presents great difficulties in practice. Indeed, such a connexion is only practicable where it can be constantly watched, as, for instance, in the vicinity of railroads.

For very considerable distances without intermediate stations, galvanic or electric excitation must, on account of their rapidity, be always the best power to have recourse to. For less distances it yet remains open to inquiry whether, with proper modifications, some of the other methods we have pointed out would not be preferable, as they dispense with a metallic connexion.

Dr. Steinheil's Magnetic Telegraph.

This telegraph is composed of three principal parts. 1, A metallic connexion between the stations. 2, The apparatus for exciting the galvanic current. 3, The indicator.

1. *Connecting Wire.*—The so called connecting wire may be looked on as the wire completing the circuit of a voltaic battery extended to a very great length. What applies to the one holds good of the other. With equal thicknesses of the same metal, the resistance offered to the passage of the galvanic current is proportional to the length of the wire. With equal lengths of the same metal, however, the resistance diminishes inversely with the section; but the conducting power of metals is very different. According to Fechner, copper conducts six times better than iron, and four times better than brass. The conducting power of lead is even lower, so that the only metals which can well vie with each other in their technical use are copper and iron. But now, though iron is about six times as cheap as copper, it will be requisite to give the iron wire six times the weight of a copper one, to gain the same conducting power with equal lengths. We thus see, that as far as the expense is concerned, it comes to the same thing whichever of these metals is chosen. The preference will, however, be given to copper, as this metal is less liable to oxidization from exposure to the atmosphere. This latter difficulty may nevertheless be surmounted by simple means, namely, by galvanising it. It would even appear that the simple transmission of the galvanic current when the telegraph is in use, is sufficient to preserve the iron from rust; such at least is observed to be the case with the iron portion of the wire used for the telegraph here, and which has already been exposed in all weathers.

If the galvanic current is to traverse the entire metallic circuit without any diminution of intensity, the wire during its whole course must not be allowed to come into contact with itself; neither should it be in frequent contact with semi-conductors, inasmuch as a portion of the power called into action takes its course by the shortest way in consequence thereof, whereby the remotest parts are deprived of a portion of the power.

Numerous trials to insulate wires, and to conduct them below the surface of the ground, have led me to the conviction that such attempts can never answer at great distances, inasmuch as our most perfect insulators are at best but very bad conductors. And since in a wire of very great length, the surface in contact with the so-called insulator is uncommonly large, when compared with the section of the metallic conductor, there necessarily arises a gradual diminution of the force, inasmuch as the out and the home wire, although but slightly, yet *do* communicate in intermediate points. It would be wrong to think that this difficulty would be got over by placing the out and the home wire very far apart. The distance between them is, as we shall see in the sequel, almost a matter of indifference. And as we shall never succeed in laying down conductors that are sufficiently insulated beneath the surface of the ground, which is always damp, there is but one other course open to us, namely, leading the wire through the air. Upon this plan, it is true, the conductor must be supported from time to time; it is liable to be injured by the evil disposed, and is apt to suffer from violent storms, or from ice which forms upon it. As we, however, have no other method that we can avail ourselves of, we must endeavor by suitable arrangements to get the better of these, not immaterial, faults in the best way that we can.

The conducting chain of the telegraph erected here, consists of three parts: one leads from the Royal Academy to the Royal Observatory, at Bogenhausen, and back, and the total length of its wire is 32,506 feet. The weight of the copper wire employed amounts to 260 pounds. Both wires (there and back) are stretched across the steeples of the town, at a distance of four feet one inch. The greatest distance from support to support is 1279 feet: this is undoubtedly far too great for a single wire, inasmuch as the ice that forms upon it materially increases the weight of the wire itself, and considerably augments its diameter, so that it thus becomes liable to be torn asunder by high winds. Over those places where there are no high buildings, the connecting wire is supported upon tall poles forty or fifty feet long, which are let five feet into the ground, and to the top of which the wire is fastened to a cross bar. At the point where the metal rests there is simply a piece of felt laid, and the wire is made fast by twisting it round the wooden bar. The distance from pole to pole ranges between 640 and 650 feet; but this is far too great, for experience has shown that the wires become considerably stretched by high winds and other causes, and have, in consequence, had to be taken up more than once. All these evils would be overcome by making the connexion by at least a triple strand of metal, and not by a single wire, supporting it at intervals of 300 feet, and giving it a tension not exceeding one-third of what it will bear without giving way. This, however, in the experimental telegraph erected here, was not practicable, for reasons into which we cannot enter.

The conducting wire thus mounted, is by no means completely insulated. When, for example, the circuit is broken at Bogenhausen, an induction shock given in Munich ought to produce no galvanic excitation whatever in the parts of the chain then disconnected. Gauss's galvanometer, however, even then gives indication of a weak current; measurements indeed go to show that this current goes on increasing as the point at which the interruption of the stream is made recedes from the inductor. The absolute amount of this current is not constant. Generally it is strongest when the weather is damp. When there are heavy showers of rain, it may be fairly said to be five times as strong as when the weather is settled dry. At moderate distances of a few miles, this small loss of power is of almost no importance, and that the more as the construction of the inductor places currents of almost any strength we choose at our command. When the distance, however, amounted to upwards of 200 miles, the greatest part of the effect would be dissipated. In such cases much greater precaution must be taken with regard to the points of support of the metallic circuit.

When thunder storms occur, atmospheric electricity collects on this semi-insulated chain as upon a conductor, but the passage of the galvanic current is not at all affected thereby. An occurrence may be mentioned here as a warning for the future. During a severe thunder storm on the

7th July, 1838, a very strong electric spark darted at the same instant through the entire conducting chain, and there was simultaneously produced at the indicator, that is fitted up in my room, a sound like the cracking of a whip. At the same time the lower toned bell of the indicator emitted a sound owing to the deflexion of the needle, and the blow was so hard that the points on which the magnetic bar plays were injured. The same phenomenon was observed also at one of the other stations. As the deflecting power of frictional electricity is very inconsiderable with respect to magnets, the above occurrence indicates the presence of a vast quantity of electricity. It can only have arisen from the electricity of the earth having at that moment made its way to that collected in the wire. Whether this was brought about through the lightning conductors in the neighborhood, or the imperfect insulation of the points of support, cannot be well made out.

Quite recently I made the discovery, that the ground may be employed as one-half of the connecting chain. As in the case of frictional electricity, water or the ground may with the galvanic current form a portion of the connecting wire. Owing to the low conducting power of these bodies, compared with metals, it is necessary that at the two places where the metal conductor is in connexion with the semi-conductor, the former should present very large surfaces of contact. Taking water, for instance, to conduct two million times worse than copper, a surface of water proportional to this must be brought in contact with the copper, to enable the galvanic current to meet with equal resistance, in equal distances of water and of metal. For instance, if the section of a copper wire is 0·5 of a square line, it will require a copper plate of 61 square feet surface in order to conduct the galvanic current through the ground, as the wire in question would conduct it. But as the thickness of the metal is quite immaterial in this case, it will be always within our reach to get the requisite surfaces of contact at no great expense. Not only do we by this means save half the conducting wire, but we can even reduce the resistance of the ground below what that of the wire would be, as have been fully established by experiments made here with the experimental telegraph.

A second portion of the conducting chain leads from the Royal Academy to my house and observatory in the Lerchenstrasse. This conductor is of iron wire; its length, there and back, is 5745 feet, and it is stretched over steeples and other high buildings, as has already been described. Lastly, a third portion of the chain, running through the interior of the buildings connected with the Royal Academy, leads to the mechanical workshop attached to the cabinet of Natural Philosophy. It is composed of a fine copper wire, 958 feet long, let into the joinings of the floor, and in part imbedded in the walls. These three portions together compose a line, returning into itself, and into which the apparatus for generating the galvanic current, and also the indicator, are inserted.

2. *Apparatus for Generating the Galvanic Current.*—Hydro-galvanism, or the galvanic current generated by the action of the voltaic pile, is by no means fitted for traversing *very long* connecting wires, because the resistance in the pile, even when many hundred pairs of plates are employed, would be always inconsiderable compared with the resistance offered by the wire itself.

The principal disadvantage, however, attendant on the use of the pile or trough apparatus, is the fluctuations of their current, joined to the circumstance of their becoming very soon quite powerless, and requiring to be taken to pieces and put together again. The extremely ingenious arrangement of Morse is likewise subject to this inconvenience. (All these inconveniences have been obviated by Morse's local circuit and the improved form of battery employed since Steinheil's experiments.—T.) All this, however, is got over when one, to generate the current, has recourse to Faraday's important discovery of induction, that is to say, by moving magnets placed in the neighborhood of conducting wires. The better way, however, is, not to move the magnets as Pixii does in his electro-magnetic apparatus, but rather to give motion to the multipliers placed close to a fixed magnet. The arrangement that Clarke has given to the multiplier is the one which, with some modifications, has been adopted. Assuming on the part of our readers a general knowledge of the principles of the apparatus, we here confine ourselves to explaining how it has been adapted to purposes of telegraphic intercourse.

The magnet is composed of 17 horse-shoe bars of hardened steel. With its iron armature its weight is about 74 lbs., and it is capable of supporting about 370 lbs. Between the arms of the magnet there is fastened a piece of metal, supporting in its centre a cup provided with adjusting screws, and which serves as a support for the axis of the coils of the multiplier. The coils of the multiplier have in all 15,000 turns of wire. A metre (3 feet 3·3708 inches English) of this wire weighs 15½ grains, and it is twice bespun with silk. Its two ends, which are insulated, are passed up through the interior of the vertical axis of the multiplier, and then terminate in two hook-shaped pieces, as may be seen in Plate I. figs. 8 and 9. In order to secure perfect insulation, the vertical axis, fig. 8, was bored out hollow. Into this hole there are let in from above two semicircular rods of copper, which are prevented touching by a strip of taffeta fastened between them with glue; and these again are kept from touching the metallic axis by winding taffeta round them. In each of these little strips of metal there is, above and below, a female screw cut. In the lower holes small metal pins are screwed in, to which the ends of the multiplier are soldered securely on. While in the upper holes, as may be seen distinctly in figs. 9 and 10, there are iron hooks screwed in. These hooks therefore form the terminations of the multiplier wires of the coils of the inductor. They here turn down, fig. 15, into two semicircular cups of quicksilver, that are separated by a wooden partition. From these cups of quicksilver there proceed connexions, J J, figs. 8 and 13, towards the wires, and they therefore may be considered as forming part of the chain. The quicksilver, owing to its capillarity, stands at a higher level in these semicircular cups than are the partitions, so that the terminal hooks of the wires of the multiplier pass over these partitions without touching them when the multiplier is made to turn on its axis. One sees that the hooks thus are brought into other cups of quicksilver at every half turn of the multiplier, in consequence of which the galvanic current preserves its sign as long as the multiplier is turned in one direction, but it changes its sign on the motion being reversed. This commutation, which it may be remarked may be established without the use of mercury, by the contact of strips of copper that act like springs, is found to answer completely. There are besides two other arrangements which we must not allow to pass unnoticed.

The galvanic current, as we shall see in the sequel when treating of the indicator, should only be permitted to be in action during as short a period as possible, but during that interval should have the greatest intensity we can command. The terminal hooks of the wires dip into the quicksilver only at the place where it forms pools that advance towards each other at the centre, and where the current is at its greatest intensity, see figs. 13, 14, and 15. Fig. 15 shows the position that the inductor has when the terminal hooks first dip into the cups. In all other positions of the inductor it should however form no part of the chain, otherwise the signals made at the other stations will be repeated by its own multiplying wire; and this becomes of the more moment the greater the resistance in the inductor is. In order therefore to cut off the inductor when in any other position than shown at fig. 15, there is a wooden ring adapted to the axis of rotation of the inductor, see figs. 11 and 12. This ring is encircled with a copper hoop, and into this latter two iron hooks are screwed. These hooks dip down into the semicircular cups of quicksilver, as shown at fig. 14. At the moment, however, that they are passing across the wooden partition, the hooks of the inductor, which are at right angles to them, dip into the cups. When the hooks of the multiplier are in contact with the quicksilver, the connexion with the hooks for diverting the current is broken. In every other position the connexion through the hooks of the multiplier is interrupted, while it is established through the others; whence it naturally follows that the current, on being transmitted from any other station, passes directly through the latter hooks, or, in other words, crosses directly from one quicksilver cup to the other, and is not forced to traverse the wire of the inductor for that purpose. In order to put the inductor in motion without trouble, there is a fly bar terminating in two metal balls fastened horizontally on to its vertical axis, (annexed cuts,) figs. 39 and 40. To prevent the quicksilver being scattered about, owing to the motion of the hooks as they dip into it when the multiplier is turning rapidly, a glass cylinder is fitted on to this part of the apparatus, fig. 1. At every half turn is seen the passage of the spark, as the hooks of the multiplier leave their cups of quicksilver.

If we choose to give up the phenomena of these sparks, a thing noways necessary to the employment of the instrument as a telegraph, the inductor will admit of a far more simple construction. It will then merely be necessary to place the commutator directly above the anker, and to let the axis of rotation pass farther up in the neck, in the direction of the fly bar. It then becomes unnecessary to bore the axis out, but the ends of the multiplier are at once fastened by twisting on to two plates of copper, and these copper plates are let into a wooden ring directly opposite each other. The wooden ring is placed upon the vertical axis, and made fast to it by clamps. Externally this ring is, in addition to the above-mentioned plates, provided with an arc of copper let into it, which acts as a contact-breaker, and two ends of the chain that the current has to traverse have the form of permanent springs, that keep pressing against the wooden rings directly opposite each other. By this means, with this arrangement also, the ends of the inductor are in metallic communication with the chain only during a small portion of each revolution, while during the rest of the time the connecting arc brings the ends of the chain into direct contact. This construction, in which quicksilver is entirely dispensed with, is, on account of its greater simplicity and durability, preferable to the arrangement first described. The apparatus of the stations at Bogenhausen and in the Lerchenstrasse are thus constructed.

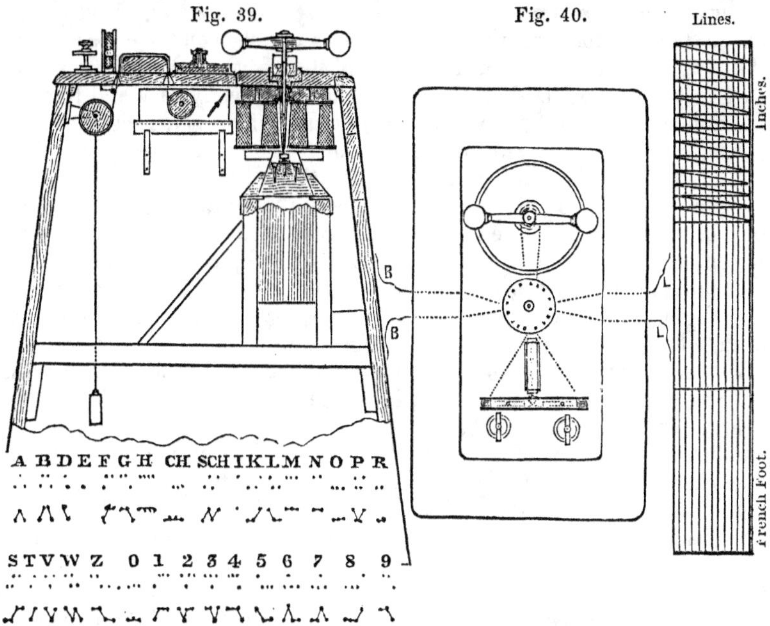

3. *The Indicator.*—We have shown in the preceding paper, that our aim is so to employ the current developed by the inductor and led through the conducting chain, that when passed across magnetic bars that are delicately suspended, it may cause them to be deflected, as was discovered by Œrsted. These deflexions, if we wish to give the signals in quick succession, must follow each other with the greatest rapidity, and should therefore be powerful. This points out to us the size we should give the magnetic bars we wish to deflect. They must not however be made too small, as in that case the mechanical force arising from their deflexion is not strong enough to be directly applied to striking upon bells, or any other similar purpose. The deflexions are, as is well known, taking the force of the current to be the same, the stronger, the greater the number of turns in the multiplier, or, in other words, the oftener the wire is led along the magnetic bar. The size of the diameter of the separate turns, as we know, only exerts an influence inasmuch as it adds to the entire length of the connecting wire. The indicator therefore is a multiplier, whose two ends connect it with the conducting chain, and within which the bar to be deflected is placed. It must be borne in mind, that the thinner the wire of the multiplier is, the larger its coils are; and the more turns they make, the greater is the resistance to the current throughout the entire chain.

Figs. 16 and 17, Plate I., represent the vertical and horizontal sections of an indicator containing two magnets, movable on their vertical axis, and which from their construction are applicable both to striking bells and also to noting down a type composed of dots. Into the frames of the multiplier, which are made of soldered sheet brass, fig. 16, there are soldered two smaller cases for the reception of the magnets, and which allow of the free motion of their axes. Above and below they have threads cut in them for the reception of four screws in holes, on the ends of which the pivots of the axes turn. By means of these screws the position of the bars may be so regulated that their motion is perfectly easy and free. In the frames of the multiplier there are 600 turns of the same insulated copper wire as was employed for the inductor. The commencement and the end of this wire are shown at M M, fig. 16. The magnetic bars are, as the figure shows, so situated in the frame of the multiplier, that the north pole of the one is presented to the south pole of the other. To the ends which are thus presented to each other, but which, owing to the influence they mutually exert, cannot well be brought nearer, there are screwed on two slight brass arms supporting little cups, figs. 17 and 18. These little cups, which are meant to be filled with printing ink, are provided with extremely fine perforated beaks that are rounded off in front. When printing ink is put into these cups, it insinuates itself into the tube of these beaks, owing to capillary attraction; and without running out forms at their apertures a projection of a semi-globular shape. The slightest contact suffices therefore for noting down a black dot. When the galvanic influence is transmitted through the multiplying wire of this indicator, both magnetic bars make an effort to turn in a similar direction upon their vertical axes. One of the cups of ink would therefore advance from within the frame of the multiplier, while the other would retire within it. To prevent this, two plates are fastened at the opposite ends of the free space that is allowed for the play of the bars, and against which the other ends of these bars press. Only the end of one bar can therefore start out from within the multiplier at a time, the other being retained in its place. In order to bring the magnetic bars back to their original position as soon as the deflexion is completed, recourse is had to small movable magnets, whose distance and position is to be varied till they produce the desired effect. This position must be determined by experiment, inasmuch as it depends upon the intensity of the current called into play.

If this apparatus be employed for producing two sounds easily distinguishable to the ear by striking on bells, it will be right to select clock bells or bells of glass, both of which easily emit a sound, and whose notes differ about a sixth. This interval is by no means a matter of indifference. The sixth is more easily distinguished than any other interval; fifths and octaves would be frequently confounded by those not versed in such matters. The bells are to be supported on little pillars with feet, and their position with respect to the bars, and likewise their distance from them, is to be determined by experiment. The knobs let into the bar that strike on the bells must give the blow at the place which most easily emits a sound. These hammers, however, are not to be too close to the bells, as in that case a repetition of the signal can easily ensue. A few trials will soon get over this difficulty. If the indicator is to write down

Plate I.

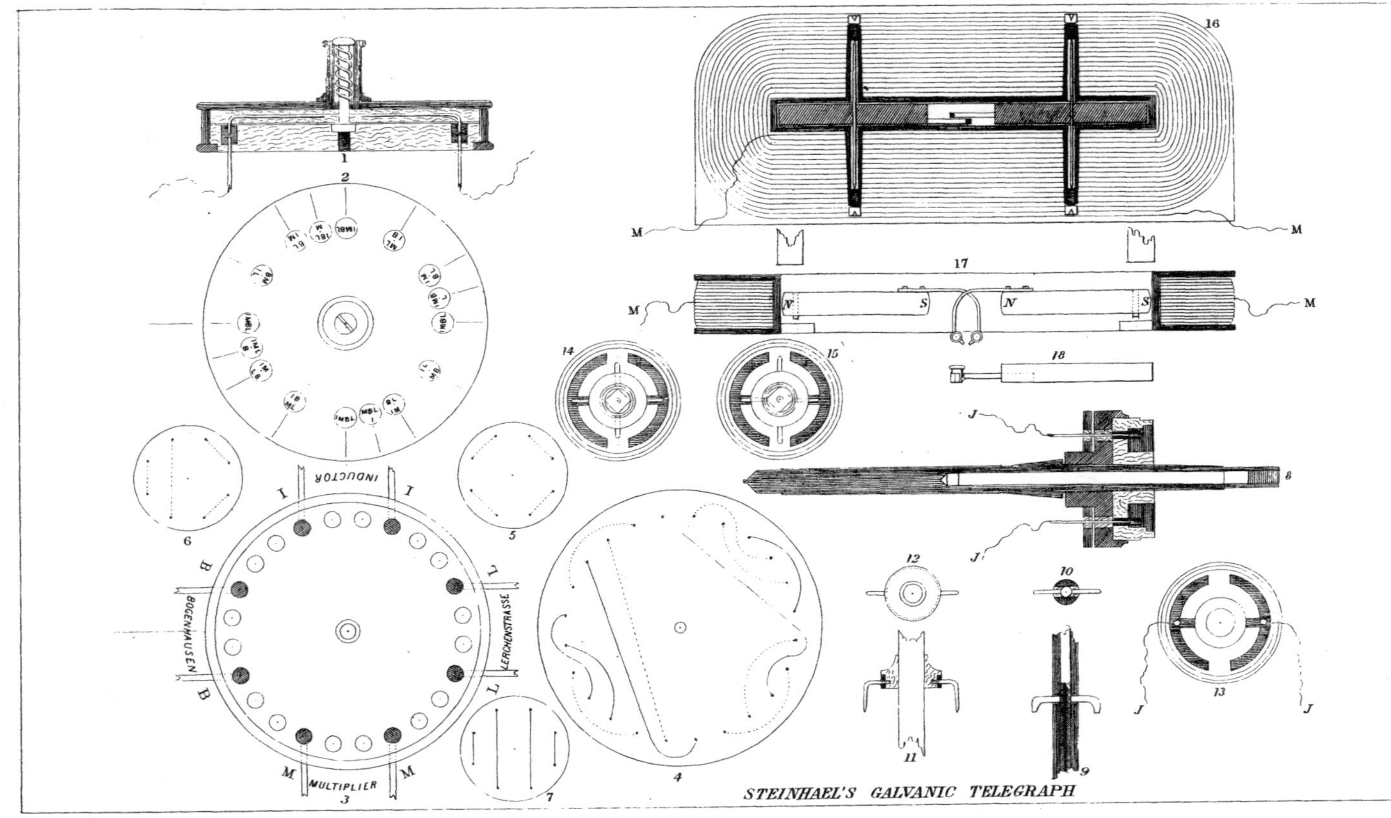

STEINHAEL'S GALVANIC TELEGRAPH

the signals, a flat surface of paper must be kept moving with a uniform velocity in front of the little beaks above mentioned. The best way of doing this is to employ very long strips of the so-called endless paper, which is to be wound round a cylinder of wood, and then cut upon the lathe into bands of the suitable width. One of these strips of paper must be made to unwind itself from a cylinder, pass close in front of the cups, run along a certain distance in a horizontal position, so that the dots noted down may be read off, and lastly, wind itself up again on to a second cylinder. This second cylinder is put in motion by clock work, the regularity of whose action is insured by a centrifugal fly-wheel. A longitudinal section of the entire arrangement is shown at fig. 39, (p. 79.) Fig. 40 represents it as seen from above. At the corners of the frame over which the ribbon of paper is led, there are placed two movable rollers, to diminish the friction. This frame moreover admits of being advanced towards the cups or withdrawn from them, so that the most proper position to give it can be ascertained by experiment. It is evident that the same magnetic bars cannot be at once employed for striking bells and for writing, the little power they exert being already exhausted by either of these operations. But to combine them both, all we have to do is to introduce a second indicator into the chain. By thus increasing the number of the indicators, the loudness of the sounds of the bells can be augmented at pleasure; this can, however, only be done at the cost of an increased resistance in the chain. In order that this may be increased by the indicator as little as possible, it would in future be better that its coils should be made of very thick copper wire, or of strips of copper plate.

The above description will enable those who are familiar with such subjects to construct the apparatus for themselves. We have yet to add a few words upon

The Way of putting the Apparatus together.—Fig. 39, (p. 79,) represents the longitudinal section of a pyramidal table, standing on the floor of the room, and containing the whole apparatus. Fig. 40 shows the same as seen from above. The wires from Bogenhausen, those from the Lerchenstrasse, the ends of the indicator, and the wires from the quicksilver cups of the inductor, or, in other words, the two ends of its multiplier, all meet together at the centre of the table, as seen at fig. 40. They are here brought into connexion with eight holes filled with quicksilver, made in a disk of wood, as shown at fig. 3, Plate I. The course that the current we call forth will take depends upon the respective connexion of these eight holes with each other. For instance, supposing them to be connected together by four pieces of bent copper wire, as shown at fig. 3, the current would pass through the whole apparatus, and also the entire chain. Establishing, however, the connexion as shown at fig. 6, would cut off the Bogenhausen station, and would at once transmit the current direct from the inductor, through the multiplier of the indicator and through the Lerchenstrasse station. Supposing this figure turned round 180 degrees, we should have the Lerchenstrasse station cut off, and the current would pass through Bogenhausen. A third system of connexions is shown by the copper wires represented in fig. 7. In this position of the sketch, the inductor and the multiplier would be in direct communication, while the two stations at Bogenhausen and in the Lerchenstrasse would be cut off.

But by turning this figure 90 degrees, we should connect these two stations, while we broke off the station in the Academy. Copper wires, serving to establish these three systems of connexion and the combinations, are laid down upon the under surface of the wooden cover of the commutator, as seen at fig. 4. There are 24 wires projecting downwards from this lid. Only eight of them, however, ever come into use at once, so that there must be sixteen other holes made in the lower disk of wood, for the reception of the wires not in use, and having no quicksilver poured into them. It is thus in our power to direct the course of the current as we choose, and the systems concerned are indicated upon the upper surface of the cover of the commutator by engraved letters, see fig. 2, Plate I.; this cover containing the different modifications of the systems of connexion, as shown at fig. 4. Changing the position of this cover round the central pin springing from the table, enables us to vary the direction of the current in any manner we like. The use of quicksilver cups in the commutator may of course be replaced by conically turned copper pins. This has indeed been done at the Lerchenstrasse and the Bogenhausen stations.

We shall conclude by a few remarks upon

The Application of this Apparatus to Telegraphic Communication.—We know from what has preceded, that at every half turn of the fly-bar from right to left, one of the bars is deflected. I have so connected the terminations of the wires, that every time this movement is repeated the high toned bell should be struck at all the stations. Standing at the side B B, and turned towards the indicator, one immediately perceives the beak imprint a dot upon the ribbon of paper as it moves along. The intervals of time between the successive repetitions of this sign, are represented by the respective distances between the dots that follow in a line upon the paper. On turning the fly-bar from left to right towards the operator, the deep toned bells ring, and the second ink cup marks down a dot upon the paper as before; not, however, upon the same line with the former dots, but upon a lower one. *High* tones are therefore represented by the *upper* dots, and *low* tones by the dots of the *lower* line, as in writing music. As long as the intervals between the separate signs remain equal, they are to be taken together as a connected group, whether they be pauses between the tones, or intervals between the dots marked down. A longer pause separates these groups distinctly from each other. We are thus enabled, by appropriately selected groups thus combined, to form systems representing the letters of the alphabet or stenographic characters, and thereby to repeat and render permanent at all parts of the chain, where an apparatus like that above described is inserted, any information that we transmit. The alphabet that I have chosen represents the letters that occur the oftenest in German by the simplest signs. By the similarity of shape between these signs and that of the Roman letters, they become impressed upon the memory without difficulty. The distribution of the letters and numbers into groups consisting of not more than four dots, is shown at fig. 39, (page 79.)

Printing Telegraph of Alfred Vail.

The printing telegraph of Alfred Vail was proposed in September, 1837.

It consists of a type wheel having on its surface the twenty-four letters of the alphabet. On the side of the wheel are twenty-four holes. The type wheel is moved circularly by means of a spring that the electro-magnetic key causes to advance at each interruption and return of the current. The paper advances under the type wheel by means of an independent clock movement.

The precision of the operation depends on the exact correspondence of the machinery, situated at the two extremities of the telegraphic lines. It is necessary that the type wheel presents the same letter at both stations, and that the clock moves at the same rate. But I believe that this system has never been put in execution. I copy from p. 169 of his work on the telegraph, the conclusions he comes to in regard to this form of telegraph:

"All electro-magnetic telegraphs require as their basis, the adoption of the *electro-magnet*, when recording the intelligence is an object, and it would seem, must be applied in a manner equivalent to the mode adopted by Prof. Morse; that is, the application of the armature to a lever, and its single movement produced by closing and breaking the circuit. It is, therefore, safe to assume that, whatever improvement in one plan may be made to increase the rapidity of the movements of those parts of the telegraph which belong to the electro-magnet, is equally applicable to any other plan, provided too much complication, already existing, does not counteract and defeat the improvement.

"Some plans, however, use an extra agent besides the electro-magnet, which is employed for measuring the time of the revolution of the type wheel, and the electro-magnet is only called in, occasionally, to make the impression. In such plans the rapidity of communication demands the combined action, alternately, of both magnets. This, of course, increases the complication, and must certainly be considered a departure from other more simple arrangements. Whatever will reduce the inertia of mechanical movements and bring them to act with an approximate velocity, at least of the fluid itself, will increase the rapidity of transmission. The more the instrument is encumbered with the sluggish movements of material bodies, the less rapid, inevitably, must be its operation, even where several co-operating agents are assisting, in their respective spheres, to increase the rapidity of the motion. Such is the case with the several kinds of letter printing telegraphs: very weighty bodies, comparatively speaking, are set in motion, stopped, again set in motion, and along with this irregular motion, other parts perform their functions. There must be a courtesy observed among themselves, or matters do not move on as harmoniously as could be desired. This is not always the case, especially where time is the great question at issue.

"All printing telegraphs which use type, arranged upon the periphery of a wheel, must have, of necessity, these several movements, viz: the irregular revolution of the type wheel, stopping and starting at every division or letter; the movement of the machinery, called the printer; the irregular movement of the paper, at intervals, to accommodate itself to the letter to be printed; the movement of the inking apparatus, or what is not an improvement in cleanliness, paper of the character used by the manifold letter writer. So many moving parts, are so many impeding causes to increased rapidity, and are, to all intents and purposes, a *complication.*

"The requirements of a perfect instrument are: economy of construction, simplicity of arrangement, and mechanical movements, and rapidity of transmission. To use one wire is to reduce it to the lowest possible economy. If there is but one movement, and that has all the advantages which accuracy of construction, simplicity of arrangement, and lightness, can bestow upon it, we might justly infer that it appeared reduced to its simplest form.

"The instrument employed by Prof. Morse has but a single movement, and that motion of a vibratory character; is light and susceptible of the most delicate structure, by which rapidity is insured; the paper is continuous in its movement, and requires no aid from the magnet to carry it.

"The only object that can be obtained by using the English letters, instead of the telegraphic letters, is, that the one is in common use, the other is not. The one is as easily read as the other; the advantage then is fanciful, and is only to be indulged in at the expense of time, and complication of machinery, increasing the expense, and producing their inevitable accompaniments, liability of derangement, care of attendance, and loss of time."

Alexander's Electric Telegraph.

I copy this account of Alexander's telegraph from the *London Mechanics' Magazine*, of November, 1837, but it was copied originally from the *Scotsman*, a paper published in Edinburgh, perhaps a month before, and a model to illustrate the nature and the operation of the telegraphic machine, was exhibited at a meeting of the Society of Arts in Edinburgh, in October, 1837.

The model consists of a wooden chest, about five feet long, three feet wide, three feet deep at the one end, and one foot at the other. The width and depth in this model are, those which would probably be found suitable in a working machine; but it will be understood that the length in the machine may be a hundred or a thousand miles, and is limited to five feet in the model, merely for convenience. Thirty copper wires extend from end to end of the chest, and are kept apart from each other. At one end, (which for distinction's sake, we shall call the south end,) they are fastened to a horizontal line of wooden keys, precisely similar to those of a piano forte; at the other, or north end, they terminate close to thirty small apertures equally distributed in six rows of five each, over a screen of three feet square, which forms the end of the chest. Under these apertures on the outside, are painted in black paint upon a white ground, the twenty-six letters of the alphabet, with the necessary points, the colon, semicolon, and full point, and an asterisk to denote the termination of a word. The letters occupy spaces about an inch square. The wooden keys at the other end have also the letters of the alphabet painted on them in the usual order. The wires serve merely for communication, and we shall now describe the apparatus by which they work. This consists, at the south end, of a pair of plates, zinc and copper, forming a galvanic trough, placed under the keys; and at the north end of thirty steel magnets, about four inches long, placed close behind the letters painted on the screen. The magnets move horizontally on axes, and are poised within a flat ring of copper wire, formed of the ends of the communicating wires. On their north ends they carry small square bits of black paper, which project in front of the screen, and serve as opercula or covers to conceal the letters. When any wire is put in communication with the trough at the south end, the galvanic influence is instantly transmitted to the north end; and in accordance with a well known law discovered by Œrsted, the magnet at the end of that wire instantly turns round to the right or left, bearing with it the operculum of black paper, and unveiling a letter. When the key A, for instance, is pressed down with the finger at the south end, the wire attached to it is immediately put in communication with the trough; and the same instant the letter A at the north end is unveiled by the magnet turning to the right, and withdrawing the operculum. When the finger is removed from the key, it springs back to its place, the communication with the trough ceases, the magnet resumes its position, and the letter is again covered.

Thus, by pressing down with the finger, in succession, the keys corresponding to any word or name, we have the letters forming that word or name exhibited at the other end; the name, *Victoria* for instance, which was the maiden effort of the telegraph on Wednesday evening. In the same way we may transmit a communication of any length, using an asterisk or cross, to mark the division of one word from another, and the comma, semicolon, or full point, to make a break in a sentence, or its close. No proper experiment was made while we were present to determine the time necessary for this species of communication, but we have reason to believe, that the letters might be exhibited almost as rapidly as a compositor could set them up in type. Even one-half or one-third of this speed, however, would answer perfectly well.

Galvanism, it is well known, requires a complete circuit for its operation. You must not only carry a wire to the place you mean to communicate with, but you must bring it back again to the trough. (The writer of this communication, and even Mr. Alexander, was not aware of the discovery of Steinheil, that the earth would conduct so as to return the current without the use of the second wire.—L. T.) Aware of this, our first impression was, that each letter and mark would require two wires, and the machine in these circumstances having sixty wires instead of thirty, its bulk and the complication of its parts would have been much increased. This difficulty has been obviated, however, by a simple and happy contrivance. Instead of the return wires, extending from the magnet back to the keys, they are cut short at the distance of three inches from the magnet, and all form a transverse copper rod, from which a single wire passes back to the trough, and serves for the whole letters. The telegraph, in this way, requires only thirty-one wires. We may also mention, that the communication between the keys and the trough is made by a long narrow basin filled with mercury, into which the end of the wire is plunged when the key is pressed down with the finger.

The telegraph thus constructed, operates with ease and accuracy, as many gentlemen can witness. The term model, which we have employed, is, in some respects, a misnomer. It is the actual machine, with all its essential parts, and merely circumscribed as to length by the necessity of keeping it in a room of limited dimensions. While many are laying claim to the invention, to Mr. Alexander belongs the honor of first following out the principle into all its details, meeting every difficulty, completing a definite plan, and showing it in operation. About twenty gentlemen, including some of the most eminent men of science in Edinburgh, have subscribed a memorial, stating their high opinion of the merits of the invention, and expressing their readiness to act as a committee for conducting experiments upon a greater scale, in order fully to test its practicability. This ought to be a public concern; a machine which would repeat in Edinburgh, words spoken in London, three or four minutes after they were uttered, and continue the communication for any length of time, by night or by day, and with the rapidity which has been described; such a machine reveals a new power, whose stupendous effects upon society no effort of the most vigorous imagination can anticipate.

The principle of Alexander's telegraph is represented in the following illustration from the work of Alexander Bain, Esq., fig 41. It consists of but one circuit, so as to make the operation intelligible.

Fig. 41.

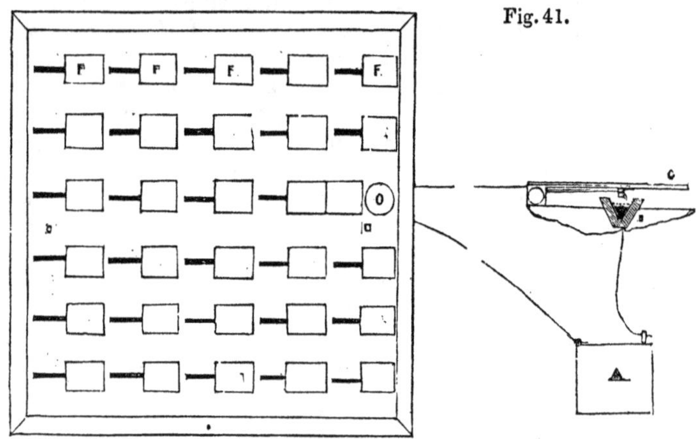

A is a voltaic battery; B, a trough filled with mercury; C, a key to be pressed down by the finger of the operator; E, is the end of a conducting wire, which dips into the mercury when the key is depressed, and completes the electric circuit; D D, is the distant dial upon which the signals are to be shown; F F, are screens, thirty in number, each being fixed to a needle, corresponding to the finger keys before described. When no electricity is passing, these screens remain stationary over the several letters, &c., and conceal them from view; but when a current is made to flow, by the depression of a key, the corresponding needle, in the distant instrument, is deflected, carrying the screen with it, and uncovering the letter, which becomes exposed to view, as at O.

In the same Magazine, there is an improvement suggested by a correspondent, which is obviously a good one, namely, the use of fifteen wires to represent the whole number of letters, thus: let each of the letter screens affixed to the movable magnets be wide enough to cover two letters. Then the positive end of the galvanic battery being connected with the inducing wire, by a touch of the keys, the magnet and screen will move in one direction and discover one letter. The negative end of the battery being thus connected with the same wire, the magnet will move in the contrary direction, and discover the other letter. There must, of course, be something fixed to prevent the magnet going so far in either direction as to discover both letters. The returning wire connected with all the other thirty, must of course have its connexion with the battery poles reversed, at the same time as the lettered wire. To prevent oscillation, let each wire act upon two magnets and screens, one magnet and screen moving in one direction, but prevented from moving in the other as now. The current of electricity if reversed, would, on account of this prevention, not move this magnet and screen in the opposite direction, but it might the other magnet and screen having a similar stop or prevention, but placed on the other side of the pole.

Davy's Needle and Lamp Telegraph.

This telegraph is called the needle and lamp telegraph, to distinguish it from the telegraph of Edward Davy, which I will describe in a future lecture.

"There is a case, which may serve as a desk to use in writing down the intelligence conveyed; and in this, there is an aperture about sixteen inches long, and three or four wide, facing the eyes, perfectly dark. On this the signals appear as luminous letters, or combinations of letters, with a neatness and rapidity almost magical. The field of view is so confined, that the signals can be easily caught and copied down without the necessity even of turning the head. Attention, in the first instance, is called by three strokes on a little bell; the termination of each word is indicated by a single stroke. There is not the slightest difficulty in deciphering what is intended to be communicated.

"In front of the oblong trough, or box, described by your correspondent, a lamp is placed, and that side of the box next the lamp is of ground glass, through which the light is transmitted for the purpose of illuminating the letters. The oblong box is open at the top, but a plate of glass is interposed between the letters and the spectator, through which the latter reads off the letters as they are successively exposed to his view. At the opposite side of the room, a small key board is placed, (similar to that of a piano forte, but smaller,) furnished with twelve keys; eight or these have each three letters of the alphabet on their upper surfaces, marked A, B, C; D, E, F; and so on. By depressing these keys in various ways, the signals or letters are produced at the opposite desk, as previously described; how this is effected is not described by the inventor, as he *intimated* that the construction of certain parts of the apparatus *must remain* SECRET.

By the side of the key board, there is placed a small galvanic battery, from which proceeds the wire, 25 yards in length, passing round the room. Along this wire the shock is passed, and operates upon that part of the apparatus which discloses the letters or signal. The shock is distributed as follows: The underside of the signal keys are each furnished with a small projecting piece of wire, which; on depressing the keys, is made to enter a small vessel, filled with mercury, placed under the outer ends of the row of keys; a shock is instantly communicated along the wire, and a letter, or signal, is as instantly disclosed in the oblong box. By attentively looking at the effect produced, it appeared as if a dark slide were withdrawn, thereby disclosing the illuminated letter. A slight vibration of the (apparent) slide, occasionally obscuring the letter, indicated a great delicacy of action in this part of the contrivance, and although not distinctly pointed out by the inventor, is to be accounted for in the following manner: when the two ends of the wire of the galvanic apparatus are brought together, over a compass needle, the position of the needle is immediately turned, at right angles, to its former position; and again, if the needle is placed with the north point southward, and the ends of the wire again brought over it, the needle is again forced round to a position at right angles to its original one. Thus, it would appear, that the slide or cover over the letters, is poised similarly to the common needle, and that by the depression of the keys, a shock is given in such a way as to cause a motion from right to left, and *vice versa*, disclosing those letters, immediately, under the needle so operated upon."—*London Mech. Mag. Vol.* xxviii., 1837.

Masson's Magneto-Electric Telegraph.

In 1837, Prof. Masson, of Caen, addressed a letter to the French Academy, in which he announced that he had made several trials with a magneto-electric telegraph, for the distance of 1800 feet. He employed for the development of the current, the magneto-electric machine of Pixü, to produce the deflexion of magnetic needles placed at the extremities of the circuits. These trials were repeated in October, 1838, with Bréquet, who was at that time one of the members of the Commission on the Telegraph from Paris to Rouen, but the results obtained were not as satisfactory as those of Steinheil, Morse, and others; afterwards Masson and Bréquet associated themselves together, and invented a new form of telegraph, a description of which is not given.—*Moigno Traité de Telegraphie, p.* 30.

Amyot's Telegraph.

In a letter addressed to the Academy of Science of Paris, in July, 1838, Amyot proposed the construction of a needle telegraph. It was to consist of a single circuit, which would move a single needle, which needle was to write on paper, with mathematical precision, the correspondence which was to be transmitted to the other extremity, by a simple wheel, on which it should be written by means of points differently spaced, the same as they are on the barrels of portable organs, the wheels to be regulated by clock work.—*Moigno, p.* 31.

Edward Davy's Telegraph.

The next telegraph in chronological order is that of Mr. Edward Davy, of London. The patent for this telegraph was sealed July, 1838, and published in the *Repertory of Patent Inventions*, London, July, 1839. The specifications are very voluminous, and not very intelligible. I have therefore studied it carefully, and have given the important points, and a drawing, which fully illustrates the improvements which Davy proposed, being careful not to omit any vital part of his machine. In this method of treating it, I have followed the examples of Moigno and Shellen, two of the latest writers upon the subject of the history of the telegraph.

In the telegraph of Edward Davy, the decomposing action of the galvanic current is employed to produce marks upon chemically prepared cloth, or other material; the cloth preferred by the inventor was *calico*, and the chemical substance employed by him to prepare the cloth was a salution of the iodide of potassium and muriate of lime.

He employed a local battery to produce the telegraphic signs by chemical decomposition. This battery also operated an electro-magnet, whose armature regulated the movement of the registering instrument. This battery is also connected with a short independent circuit, which is closed and opened by the movement of a magnetic needle, surrounded by a coil of copper wire, which forms part of the main circuit. He employed finger-keys to open and close the circuit; his receiving instrument being similar in principle to Cook and Wheatstone's, only closing his circuit like Mr. Morse, by the contact of solid metals, instead of mercury. When the main circuit is closed by the finger-keys, the needle is deflected which closes the short circuit; but when the main current is interrupted, the needle opens the short circuit by returning to its original position.

The cloth or other chemically prepared material is drawn between a metallic cylinder and a series of platinum rings surrounding a wooden cylinder; by these rings the current from a local battery is passed through the chemically prepared cloth to the metallic cylinder beneath, producing signs consisting of simple dashes arranged in six rows. The calico is moved by clock-work, and this clock-work is regulated by a U electro-magnet, with an armature and lever, which at each motion withdraws the stop from a fly-wheel for the space of a semi-revolution, during which a single sign is made upon the calico, the clock-work moving always in proportion to the number of signs transmitted. The platinum rings were so arranged as to be connected separately or together, at will, with the other poles of the battery, but insulated from each other.

In his patent three telegraphic wires are represented, which are made by means of his commutator to connect a local circuit with either of the six platinum rings, so as to simplify the system of marking necessary to form the signs for the different letters of the alphabet.

There cannot be a doubt that Davy was informed of the telegraphs of Morse and Steinheil, by the following remarks at page 12 of his Specifications:

"I am aware that it has been proposed to use a marking instrument with lead or ink, by the aid of an electro-magnet, to make a number of dots or marks in immediate succession, to indicate the signification of such communication; I do not, therefore, claim the use of marking instruments generally, but only when they are adapted to make communications by marks across and lengthwise of the fabric which receives them, as above described."

The most ingenious portion is the escapement. The figure represents the principle of the escapement, and the electro-magnet. A is the voltaic battery; B lever; N metallic button, to which is fixed the wire conductor of the battery; C an electro-magnet; D the armature; I is a clock-weight; H the band of the wheel that carries the revolving cylinder of the signs, K; G is a van or regulator of motion; E a pair of pallets fixed to the armature D. On the side opposite the axis of motion, is fixed a spring, F, to separate the armature from the electro-magnet, by which the electric current is broken, and magnetism destroyed. The arrangement is such that for every revolution of the van G, the cylinder K advances one division, and a letter is impressed. If the lever B rests against the metallic button N, the metallic circuit of the voltaic battery is immediately established, the electric current passes along the conducting wires of the electro-magnet C, which instantly attracts the armature D, forces the superior pallet E to abandon the lever O, and permits the van to turn. As soon as it turns half a revolution, it is arrested by the inferior pallet,

Fig. 42.

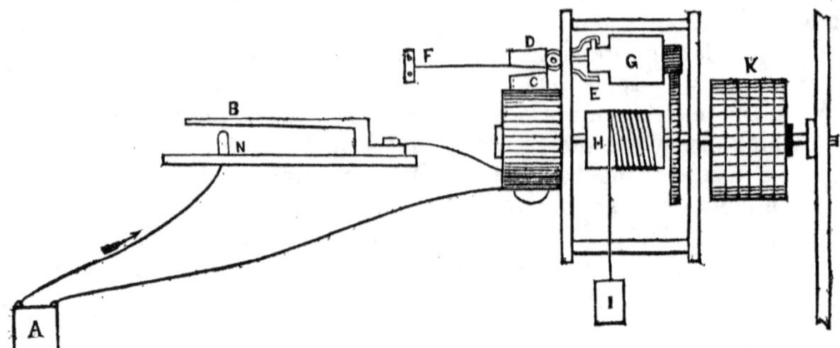

gainst which the lever touches. The contact of this lever, being abandoned, the voltaic circuit is instantly broken, magnetism destroyed, and the spring F leaves the armature in its first position. This movement lowers the inferior pallet, sets at liberty the lever O, and the second half of a revolution is performed, bringing it into a new position, and arrests it against lever O, or superior pallet. For each complete revolution, a character successively appears. The operation of successively elevating and depressing the key, gives the cylinder of signs a circular motion, in the same manner that the hand of a clock is made to revolve by means of balancing and escapement. On some cotton fabric are some longitudinal lines, intersected by transverse ones, dividing the surface into little squares. It is impregnated with iodide of potassium and chloride of lime, and wound on a cylinder that turns by a weight at each magnetic pulsation. The current traverses this prepared material, and leaves a well marked trace in the square indicated by the touch of the director. The position of the square in the net-work marked on the stuff, determines the letter or signal. This mode requires seven or eight lines, and has never been put in practical operation, though patented in January, 1839.

The following are the claims in full, as given in the original publication:

"First, The mode of obtaining suitable metallic circuits for transmitting communications or signals by electric currents, by means of two or more wires, which I have called signal-wires, communicating with a common communicating-wire, and each of the signal-wires having a separate battery, and, if desired, additional batteries, for giving a preponderance of electric currents through the common communicating-wire, as above described.

"Secondly, I claim the employment of suitably prepared fabrics for receiving marks by the action of electric currents for recording telegraphic signals, signs, or communications, whether the same be used with the apparatus above described or otherwise.

"Thirdly, I claim the mode of receiving signs or marks in rows across and lengthwise of the fabric, as herein described.

"Fourthly, I claim the mode of making telegraphic signals or communications from one distant place to another, by the employment of relays of metallic circuits, brought into operation by electric currents.

"Fifthly, The adapting and arranging of metallic circuits in making telegraphic communications or signals, by electric currents, in such manner, that the person making the communication shall by electric currents and suitable apparatus, regulate or determine the place to which the signals or communications shall be conveyed.

"Sixthly, I claim the mode of constructing the apparatus which I have called the escapement, whether it be applied in the manner shown, or for other purposes, where electric currents are used for communicating from one place to another.

"Seventhly, I claim the mode of constructing the galvanometer herein described.

"And lastly, I claim such parts as I have herein pointed out, as being useful for other purposes, as above described."—[*Repertory of Patent Inventions*, *July*, 1839.

Bain's Printing Telegraph.

The following extract of a letter is taken from a work, entitled "An Account of some remarkable applications of the Electric Fluid to the Useful Arts: by Alexander Bain: edited by John Finlaison, Esq. London, 1843," which gives us the date of Mr. Bain's first telegraph:

"*Percival Street, Clerkenwell, Aug.* 28, 1842.

"Dear Sir:—I recollect visiting you early in June, 1840, when you showed me a model of your electro-magnetic telegraph.

"Robert C. Pinkerton."

In July, 1841, it was exhibited and lectured on at the Polytechnic Institution, London. It consists of three principal parts.

1st, The rotary motion given to the type wheel, step by step motion, like the second-hand of a clock, until the required letter arrives opposite the paper.

2d, The means of inking the types, or otherwise making permanent the imprint of the types upon the paper.

3d, The motion communicated to the paper, so as to bring a fresh surface under the types, and receive the printed intelligence in a continuous spiral line, until the book is filled.

He uses wire coils freely, suspended on centres, for electro-magnets. These coils, within and in the vicinity of which are fixed powerful permanent magnets, are deflected as long as the electrical current is passing through them; but when the electric current is broken, they are drawn upwards by the force of the spiral springs, the levers are released, and the machinery of the telegraph, worked by main springs, are left free to rotate. The only battery proposed by Mr. Bain is a pair of copper and zinc plates, one of which is to be buried in the earth at one station, and the other at the distant station, where there is to be a telegraph the exact counterpart of the first.

I have considered it entirely unnecessary to give a drawing of this telegraph, as it never could be of very great service; and as to the form of battery, it was entirely out of the question. The best evidence of this was, that an entire change was made in it by Mr. Bain in 1846, a description and drawing of which will be found in my article on Galvanic or Electro-Chemical Telegraphs.

I find in the same work the following account of some interesting experiments on the earth as a source of permanent voltaic electricity:

"In prosecuting some experiments with an electro-magnetic sounding apparatus, in the year 1841, it was found that if the conducting wires were not perfectly insulated from the water in which they were immersed, the attractive power of the electro-magnet did not entirely cease where the circuit was broken. For the purpose of investigating the nature of this phenomenon, a series of experiments took place, with great lengths of wire, in the reservoir of water at the Polytechnic Institution, when similar results were obtained. While reflecting upon these experiments, some few months after they had been performed, Mr. Bain was led to infer, that if a surface of positive metal was attached to one end of a conducting wire, and an equal surface of negative metal to the other end, and the two metallic surfaces put into water, or into the moist earth, (the wire being properly insulated,) an electric current would be established in the wire."

This proposition was soon tested by experiment. A surface of zinc was buried in the moist earth, in Hyde Park, and at rather more than a mile distance a copper surface was similarly deposited; the two metals were connected by a wire suspended on the railing, and on placing a galvanometer in the circuit, an electric current was produced, which passed through the intervening mass of earth from one plate to the other, and returned by the wire. In the first experiment, the metallic surfaces being small, the electric current produced was feeble; but on using a large surface of metal, a corresponding increase in the energy of the current was obtained, with which an electrotype process was conducted, and various electro-magnetic experiments performed with universal success.

It is essential to success, that the earth wherein the plates of metal are deposited should be of a moist nature. A current has indeed been obtained in dry soil, but of such small energy as to be of no practical utility.

A patent was solicited for the application of this mode of producing electric currents to his printing telegraph, and obtained in April, 1841.

This form of battery could never have been of any useful application to great distances, without an increase of the number of plates and of the exciting fluid.

Sturgeon's Electro-Magnetic Telegraph.

In the *Annals of Electricity* for October, 1840, is published a description and drawings of a form of electro-magnetic telegraph, proposed by William Sturgeon, of London, a man who has by his numerous experiments and researches into the subject of electricity and magnetism, conferred signal benefits on these important sciences, and has not received the full award of merit even from his own countrymen. The publication of the *Annals of Electricity* alone deserves the thanks of all interested in these important subjects, containing as they do a mass of valuable information not to be found elsewhere in our language.

"In describing a new electro-magnetic telegraph, I am necessarily impelled by a similar feeling to that which urged my predecessors to bring their respective inventions before the public; and I cannot resist the idea that there will be found a peculiar simplicity both in the structure and management of the telegraph I am about to describe. Indeed, I shall point out the structure of two distinct telegraphs, having the sign common to both. Also, a third, differing very materially from the other two.

"In one of these telegraphs I use six soft iron bars, bent into the form of horse-shoe magnets, and covered with copper wire spirals, in the usual way, for converting them into occasional magnets by electric currents. To each magnet is a short bar of soft iron for a keeper or cross-piece, which is attached to the shorter arm of a lever, of the first order; and to the extremity of the longer arm of the lever is attached a circular card. The arrangement of one of these pieces of apparatus is shown by figs. 44 and 45, the former being a side view, and the latter an end view of it: *m*, in both figures, represents the magnet, *i* the cross-piece, *a b* the lever, and *f* the fulcrum. The cards at the longer extremities of the six levers are numbered 1, 2, 3, 4, 5, 6, which, individually, and by a series of simple combinations, form all the signals that are required.

Fig. 43.

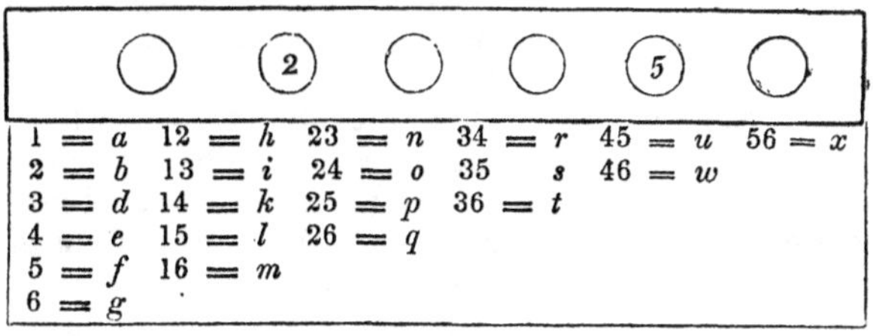

1 = *a*	12 = *h*	23 = *n*	34 = *r*	45 = *u*	56 = *x*
2 = *b*	13 = *i*	24 = *o*	35 *s*	46 = *w*	
3 = *d*	14 = *k*	25 = *p*	36 = *t*		
4 = *e*	15 = *l*	26 = *q*			
5 = *f*	16 = *m*				
6 = *g*					

Fig. 44.

Fig. 45.

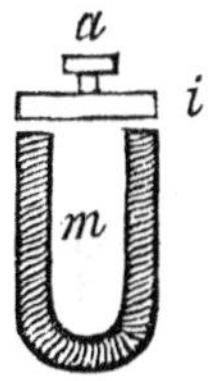

"When the levers are in the position shown in figs. 44 and 45, the magnet is out of action, in consequence of the battery circuit being interrupted. If, now, the battery circuit were to be closed, the magnet *m* would immediately be brought into action, and its attractive force would bring down the cross-piece *i*; which, being attached to the shorter arm of the lever, would raise the longer arm with its card and sign, into the position of the upper dotted circle, where it becomes visible through a circular opening in the face of the instrument, as at (5) in fig. 43. When that particular sign has appeared the required time to be observed, the battery circuit is opened, the magnet *m* loses its power, and the longer arm of the lever preponderating, again falls down to its first position, and the card with its sign disappears.

"The face or dial of the telegraph is represented by fig. 43, which may be either of painted wood or metal, silvered in the manner of clock faces, or barometer scales. On the upper part of the dial there are six circular openings, for the occasional appearance of the cards, with their figures, which are attached to the longer arms of the six levers. (See fig. 44.) Below the circular openings in the dials plate there are arranged the signals which are to represent all the alphabetical letters that are necessary for the spelling of words. The signals are thus continually before the eyes of the operator, and are too simple to miss being understood. These levers, with their magnets, &c., figs. 44 and 45, are placed behind the dial in a suitable case, and in such a manner that the figures on the cards may appear at the circular openings whenever their levers move upwards by the attractions of their respective magnets at the other, or shorter arms; and to disappear below those circular openings, when the magnets are out of action. To accomplish this latter effect, the face of the cross-piece of iron, which is attached to the short arm of each lever, must be covered by a card, or a film of some non-ferruginous matter, which will prevent close contact of the iron and magnet. By this arrangement of the apparatus, it is a matter of no consequence in what way the magnetic poles are arranged, because the attraction of the cross-pieces, attached to the shorter arms of the levers, will take place as well with one arrangement as with another. But for uniformity, we will suppose that the coils on the magnets are all of the same kind, and that the north poles are to be in one and the same direction, towards the left hand for instance, to a person facing them, then those extremities of all the coil wires which were situated in one direction, might be collected together in one bundle, and either continued to the station where the battery is situated, or soldered to one stout copper conductor, at some short distance from the magnets, which conductor would become a general *fixed channel* between all the magnets at this station, and the battery at the other station. The other six ends of coil wires must be insulated by silk covering, and continued to the battery without metallic contact with each other. At the battery station these six insulated wires are to be attached to six wooden or ivory keys with springs, like the keys and springs of a piano forte; by the downward motion of which, the extremities of the wires become immersed in a long trough of mercury, connected with the opposite pole of the battery to that which the other conductor is attached to. On the top of each key is to be a conspicuous figure, corresponding to the figure which is to appear in the dial plate at the other station, so that when one finger is placed on key 2, and another finger on key 5, the magnets 2 and 5 at the other station are brought into play,and by attracting their respective pieces of iron, the figures 2 5 make their appearance on the dial as seen in fig. 43, and the letter p is understood. By these means, twenty-one of the letters of the alphabet can easily be represented without a possibility of error, either in the manipulation at the one station, or in the reading at the other; unless, indeed, there be a deficiency of attention which would incapacitate the attendants for employment at any telegraph whatever.

"The keys of this telegraph are sufficiently near to each other to permit the fingers to press on any number of them at one time, and, if necessary, the whole of the magnets may be brought into play at once, by the application of three fingers of each hand to the keys. By these means, the numerals may be grouped into combinations of three, four, five, and six, and thus, without the slightest confusion, a considerable number of signals would be obtained, which might represent words, or whole sentences, which would greatly expedite the transmission of intelligence from one end of the line to the other.

"There is a very great advantage in employing the numerals for signals. Not only because they are not so liable to lead to confusion as by the employment of the alphabetical letters, when used in combinations or groups; but because the subject of communication may be kept a perfect secret from one end of the line to the other; which is a most essential consideration in government expresses, and very often in those of mercantile affairs also.

"In this telegraph a seventh magnet is employed to ring a warning bell, as first proposed by Professor Steinheil.

"Although in the telegraph already described I employ soft iron magnets and levers to bring the signals into view, I am of opinion that magnetic needles in coiled conductors, or electro-magnetic multipliers, will be somewhat more prompt in their motions than the lever, at great distances from the battery. I therefore propose to make the necessary signals by means of magnetic needles, which can be moved with the same arrangement of conductors as that already described. And although I have only used six numerals for the signals, I am very far from supposing that the working of an electro-magnetic telegraph is facilitated or simplified by using a small number of original signals, or by having a small number of conductors. The simplest method of *spelling* words would be to have a needle for each letter of the alphabet, and the telegraph could be *made* and *worked* as easily by 24 needles as by a smaller number. And the words and sentences, which could be signified by combining them in pairs, or in groups of two each, would afford great facilities for the rapid transmission of ideas from one end of the line to the other. The needles could be placed in three horizontal rows, one above another, on a vertical dial plate.

Fig. 46.

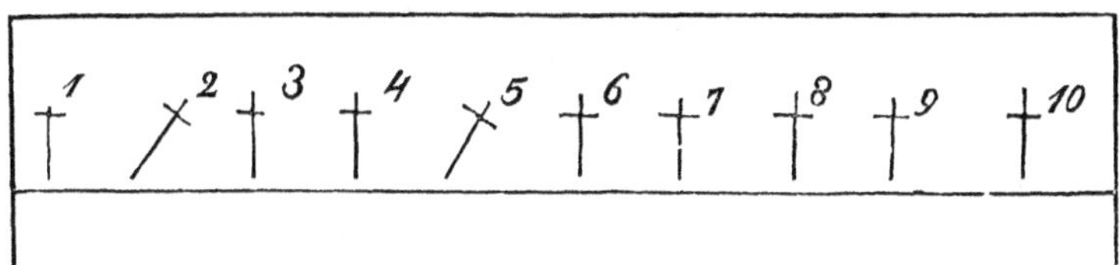

"I have shown a dial plate in fig. 46, on which are placed 10 needles, with their respective figures or signs. As the needles can be deflected in only one direction, viz., with the north end towards the figure which belongs to it, there can be no mistake in understanding what sign is to be understood. I believe that any of these telegraphs will be found much simpler than those already before the public. They are capable of producing many more signs than any other known, and may be made at a less expense."

The House Printing Telegraph.

This instrument has been appropriately termed one of the wonders of the age; its apparent intricacy of construction arises not so much from the use of electricity and magnetism, as from the number of minute physical contrivances, and the various methods by which they are brought into action.

Of the origin and life of the inventor, Mr. Royal E. House, it seems difficult to obtain any definite or conclusive information; while the results of his labors are spread before the public, form a prominent object of its curiosity, and are made subservient in a high degree to its utility, the man himself seems almost a recluse, and veiled, as it were, from the sight of the world. If some tell us that he originated in New York, more authentic sources affirm that he was born in Pennsylvania, and reared among the Green Mountains of Vermont. To the old Keystone, then, may we ascribe the honor of having given birth to one who has achieved so much in the progress of American artizanship.

To converse and carry on intelligent discourse at the distance of many hundreds of miles, is not new; nay, it has become common; but to impress with the subtile electric spark through vast space, solid material, with the symbols of our language in the fulness of their proportionate beauty; to make the cold, dull, inanimate steel speak to us in our own tongue, surpasses the mythological narratives of ancient Greece and Rome, throws into the shade the fabulous myths of superstitious Arabia, and sinks into insignificance the time honored traditions of the Oriental World.

A letter dated Boston, Dec. 23, 1850, received in reply to some inquiries, relative to Mr. House, affords the following interesting information: "Mr. House is a self-educated man, and was engaged nearly six years in perfecting his instrument; he is decidedly scientific, but not learned, having devoted much attention to electricity and its kindred sciences; observing the property of a helix or coil of wire to attract an iron bar to its centre, he proceeded to make some practical application of the fact, and succeeded in constructing what is termed an axial magnet; his principal object then, was the construction of a machine adapted for its use, which he fabricated after many attempts and much perseverance.

Such is the cast of his intellect, that he could form the entire object in his mind, and retain it there until he had completed its whole arrangement, without committing any thing to paper; somewhat abstract in disposition, he is careless about money, little communicative concerning himself, capable of long protracted thought, and completely absorbed in his hobby, the telegraph; to such an extent is this abstraction carried, that he often forgets his most faithful and puctilious business promises, and when sought after to comply with them, is found investigating some interesting object of science, or deeply engrossed in thought; even with particular friends he is very reserved about himself.

From some affection of the eyes he was confined to his dwelling during most of the time spent in contriving his instrument; he resides at present in New York. An application was made for a patent in 1845 or '46, but it was refused on the ground that some of the specifications clashed with those of Mr. Morse; one, however, was granted in October or November of 1848, to date from April 18, 1846.

The stations between which communications are conveyed, are connected by means of a circuit composed of one conducting wire, (see J, fig. 47,) and the ground; the wire is insulated to prevent escape of the electric fluid by enclosing it throughout its whole length in tubes of guttapercha: the heat of the sun melts this covering, or renders it so soft as to destroy its form, and it has been abandoned by all the lines except one; most of them employ, now as at first, the naked wire, supported on glass knobs fixed with bits of muslin to iron spikes driven into the post; they were formerly made of twisted wire and wound around glass knobs; thus exposed to the atmosphere, they soon became oxidized, requiring frequent repairs, or the lightning by striking them often played many pranks with the machines and their operators; the action of the current was also very unequal, owing to the varying electrical conditions of the atmosphere.

Notwithstanding all their precautions, a severe accident of the above nature, occurred to the House Telegraph in this City, on the 29th of May last; during a severe thunder storm in the afternoon of that day, the lightning, as was supposed, struck the line about six miles from the city; it destroyed nearly three miles of wire, melted off the helix of the magnet here, and terminated with a loud explosion at the battery; several gentlemen were sensibly and severely affected, and one of the operators, Mr. Alexander, received a heavy shock, causing vertigo, ringing in the ears, nausea, and temporary insensibility.

The posts to sustain the wire, are from 20 to 30 feet in height, set 5 feet deep, nine inches in diameter at the base, four and a half at the top, and about 15 rods distant from each other, that being the medium length which the kind of wire cited will support of itself and be durable; the Grove battery is employed to generate the current, of which about thirty cups are necessary for a distance of 100 miles.

The main constituents of his telegraph, are the composing machine, the printing machine, a compound axial magnet, a manual power which sets the two machines in motion, and a letter wheel or tell-tale, from which messages can be read when the printing machine is out of order.

A composing and printing machine are both required at every station; the printing apparatus is entirely distinct from the circuit, but all the composing machines are included in and form part of it; the circuit commences in the galvanic battery of one station, passes along the conductor to another station, through the coil of the axial magnet to an insulated iron frame of the composing machine, thence to a circuit wheel revolving in this frame; it then enters a spring that rubs on the edge of this circuit wheel, and has a connexion with the return wire, along which the electricity goes through another battery back to the station from whence it started, to pursue the same course through the composing machine and magnet there, and all others upon the line; thus the circuit is confined to the composing machines, axial magnets, conducting wires, and batteries.

The composing machine Fig. 47, is arranged within a mahogany frame H, three feet in length, two in width, and six or ten inches deep; the various parts of the printing machine are seen on the top of the same case; both are propelled by the same manual power, which is distinct from the electric current; it is simply a crank with a pulley carrying a band to drive the machine, and a balance wheel to give stable motion; one of the spokes of the balance wheel has fixed to it, an axis for the end of a vertical shaft to revolve on, that moves the piston of an air condenser G, fastened to the floor; the air is compressed in the chamber I, fourteen inches long, and six in diameter, lying beneath the mahogany case H; it is furnished with a safety-valve, to permit the escape of redundant air not needed in the economy of the machine.

Fig. 47.

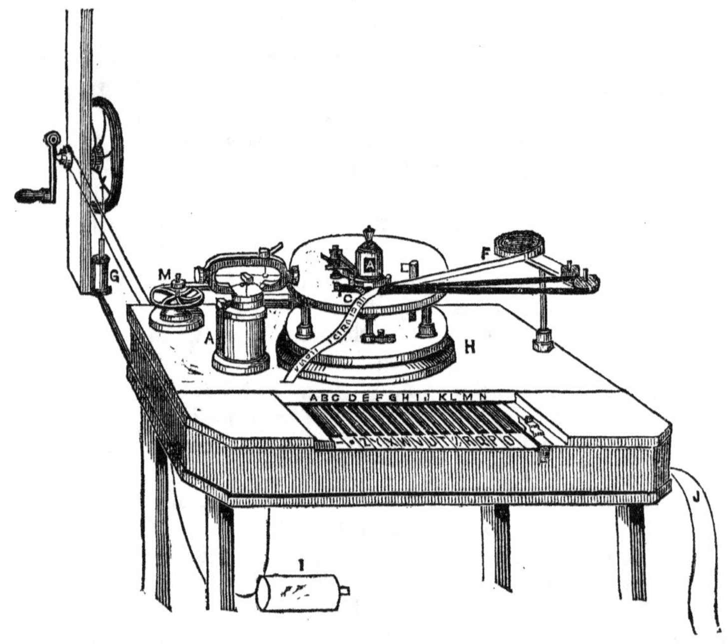

Fig. 48.

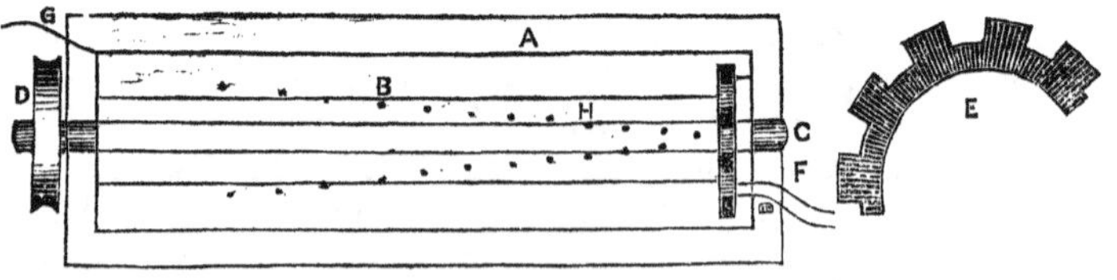

The composing system has an insulated iron frame A, Fig. 48, placed immediately below the keys, parallel with the long diameter of the case; this has within it a revolving shaft C; the shaft is enclosed for the greater part of its length by the iron or brass cylinder B; it is made to revolve by a band playing over the pulley D, fixed to the left extremity of it. The cylinder is detached from the shaft, but made to revolve with it by a friction contrivance, consisting of a spiral spring arising from the shaft and pressing against the interior of the cylinder; the spring runs the whole length of the shaft: Fig. 49, shows a transverse section of it; the object of this is to allow the shaft to revolve, while the cylinder can be arrested.

Fig. 49.

On the right end of the cylinder, is fixed the brass wheel E, Fig. 48, four or five inches in diameter, called the circuit wheel, or break; the outer edge of it is divided into 28 equal spaces, each alternate space being cut away to the depth of one-fourth of an inch, leaving fourteen teeth or segments, and fourteen spaces, Fig. 48, E; the revolving shaft and cylinder form part of the electric circuit; one point of connexion being where the shaft rests on the frame, the other through a spring F, having connexion with the other end of the circuit, pressing on the periphery of the break-wheel E, fig. 48; G, the other part of the circuit coming from the axial magnet to the frame A; when the shaft, cylinder, and circuit wheel revolve, the spring will alternately strike a tooth and pass into an open space; in the former case, the circuit is closed, in the latter it is broken.

For the purpose of arresting the motion of the circuit wheel and cylinder, the latter has two spiral lines of teeth H, fig. 48, extending along its opposite sides, having fourteen in each line, making 28, one for each tooth, and one for each space on the circuit wheel; the cylinder extends the whole width of the key board above it; the latter is like that of a piano-forte, containing twenty-eight keys that correspond with the twenty-eight projections on the cylinder, and have marked on them in order, the alphabet, a dot, and dash, Fig. 47; they are kept in a horizontal position by springs; there is a cam or stop fixed to the under surface of each key directly over one of the projections on the cylinder; these stops do not meet the teeth unless the key is pressed down, which being done, the motion of the cylinder is stopped by their contact; by making the circuit wheel revolve, the circuit is rapidly broken and closed, which continues until a key is depressed; that key being released, the revolution continues until the depression of another key, and so on; the depression of a key either keeps the circuit broken or closed, as it may happen to be at the time, so that the operator does not break and close the circuit, but merely keeps it stationary for a moment; from one to twenty-eight openings and closings of the circuit take place between the depression of two different keys, or the repetition of the depression of the same one; the object of the composing machine is to rapidly break and close the circuit as many times as there are spaces from any given letter to the next one which it is desired to transmit, counting in alphabetical order.

The rapid electrical pulsations are transmitted by the circuit of conductors to the magnet and printing machine at another station, through the wire J, fig. 47. The helix of this magnet is an intensity coil contained in the steel cylinder A, fig. 47, on the upper surface of the mahogany case; its axis is vertical.

Fig. 50.

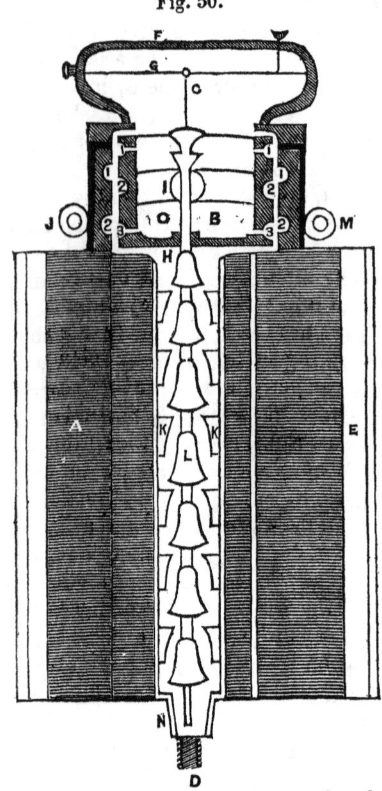

Fig. 50, A is a brass tube, eight or ten inches long, placed within the helix, and fastened at the bottom by the screw D. To the inner surface of this tube are soldered six or eight soft iron tubes, separated from each other at regular intervals. Above the steel cylinder is an elliptical ring, F, through the axis of which is extended an elastic wire, G; two screws are attached to the wire, by which it is made lax or tense, to suit the intensity of the electric current. From this is suspended the brass rod, C, that passes down within the small iron tubes before mentioned, and has strung on it six or eight small iron tubes, L; these are fastened at equal intervals and have their lower extremity expanded into a bell-like flanch; the surrounding fixed ones have their upper ends enlarged inwardly in the same manner. The tubes, L, and the wire to which they are fastened, are movable, so as to come in contact with the small exterior iron tubes K, fig. 50, but are kept separate by the elastic spring above. At E is the brass covering. On the transmission of an electric current through the helix, the tubes become magnetic. Such is the arrangement of their polarities, that they act by attraction and repulsion, overcome the elasticity of the spring, and bring the movable magnets down to the fixed ones;—the current being broken, the spring separates them. The two flanches do not come in direct contact, though the movable one acts responsive to magnetic influence. Most of the magnetism exists at the flanches, and the order is such that the lower end of the inner tube has south polarity, the surrounding one above, the same, which repels it, while the top of the surrounding one below has north polarity, and attracts it;—this movement is through a space of only one-sixty-fourth part of an inch.

On the same rod, above the movable magnets, is fixed a hollow cylindrical valve, having on its outer circumference the grooves 1, 2, 3, fig. 50. The plate represents a longitudinal half-section of the valve, magnets, and helix. The valve slides in an air chamber, H, which has two grooves, 1, 2, on its inner surface. Air is admitted through the orifice I, by means of a pipe from the air chamber beneath the case, into the middle groove of the valve. The grooves of the chamber open into the side passages J and M, which connect at right angles with a second chamber, in which a piston moves. The movement of the magnets changes the apposition of the grooves in the first chamber, by which air enters from the supply pipe, through one of the side passages, into the second chamber, at the same time that air on the other side of the piston in the second chamber escapes back into the grooves 1 and 2 of the valve, through the other side passage, and from them into the atmosphere. This causes the piston to slide backward and forward with every upward and downward motion of the valve.

Fig. 51.

This piston moves horizontally, and is connected with the lever, 8, Fig. 51, of an escapement, the pallets of which alternately rest on the teeth of an escapement wheel of the printing machine A, Fig. 51. This part of the apparatus is arranged on a circular steel plate, twelve or fourteen inches in diameter, supported by standards on the mahogany frame, H, Fig. 47. The escapement wheel revolves on a vertical shaft that passes through the steel plate, and has fixed on it there a hollow pulley. This pulley contains within it a friction apparatus, precisely similar to that in the cylinder of the composing machine, and is driven by a band running around another pulley, (M, fig. 47.) The pulley can be made to revolve constantly, while the shaft and escapement wheel may be stopped. The escapement wheel has fourteen teeth, each one of which causes two motions of the escapement, which will make twenty-eight for a single revolution of the wheel, which is shown in fig. 52.

Fig. 52.

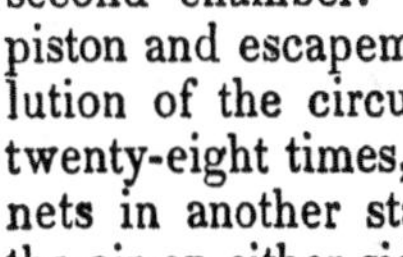

When in operation, the piston to which the escapement arm 8, fig. 51, is attached, is subjected, on one side or the other, to a pressure of condensed air; therefore the piston and escapement will only be moved by the escapement wheel when the air is removed from one side or the other of the piston. The position of the valve, fig. 50, attached to the magnet regulates the pressure of air on either side of the piston, by opening one or the other of the side passages into the second chamber. By breaking and closing the circuit, therefore, the piston and escapement move backward and forward; thus a single revolution of the circuit wheel at one station opens and closes the circuit twenty-eight times, causing an equal number of movements of the magnets in another station; they carry the valve which alternately changes the air on either side of the piston. This permits the escapement wheel to move the escapement and piston twenty-eight times, and allows one revolution of the escapement wheel for one of the circuit wheel at the transmitting station.

A steel type wheel, fig. 51, A, B, C, D, two inches in diameter, is fixed above, and revolves on the same shaft with the escapement wheel; it has on its circumference twenty-eight equi-distant projections, on which are engraved in order the alphabet, a dot, and a dash. The fourteen notches of the escapement wheel cause twenty-eight vibrations of the escapement in a revolution, that correspond to the characters on the type wheel. Every vibration of the escapement, therefore, makes the type wheel advance one letter; these letters correspond to those on the keys of the composing machine. If any desired letter on the type wheel is placed in a certain position, and a corresponding key in the composing machine is depressed, by raising that key, and again depressing it, the circuit wheel at one station, and the escapement and type wheel at the other station, all make a single revolution, which brings that letter to its former position. Any other letter is brought to this position by pressing down its key in the composing machine, the circuit being broken and closed as many times as there are letters from the last one taken to the letter desired.

To form the letters into words, it is necessary that the printing and composing machines should correspond, and for this purpose a small break and thumb screw, 9. and 10, fig. 51, can be made to stop the type wheel at any letter. In sending messages, they usually commence at the dot; if, by accident, the type wheel ceases to coincide with the distant composing machine, the printing becomes confused, the operator stops the type wheel, sets it at the dash, and the printing goes on as before.

Above the type wheel, on the same shaft, is the letter wheel, E, fig. 51, on the circumference of which the letters are painted in the same order with those on the type wheel below. It is encased in a steel hood, having an aperture in it directly over where the letters are printed, so that when the type wheel stops to print a letter, the same letter is made stationary for a moment at the aperture, and is readily distinguished; hence messages can be read, thus making it a visual telegraph.

The type wheel has twenty-eight teeth arranged on the outer edge of its upper surface; near it, on the opposite side from where the printing is done, is the shaft T, fig. 51, revolving in an opposite direction. A steel cap, X, fig. 51, two inches in diameter, is so attached to the top of this shaft that friction carries it along with it, but it can be moved in the opposite direction; it has a small steel arm, three-fourths of an inch long, projecting from its side, and playing against the teeth on the type wheel; while the latter is revolving, its teeth strike this arm, and give the cap a contrary motion to its shaft. There is a pulley on this shaft, below the plate, connected by a band to M, fig. 47; its speed is less than that of the type wheel. When the type wheel comes to rest, the arm falls between the teeth, but it has not time to do so when they are in motion. On the opposite side of the cap to where the arm is attached are two raised edges, called detent pins, against which the detent arm, U, fig. 51, alternately rests, as the position of the cap is altered by the small arm that plays on the teeth of the type wheel.

Between the type wheel and cap, is a small lever and thumb screw, 9, fig. 51, which acts as a break on the cap; its motion can be stopped by it, while the type wheel revolves; it is used merely to arrest the printing, though the message may be read from the letter wheel.

The detent arm revolves in a horizontal direction about the vertical shaft, which is also driven by a pulley beneath the steel plate; when the type wheel is at rest, the detent arm rests on one of the detent pins, but when it moves, the teeth on its upper surface give the arm and cap a reverse direction to its shaft, which alters the position of the detent points, so that the detent arm is liberated from this first pin, and falls upon the second, where it remains until the escapement and type wheels again come to rest; when this happens, the arm falls between two of the teeth, the cap resumes its first position, the detent is let loose, makes a revolution, and stops again on the first pin.

The shaft that carries the detent arm has an eccentric wheel R, fig. 51, on it, above the arm; an eccentric wheel is one that has its axis of motion nearer one side than the other, and while revolving, operates like a crank; from this eccentric is a connecting rod S, which draws a toothed wheel against the type; this toothed wheel is supported in an elastic steel arm, (shut out of view by the coloring band,) on the opposite side of the type wheel from that of the eccentric, and revolves in a vertical direction; the band E, fig. 47, carrying the coloring matter to print with, passes between this and the type; the dots seen represent small teeth that catch the paper and draw it along, as the wheel revolves, between itself and a steel clasp, operated by a spring that presses the paper against the teeth and keeps it smooth; the clasp is perforated in such a manner that the type print through it; there are two rows of teeth, one above, the other below the orifice.

The vertical wheel, fig. 51, is embraced in a ring by the connecting shaft S, and a rotary motion is imparted to it by a ratchet fixed to its lower surface, moving with it and catching against two poles fastened to the steel plate below it; the poles are pressed against the ratchet by springs as shown in fig. 53; the wheel is octagonal, and every revolution of the eccentric, turns it through one-eighth of a revolution, and therefore presents a firm, flat surface to push the paper against the type, and advances sufficient for every letter, one being printed each time the detent arm revolves.

Fig. 53.

When the type wheel stops, the detent arm revolves, that carries with it the eccentric, which through the connecting rod draws the toothed wheel having the paper and coloring band before it against the type, and an impression is made on the paper; a letter is printed if the circuit remains broken or closed longer than one-tenth of a second; about one hundred and sixty letters in the form of Roman Capitals, can be accurately printed per minute; the roll of paper L, fig. 51, is supported on a loose revolving wire frame work; on the same standard is a small pulley W, around which one end of the coloring band runs.

In transmitting a message, the machine is set in motion, a signal is given, (which is simply the movement of the magnet,) and then with the communication before him, the operator commences to play like a pianist on his key board, touching in rapid succession, those keys which are marked with the consecutive letters of the information to be transmitted; on hearing the signal, the operator at the receiving station tells his assistant to turn the crank, setting the machine in motion; then setting his type at the dash, sends back signal that he is ready, and the communication is transmitted; he can leave his machine, and it will print in his absence; when the printing is finished, he tears off the strip which contains it, folds it in an envelope ready to send to any place desired. The Governor's Message has been transmitted by this instrument, and published entire in New York, two hours after its delivery in Albany.

The function of the electric current in this machine, together with the condensed air, is to preserve equal time in the printing and composing machine, that the letters in one may correspond with the other; the electrical pulsations determine the number of spaces or letters which the type wheel is permitted to advance: they must be at least twenty-five per second to prevent the printing machine from acting; the intervals of time the electric currents are allowed to flow unbroken are equal, and the number of magnetic pulsations necessary to indicate a different succession of letters are exceedingly unequal; from A to B, will require one-twenty-eighth of a revolution of the type wheel, and one magnetic pulsation; from A to A, will require an entire revolution of the type wheel and twenty-eight magnetic pulsations.

The first line operating with this instrument was completed in August, 1850, by the Boston and New York Telegraph Company, between those cities, passing through Providence, Norwich, Hartford, and New Haven; they were incorporated with a capital stock of $27,000 by the Legislature of Massachusetts, April 20, 1849; it has also been patented in England, by Jacob Brett, who is extending the lines through that Kingdom.

In reply to an inquiry of mine in regard to the number of lines employing this form of telegraph, I received the following dispatch:—

"The Boston and New York Telegraph Company using House's Printing Telegraph; about six hundred miles of wire; two wires. Stations at Boston, Mass., Providence, R. I., Springfield, Mass., Hartford, Conn., New Haven, Conn., and New York. A line being constructed to connect with the Boston line, running from Springfield, Mass., to Albany, N. York, there intersect the New York and Buffalo line, using the same instruments, extending from New York to Buffalo, a distance of five hundred and seventy miles. One wire now in operation, connecting with Poughkeepsie, Troy, Albany, Utica, Syracuse, Lyons, Rochester, Albion, Lockport, and Buffalo; and another wire nearly completed, same distance. The same line to continue to St. Louis, Mo., connecting with Cleveland, Cincinnati, Louisville, and St. Louis; will be completed the entire distance by January, 1852, forming the longest line in the world under the direction of one company; whole length being fifteen hundred miles. The New Jersey Magnetic Telegraph Company, using House's instruments, and the first line ever put in operation, extends from Philadelphia to New York; one wire, CXXXII miles; another now being put up.

Respectfully, J. W. PHILIPS."

Subjoined is a specimen of the form of printing executed by this machine, kindly offered by the principal operator at this station, Mr. J. W. Philips, to whom, and the records of the House trial, I am indebted for most of my information.

HOUSES-PRINTING-TELEGRAPH

The Electric Telegraph between England and France. Extension to Ireland and Belgium.

The first wires for the Submarine Telegraph were sunk in the British channel on the 27th of August, 1850. The wire was thirty miles long, with a covering of gutta percha half an inch in diameter, the wire imbedded by leaden clamps of twenty and twenty-five pounds, to the bottom of the sea; the clamps were streamed out at every sixteenth of a mile, and the wire was safely sunk to a depth which was hoped would place it out of the reach of anchors or monsters of the deep; and the other end of the wire was run up the cliff at Cape Grinez, to its terminal station on the French side of the channel, and messages were passed between the two countries.

But unfortunately for the first effort, in the course of a month, the wire received so much injury on a rock off Cape Grinez, as to make it entirely useless, and upon a careful consideration, the Directors of the Company determined to lay, instead of one, "four permanent wires."

Upon an examination by divers, it has been found that where the rupture of the coil occurred, it had rested on a very sharp ridge of rocks, about a mile out from Cape Grinez, so that the leaden weights, hanging pannier-like on either side, in conjunction with the swaying of the water, caused it to part at that point; while at another place, in shore, the shingle from the beach had the effect of detaching the coil from the leaden conductor that carried it up the Cape.

The wire, in its gutta percha coating, was consequently cut in two places, representing a remnant of wire of about four hundred yards, which was allowed to drift away, till it came into the possession of a fisherman of Boulogne; and it was no wonder that it was cut, being represented as not thicker than a lady's stay-lace, while it ought to have been as thick as the cable of those placed in the Britannia tubes in position, say eight or ten inch cable, and to be submerged below five fathoms, by the aid of enormous weights, so as to avoid all currents.

In the *London Mining Journal* for November, 1850, Mr. J. J. Lake, of the Ordnance Office, Plymouth, proposes, in order to prevent injury to the telegraphic wires, from the nature of the bottom, to suspend them by corks placed at intervals, and to secure them to the bottom by anchors or a dead weight, at certain greater distances, and at each anchor, or weight, a small buoy, with a flag, could be secured, which would indicate their locality; and in the event of accident, they could readily be found.

I will now state the present condition of this communication, and the means taken to secure it from accident; and I will then describe the form of telegraph which is employed by Mr. Brett. In *L'illustration Journal Universel*, for October, 1851, it is stated that in this, the last effort, they had not calculated for the proper amount of cable, when first taken across the channel, it requiring a mile more cable, but the accident was soon repaired. The engraving is one taken from that Journal, and they remark that it is indeed a wonderful work. The cable of wire in which is enclosed the electrical conductor, was manufactured in the short space of three weeks, by means of a machine, the invention of Mr. Fenwick, an ingenious English engineer. It is hoped, that to preserve the conducting wire free from accidents which caused the first experiment to fail, by the present arrangement four wires are enveloped in a double cover of gutta percha, and each re-covered with cable lying at the bottom of the sea. The covers forming, together, a length of ninety-six miles, over which is placed a linen covering prepared in a composition of tar, tallow, &c., and crossing its length the centre of the cable.

Fig. 54.

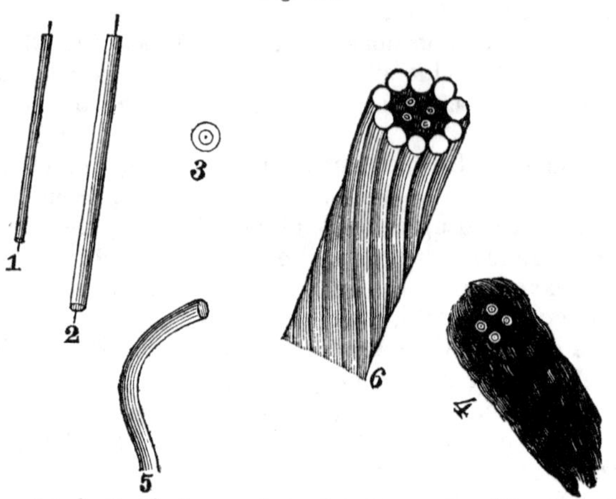

No. 1, fig. 54, is the first covering of gutta percha; No. 2, is the second covering, re-covering the first; No. 3, section of the covering No. 2; No. 4, is the wire in the covering of tarred linen; No. 5, is the simple wire of galvanized iron; the covering is that of zinc; No. 6, is a view of the arrangement of the cable, showing the galvanized iron wire, &c.

To recapitulate:—The rope is 24 miles long, and consists of four copper wires, through which the electric current will pass, insulated by coverings of gutta percha. These are formed into a strand, and bound round with spun yarn, forming a core or centre, round which are laid ten iron galvanized wires of 5-16ths of an inch diameter, each welded into one length of 24½ miles, and weighing about fifteen tons. The rope weighs, altogether, about 180 tons; it forms a coil of 30 feet in diameter outside, 15 feet inside, and five feet high, and was in good working order in September, 1851. English papers received by the arrival of the Niagara, on Friday, December 12th, 1851, state that the Submarine Telegraph is working well. Messages on the same day have been transmitted from London and Liverpool to Paris, Havre, Vienna, Trieste, Hamburg and Ostend; and in one instance, a communication was forwarded to Cracow, to be despatched thence by mail to Odessa.

The rates are, for a message of twenty words:—

From Paris to Calais.	. . . . . .	7f. 56c.
" " Dover,	. . . . . .	19f. 56c.
" " London,	. . . . . .	32f. 81c.
" " Birmingham,	. . . . .	—— ——

From Paris to Brighton, Cheltenham, Coventry, Gloucester, New Market, Norwich, Oxford, Portsmouth, Southampton, &c., 26f. 03c.

From Paris to Chester, Edinburgh, Glasgow, Holyhead, Liverpool, Manchester, New Castle, Nottingham, Sheffield, York, 29f. 31c.

Now that the English channel has been crossed in so substantial a manner, and with such perfect success, the crossing of the Irish channel must follow; for the same Company will perform this important work.

By their act of incorporation they are styled "The Submarine Telegraph Company between England and France, between England and Ireland, and the European and American Printing Telegraph," all proposed by Mr. Jacob Brett, in 1851.

Messrs. Carmichael & Brett have contracted with the Belgian Government for the formation of a submarine telegraph between Belgium and England. They are to have a monopoly of ten years, and the governments are to have priority of all messages.

Description of Brett's Printing Telegraph, Plate II.

Suppose at one extremity of *a single line* of telegraphic wire, a small key board, containing a row of ivory keys, marked with the letters of the alphabet, and other characters or words; and that it be connected by the said wire to the printing machine at the other extremity. This machine contains a type wheel, having on its circumference corresponding letters, words, or signs; a slight electric power is sufficient to regulate the motion of the whole, so that the instant a key representing any word, letter, or sign, is pressed down by the person at the key board at one end of the line, the corresponding word, letter, or sign of the type wheel prints, and the signal bells ring at the other end of the line of telegraph, without limit as to distance. The communications are printed on paper supplied from a scroll of unlimited length, from which any portion of the correspondence may be cut off at pleasure.

The motive power is simple; it being that of a weight, which sets in motion the key shaft and governor of the key board; and the circuit wheel in connexion with the shaft being put in contact with the wire of the galvanic battery, or other generator of electricity, according to the velocity of motion and manipulation at the key board, so will the motion be fast or slow at the printing end of the telegraph; the type wheel of the telegraph is set at liberty by means of an escapement, and weights in connexion with it, so as to print with a like velocity, in combination with an hydraulic or pneumatic regulator, which admits of the desired letter *only* being printed, by checking and releasing an eccentric arrangement; a rod from thence unites with the cylinder on which the paper is printed, in various modes, as may be desired, either in paragraphs—on a sheet of paper—upon a long strip of ribbon or paper—or, if for government despatches and the like, it can be printed line by line, like the column of a newspaper, of an unlimited length.

Fig. 2 represents a separate key board, of a circular form, from which communications can be forwarded to any or every station in connexion with it, the letters, words, or characters being arranged round it on the keys; and these, if depressed by the fingers, will check the motion of a pin, or shaft, and also of the circuit wheel fixed to the same axis, at such given point or key, by which means the operator may make or break the circuit of conductors at such letter or point.

The distance actually proved to act by this telegraph in one continuous line has been 230 miles, and 340 miles apart, at the rate of 100 letters per minute. This is a modification of the House Printing Telegraph.

From the year 1847 to that of 1852 there have been so many fancied improvements made in electro-telegraphs, that it is unnecessary to consume time in describing them. The most important I have noticed in full; but in the majority, I have only described a new claim, or a good modification of an old arrangement.

The three most interesting telegraphs which have been devised in that time, are those of Henley & Foster, of England; Siemens, of Berlin, and Allen, of Edinburgh. I have arranged them chronologically, and have given a list of the publications where they may be found, especially in the instances where the description given here is limited.

Nott's Improvement in Electric Telegraph, January 20, 1846.—Novel arrangement of apparatus, by which audible and visible signals can be given, through the agency of electro-magnetism.—Rep. Pat. Inventions, 1847, p. 97.—(Irish.)

Hatcher's Improvements.—First, consisting in arranging and disposing of magnets in such a way that when an electric current is transmitted through them, gives a step by step motion. The second relates to the means of forming the metallic connexions. Third, in regulating a number of clocks.—Patent, dated March 23, 1847.—(English.)

Reid's Electro-Telegraphic Improvements.—Better insulation of the wires, by laying them in channels under ground, and covering them with gutta percha, marine glue, or tar; using a modified galvanometer to sound an alarm, and earthenware insulators.—Patent, dated Nov. 23, 1847.—(English.)

Henry Mapple, Wm. Brown, and James Lodge Mapple, Telegraphic Machine, June, 1847.—They magnetized a steel dial by electricity, and thereby made a steel pointer to move over it.—Rept. Patents, Feb., 1848.

Barlow and Foster's Improvements in Electric Telegraphs, April 27, 1848.—First, coating the telegraphic wires with a compound, consisting of one part by weight of New Zealand gum, and one part of milk of sulphur, added to eight parts of gutta percha, by little and little, while in a kneading trough, at a temperature of 120° Fahr. The coating is effected as follows:—Two pairs of rollers are made to revolve by means of suitable gearing, at one uniform speed, and each pair is provided with a pipe, fitted steam-tight, to one end of their axis, through which pipe steam is admitted at pleasure, which serves to bring the rollers to a temperature sufficient to soften partially two bands of gutta percha, passed between them. Then, there is another pair of rollers, which have their surfaces cut with semi-circular grooves; the grooves of the one roller corresponding or falling right over those of the other. The wires to be covered are wound upon reels, from which they pass between the second pair of rollers. The bands or fillets of gutta percha are passed between the first pair of rollers, (and are so brought into an adhesive state,) and the two bands of gutta percha, with the wires between them, are in this state passed between the second pair of rollers, by which the fillets of gutta percha are made to adhere together, and consequently to envelope the wires.

BRETT'S
Electric Printing Telegraph.

Fig. 1.

Fig. 2.

2d, The governing the currents of electricity, so as to cause each pulsation thereof, separately or conjoined, to indicate different signs or symbols.

3d, The patentees describe an electric telegraph apparatus for indicating the passing and time of passing of a railway train.

A dial is pierced with fifty holes at regular distances, in which holes small plugs are placed. This dial is made to revolve once every hour. A metal spring presses against the face of the dial, and has the effect of thrusting back any plug that may have been protruded. Above the dial is an electro-magnet, which attracts, on the passing of an electric current from the station which the train has just passed, one end of a lever, the other end of which protrudes the plug immediately underneath beyond the face of the dial, so that the attendant is enabled, by looking at the dial, to see whether the train has passed the station, and what time has elapsed since it passed.—*London Mech. Mag. No.* 1319, *Nov.* 18, 1848.

C. F. Johnson, Oswego, Tioga County, New York.—Improvement in Electric Telegraphs, May 16, 1848.—Claim.—First, forming signs for telegraphic purposes, by the dropping of balls upon an endless belt moving with an uniform velocity. Second, I claim the taking off impressions on paper, from balls as dropped substantially in the manner described.—*Franklin Institute Journal, Vol.* xvii, 3*d series, p.* 310.

John Lewis, Recardo, Lownds Square, Middlesex, England, Sept. 18, 1848.—1st, "Improvement" to a mode of insulating wire for electro-telegraph purposes; and 2d, to an apparatus for suspending them.—*Mechanics' Magazine, March*, 1849.

Edward R. Roe, Improvements in the Machine for Operating or Manipulating Morse's Electro-Magnetic Telegraph, May, 1849.—"The invention consists, 1st, of movable metallic types as conductors of electricity or galvanism; 2d, a metallic type bed upon which they are to rest, (which is also movable to and fro, somewhat in the manner of a common printing press;) and 3d, a movable board, which is also a conductor, and is made to traverse the face of the types, thereby making, continuing, or breaking the galvanic circuit, according to the form of the types.

Claim.—"What I claim as my invention is, 1st, The combination of the body, the socket, the spiral ring, and the wand, with its conducting point and its non-conducting inclined planes, the whole constituting the traverser.

"2d, I claim the manner of giving the proper motion to the traverser, by the combination and action of the traverse wheel, the pully, and the cord which plays in it, the teeth upon the traverse wheel and the brakes operated by the type bed, in the manner set forth.

"3d, I claim the combination, for telegraphic purposes, of the types, arranged in the manner described, with the traverse and its wand, and its conducting point guarded by non-conducting inclined planes."—*Franklin Institute Journal, Vol.* xvii, 3*d series, p.* 320.

Charles Shepherd, London.—Improvements, April 16, 1849.—1st, The employment in chronometers, of apparatus actuated by electro-magnetism, for winding up the remontoir escapement, which is retained by a detent.

2d, Giving audible signals in chronometers by means of a locking plate, and apparatus connected therewith, worked by electro-magnetism.

3d, An arrangement of apparatus for making and breaking the circuit.

4th, A peculiar arrangement and adaptation of apparatus, worked by electro-magnetism to chronometers.

5th, The combination in chronometers and telegraphs, of two pallets and detents for giving the step by step motion.—*Lond. Mech. Magazine, Oct.* 20, 1849.

L. G. Curtis, Ohio.—Improvement in Indicating Telegraph, January 16, 1849.—"The basis of the American Indicating Telegraph invented by me, is upon these principles, viz: Electro-Magnetism, machinery, figures and signs, and their combinations.

"This end is obtained by means of a revolving disk or dial plate, marked with successive series of numerals, 0 1 2 3 4, arranged in a circle or otherwise, said dial plate being revolved by degrees, as the galvanic current is completed and broken by the alternate vibration of the lever, to which the pallets, armature and springs are attached."—*Franklin Institute Journal, Vol.* xviii., 3*d series, p.* 280.

Caleb Winegar, New York.—Improvement in Magnetic Telegraphs, March 20, 1849.—Claim: "Moving the paper on which telegraphic marks are made, into and out of contact with a stationary pen, by which means I avoid the danger of dispersing the ink, which happens when the pen is rapidly agitated.

"I also claim operating the magnet which effects the movement of the paper.

"I also claim the arrangement for conveying ink to the stationary pen," &c., &c.—*Franklin Institute Journal, Vol.* xviii., 3*d series, p.* 361.

M. Dugardin—Method of Insulating the Metallic Wires intended for Subterranean or Submarine Telegraph.—"This process consists of two operations. The first is the wrapping of ribbon of caoutchouc $\frac{4}{10}$ths of an inch wide, and $\frac{5}{100}$ of an inch thick, around a metallic wire, so that each turn of the wrapping shall cover about one-half of the preceding one. The second consists in wrapping spirally, and $\frac{4}{100}$ths thick, so that the edge of each turn shall touch the former, but without lapping over it. The leaden envelope serves to protect the caoutchouc from blows. (Comptes de l'Academie des Sciences, for January 2d, 1849.)—*Franklin Institute Journal, Vol.* xvii., 3*d series, p.* 284.

Henry G. Hall, Ohio.—Improvement in Posts for Telegraphs, &c., Sept. 19, 1848.—Preventing the posts from rolling, by combining the cast iron or artificial stone shoes with the posts.—*Franklin Institute Journal, Vol.* xxiii., 3*d series, p.* 102.

Improvements in Electro-Telegraphic Apparatus and Machinery. Wm. Thomas Henley, and David George Foster, of Clerkenwell, London, January 10th, 1849.—The invention consists, *Firstly*, in certain improved arrangements of electric apparatus, whereby a visible index hand or pointer is directly acted upon by a single magnet suspended within the sphere of influence of an electro or other magnet, having each of its extremities converted or resolved into two or more poles.

Secondly, Our invention consists in keeping the magnetic bar, needle, or pointer in one position for any length of time, or imparting to such bar, needle, or pointer, any number of distinct deflexions or movements, by means of the current or currents derived from magneto-electricity, and also in making use of the residual magnetism to act upon the needle on its return to its stationary position, instead of the force of gravity; that is to say, in moving the needle in one direction by the induced current, and bringing it back to its stationary position by the action of the reversed inductive current, whereby the motions of the needles are increased in rapidity, and rendered much more marked and distinct than heretofore.

Thirdly, Our invention consists in certain improved arrangements of the magneto-electro apparatus used in electric telegraphs, whereby two distinct currents may be derived from the same magnet, and the reversed current can be made of equal intensity with the primary induced current, and single or double currents may be sent, as required, through any required number of instruments at different stations.

Fourthly, Our invention consists in the improved apportionment of the signs or symbols used in electric telegraphs. [The object of this new apportionment is to reduce the number of movements requisite, and it seems very successfully carried out. We pass over the details, which would occupy more space than we can afford to them.]

Fifthly, Our invention consists of an improved compound of gutta percha, suitable for the insulation, covering, and exterior protection of wire and other metallic substances employed to transmit currents of electricity. We mix the gutta percha nearly in equal portions, by weight, with sand which has been ground or pounded to a degree of fineness exceeding that of the finest natural sand, or with the siftings of glass paper manufactories, or glass fragments and particles of any sort, reduced to a similar degree of fineness, and this either by mixing the pulverized sand or glass with the gutta percha in a state of solution, or while in a plastic state.

Sixthly, Our invention consists in the employment of a current reverser of a peculiar construction, whereby we are enabled to dispense with the use of magneto apparatuses for the purpose of deriving currents of electricity in the manner before described, and to substitute in lieu thereof, voltaic batteries, such as are commonly in use for the purpose of transmitting currents of electricity along metallic conductors, such reverser completing the circuit twice during its motion, by the transmission of a reversed current, in the manner of the magneto machines.

Seventhly, Our invention consists in the employment, in manner following, of currents of electricity to regulate and govern the motions of time-keepers, whether the same be influenced by a current from a distant station or otherwise. We make use for this purpose of the currents of either magneto or voltaic electricity; but obtained in the latter case without the aid of soft iron from two hollow coils of insulated wire affixed to the pendulum of the regulator, and surrounding the poles of two permanent horse-shoe magnets, which coils vibrate in the direction of their length alternately, off one pole on to the other, a current being induced at each vibration, but in opposite directions.

Claims.—1. We claim in respect to electric telegraphs, and to all machines or machinery, to the moving of which electricity is or may be applied, the different arrangements of apparatus described under the first head of this specification, in so far as respects the division of each pole of the magnet into two or more poles, and the direct action on the index hand or pointer, or other recipient of the magnetic influence.

2. We claim the mode of causing the index hand or pointer to be permanently deflected (that is, for any length of time required) in one direction, and bringing it back by the reversed current to its original stationary position, and keeping it there, as before described.

3. We claim the three several magneto-electric apparatuses described under the third head of this specification, in so far as regards the peculiar arrangements and combinations, whereby two distinct currents are obtained from the same magnet, the reversed current is obtained of equal intensity with the primarily induced current, and either single or double currents may be sent as required through any number of instruments at different stations.

4. We claim the improved system of visible symbols suitable for electric telegraphs, before described and exemplified.

5. We claim the employment in electric telegraphs, and in all other machines and machinery to the moving of which electricity is applied, of the peculiar compound of gutta percha, before described, for purposes of insulation and protection.

6. We claim the improved current reverser, before described, in so far as respects the effecting by a single depression of the lever or key, the completing, reversing, and breaking of the electric current.

7. We claim the application of currents of magneto-electricity to regulate the motion of time-keepers in the peculiar manner described under the seventh head of this specification; that is to say, in so far as regards the obtaining of the currents from the inductive action of permanent magnets and coils of insulated wire without the aid of soft iron. And,

8. We claim the application to the regulating of time-keepers of currents of electricity (whether magneto or voltaic) transmitted from a primary or standard clock by the improved apparatuses and instruments, and by the peculiar modes before described, that is to say, in so far as regards the alternate transmission of the current in opposite directions, and the different mechanical arrangements whereby that is effected.—*London Mech. Mag.*, *Vol. L*, *p.* 148.

Henley's Magneto-Electric Telegraph.—An experiment has been made under the direction of the French Government, to test the efficacy of Mr. Henley's Magneto-Electric Telegraph, which is worked without batteries of any kind, and at a fraction of the cost of the voltaic system. The line of railway assumed for the trial was that from Paris to Valenciennes. The persons present at the two stations were, the Director of the French telegraph, a Commissioner appointed by the Belgian Government, and a few others. The distance is 180 miles, being the longest telegraph line in France. After a most satisfactory series of trials on the single distance, first with full power, and afterwards with one-twentieth of the power, the wires were connected so as to treble the total length of wire, making 540 miles to and from Paris and back; the magnetic message being communicated through the first wire, back by the second, through the third, and back again by the earth. It was not anticipated that the magnet could possibly work through this resistance; but in fact, it is alleged it was worked as directly and rapidly as when only made to traverse the 180 miles with full power. The ordinary telegraph, with battery power, used by the French Government, was then put in requisition, but not the slightest effect was produced. On the single distance even, a signal was not obtained for several minutes, owing, it is said, to some fault in the batteries. The Government officers and others inspecting the working operation, expressed themselves thoroughly satisfied with the series of trial.—*London Mining Journal*, 1850.

Highton's Improvements in Electric Telegraphs.—On February 7, 1850, Mr. Edward Highton, Engineer, Middlesex, England, patented the following arrangement of telegraphic circuits: "Two or more signalizing instruments, and to each instrument two batteries are connected, so placed in regard to their poles as to work in opposite directions. A method of working electric telegraphs by the inductive influence of electro-magnets, making the dials, which carry the letters or characters, movable, instead of the pointers. As many of his claims are old, I only notice such as are important. He incloses his wires in flexible materials, such as lead; this was done in 1844, by Prof. Morse. The protecting the telegraphic wires by enveloping them in masonry; also, enameling the exterior surface of gutta percha coating of electric wires by rubbing the surface over with naphtha, or other solvents, and then smoothing it down by a cushion or brush.

A method of constructing the supporting posts out of a number of planks firmly united together, instead of out of one piece of timber, cut taperingly, as has hitherto been the custom.

Removing the atmospheric electricity which is collected during storms or other atmospheric disturbances, by causing the line wire, or a bar of iron connected thereto, previously enclosed in bibulous paper, or other fabric, to pass through a mass of iron filings.—*London Mech. Mag.*, *No.* 1413, *Sept.* 1, 1850.

Brown and Williams's Improvements in Electric and Magnetic Telegraphs, *March* 17, 1850.—The only new claim is a method of protecting the conducting wires of electric telegraphs by strands of hemp put on by a braiding engine, and then coating the whole by gutta percha. And a method of connecting the transmitting wires by screwing one end of a wire into a nut formed on the corresponding end of the next wire.—*Lond. Mech. Mag.*, *March* 7, 1850.

W. S. Thomas's Improvements in Electric Telegraphs, *patented Feb.* 12, 1850. *Claim.*—What I claim as new is, the making of signals or marks for telegraphic purposes, by the agency of heat, generated, induced, or controlled by a current of electricity passed along attenuated conductors, wires, or points; the signals being the flashes of light emitted by the heated conductor or points, are manifest to the eye of the operator; the marks being produced on the paper by the heated point or conductor are the record of the message.—*Journ. Frank. Inst.*, *Sept.* 1850.

Mr. J. L. Palvermacher, C. E., of Vienna. Improvement in Galvanic Batteries, in Electric Telegraphs, and Electro-Magnetic and Magneto-Electric Machines.—I only notice his improvements in electric telegraphs, that is to say, in so far as regards, 1st, A method of varying the intensity of the current, either by increasing or diminishing the number of elements employed, or by interposing more or less powerful resistance to the current. 2d, The imprinting letters or signs by one completion of the current. 3d, The substitution of a letter cylinder for the letter wheel ordinarily employed, and a method of arranging the letters and signs on each cylinder. 4th, The application of a double escapement, each capable of assuming four directions, and each producing effects different from those produced by the others. 5th, The employment of four electro-magnets, to act on two soft iron bars, and thereby render a weak galvanic current available in two directions, and productive of two separate and distinct effects. And, 6th, The method of gradually detaching the keeper from the electro-magnet, by causing the springs which act upon the keeper magnet, to come only successively into operation.—*Lond. Min. Journ. Vol. XX, p.* 323, *July*, 1850.

Mitchell's Electric Telegraph.—At a recent meeting of the Philosophical Society of Glasgow, Alexander Mitchell, in a lecture on the electric telegraph, introduced some improvements stated to have been made by him in the general arrangement of the instrument, in the use of only one wire, and in the great facility by which the instruments can be worked. As given in a Glasgow paper, it appears that letters are arranged in a segment in front of the operator, and corresponding ones inscribing on keys similar to those of a piano-forte. On pressing down a key, the corresponding letter is immediately pointed to by a needle, a similar movement taking place at every station throughout the circuit. We know not if Mr. Mitchell was the first constructor of this kind of telegraph, but we do know that a similar one was exhibited two years since at the Society of Arts; and we also know that several inventors of telegraphs have been content to use only one wire, employing the earth for the return circuit.—*Lond. Mining Journ. Vol. XX, April* 13th, 1850.

Austin F. Park's Improvements in Electric Telegraph Manipulators, Troy, New York, August 27, 1850.—"The nature of my invention consists in arranging machinery for closing and breaking an electric telegraph circuit in transmitting intelligence, whereby the operator, by giving a finger key one instantaneous touch, as distinguished from the prolonged touch applied to the key in ordinary machines, closes and breaks the electric circuit, at and during such time as is required to signal or record a telegraphic sign for a letter, figure, or other character."—*Journ. Frank. Inst., Vol. XX, p.* 245.

The machine is stated to be ingenious, but unfortunately it is too complicated; the advantages of its use are to prevent mistakes from being made by telegraphic operators. I have not given the claims, as it could not be understood without a drawing.

Charles S. Bulkley's Improvements in Repeaters for Electro-Magnetic Telegraphs, Macon, Bibb Co., Georgia, Nov. 12, 1850. *Claim.*—"What I claim as my invention is, the manner of connecting two galvanic circuits with the two electro-magnets, (*a a*, and *d d*, in the said repeater,) each of the said galvanic circuits, as it passes through my said telegraphic repeater, embracing in its course the armature of the opposite electro-magnet, in the said instrument, previous to its passing through the helices in the electro-magnet, embraced in its own respective circuit.

"In combination with the above, I also claim the connecting the points with the galvanic battery (or batteries), when the said points are placed in such positions in relation to the armatures of the electro-magnets in my said telegraphic repeater that when either one of the said electro-magnets is charged, it will, by attracting its armature against one of the points *l* or *i*, close the poles of the galvanic current in which the opposite electro-magnet (in the instrument) is in connexion, and thereby throw the battery into said circuit."—*Journ. Frankl. Inst., Vol. XXI*, 3*d series.*

The object of this repeater is for the purpose of repeating or recording a communication in several places at once along a line, and at the same time allowing the galvanic circuit to remain open when the line is not in use.

Siemens' Improvements in Electric Telegraphs.—Ernst Werner Siemens, of Berlin, patented in England, April 23, 1850, the following improvements: *Claims.*—"1st, The constructing electro-magnets for telegraphic purposes, of longitudinally divided tubes of iron or other magnetic metal, or of bundles of wire of iron or other magnetic metal.

"2d, The construction of instruments, for obtaining motion for telegraphic purposes, by means of one or two-electro magnets revolving on their axes within the fixed coils, by which they are rendered magnetic, or mounted on a transverse axis, and vibrating from side to side within the coils, by which they are magnetized.

"3d, The construction of instruments for producing motion for telegraphic purposes by means of metallic spiral coils or bands traversed by electric currents, and attracting or repelling each other; also producing motion in such spirals by the proximity of permanent magnets, which at the same time serve to produce electric currents by induction for working telegraphic apparatus.

"4th, The construction of the conducting contact pieces of alloys of platinum, iridium, or palladium with gold or silver, whether such alloys be further alloyed by the admixture of other metals or not.

"5th, The construction of electric telegraphic printing apparatus in such manner that the magnet which works the step by step motion, breaks and restores the circuit by the oscillation of the armature, or of the moving magnet itself.

"6th, The combining of electric telegraphic printing apparatus in the same circuit with indicating apparatus, when the magnets which work the step by step motion of either or both instruments break and restore the circuit by the oscillation of the armatures, or of the magnets themselves.

"7th, The impression of the types on the paper at the instant that the type-wheel stops, by arranging the electro-magnet which acts on the hammer, so that the short intermittent currents which work the electro-magnet of the type-wheel traverses the coils of this magnet without producing motion of the armature, which, however, is set in motion when the current is rendered continuous by the stoppage of the type-wheel.

"8th, The arrangement of the magnet which acts on the hammer in electro-telegraphic printing apparatus, so that its own circuit is broken by the magnet itself towards the end of its stroke.

"9th, The arrangement of apparatus in electric printing apparatus in such manner that the printing is effected by pressing the type against paper, in contact with an inked roller.

"10th, An arrangement for retaining the moving piece which breaks and restores the electric circuit in its respective positions.

"11th, The application of a small pin for preventing the overrunning of the ratchet-wheel in electric telegraphic apparatus, with the step by step motion.

"12th, The arrangement of a transmitting apparatus with an indicating or printing electric apparatus worked by step by step motion, or with both together, in such manner that the transmitting apparatus breaks and restores the circuit of the telegraphic apparatus, which reciprocally breaks and restores the circuit of the transmitting instrument.

"13th, The combination of a self-acting alarum, with a transmitting apparatus.

"14th, The combination of a self-acting alarum with a transmitting instrument, which breaks and restores the circuit of the alarum magnet, which in its turn reciprocally breaks and restores the circuit of the transmitting instrument.

"15th, The combination of one or two cylinders carrying pins, with a series of springs and keys, for making contacts for transmitting a distinct determinate succession of electric currents in one or both directions by the depression of each key.

"16th, The employment of an implement of the nature of a plough, and revolving cutters for making trenches or channels to receive underground line wires.

"17th, The application of the propelling power of a locomotive engine to giving motion to such implements.

"18th, Conducting under-ground line wires into the ground, by means of suitable guides, which either form part of, or immediately follow, the cutting instruments.

"19th, The following improvement in the manufacture of coated wire for electric telegraphic purposes: first, an arrangement of machinery for coating the wire, with two cylinders and pistons, by which the pressure of the semi-fluid mass against the wire is equalized; 2d, arranging these cylinders, (or cylinder when only one is used,) so that they may be removed and replaced by others, while the former are being discharged; and, 3d, the consolidating of gutta percha or its compounds within these cylinders in vacuo.

"20th, The testing of coated wire for telegraphic purposes, by passing it through water, with which is connected an apparatus capable of producing electric shocks, so that the circuit may include the person of the operator, and may be completed by the passage of the electricity through the defects in the coating in the wires.

"21st, The covering of insulated under-ground line wires with strips of sheet lead.

"22d, Establishing a direct communication between under-ground line wires and the earth, by means of a thin wire of German silver, or some other imperfectly conducting substance, so that the resistance to the passage of the electricity may be capable of being regulated at pleasure. *London Mechanics' Magazine, No.* 1421, *Nov.* 2, 1850.

An interesting report of M. Siemens' telegraph to the Academy of Science, Paris, will be found in VOL. XXI, Third Series, of this Journal, p. 209 and 255-15, 1850.

The commission conclude their report of M. Siemens' apparatus in the following words: "The commission have examined M. Siemens' apparatus with great interest, and remarked throughout, an evidence of a perfect intelligence of the theory, as M. Siemens appears to have taken into account all the complicated phenomena which are manifested in the conductors and electro-magnets, especially when the actions are of short duration.

"M. Siemens' system, if worked with care and attention, appears to possess incontestible superiority over all other apparatus of the like nature, that is to say, the ordinary arrangement of alphabetic apparatus; as the latter do not work with the same degree of precision and accuracy. With regard to speed, the commission are led to believe that M. Siemens' apparatus surpasses all other alphabetic apparatus; their opinion is, also, that M. Siemens' improvements in the construction of electro-magnets will prove advantageous."

Horn's Igniting Telegraph, patented June 25, 1850.—The register invented by G. H. Horn, of Boston, employs a principle, namely, the heating or igniting effect of electricity. When an electrical current flows through a fine platinum wire it ignites it, or brings it to a red heat. If this wire is bent, as at A, in figure 55, so as to be in contact, for a short distance, with a moving fillet of paper, it will burn a hole through the paper when the current passes. This can be done with great rapidity, so as to represent probably a hundred linear letters per minute.

Fig. 55.

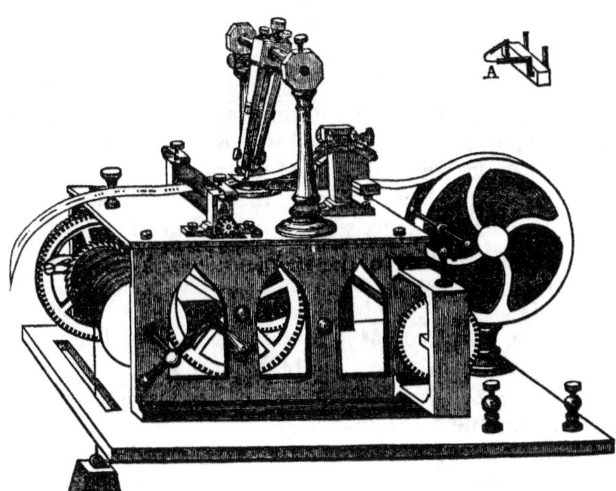

This instrument, the greater part of which consists of the clock-work, spool, &c., required for moving the paper. Above the clock-work are two pillars, supporting an axis, upon which is the adjustable wire-holder, the lower extremity of which is seen touching the fillet of paper. By means of the connexions and insulations of the pillars, axis, and wire-holder, the platinum wire, which passes over a little slip of porcelain at the end of the wire-holder, becomes part of the circuit, with which the two screw-cups on the right of the base-board are connected. When the wire needs adjustment, the wire-holder can be turned up on its axis. The bed supporting the fillet of paper is also adjustable, so as to regulate the contact between the wire and the paper.

This register requires a quantity current to produce the effect of ignition, and therefore needs a receiving instrument and local battery, to be operated by the telegraphic circuit.—*Book of the Telegraph, p.* 37.

This telegraph is the same in principle with that patented by Wm. S. Thomas, Feb. 13, 1850.

Before concluding these lectures I will here notice two telegraphs which I have omitted in their regular order, and first of

The Telegraph of Brett and Little of London.—The magnet employed in this telegraph is in the form of a ring or horse-shoe, and is suspended in the centre of helices of copper wire, which are double and of a circular form. This magnet is deflected either to the right hand or to the left, according to the direction of the current. The indicators are not magnets, but are moved by the agency of the magnets, by which a distinct and certain indication is insured.

Another modification of this instrument has been made by Mr. Little, which is as follows: the patent instrument is of the form of a disk of mahogany, about 1 foot high by 8 inches broad, standing in a vertical position on a pedestal; the only appliances at the back being the metallic buttons, or binding screws, necessary to convey the galvanic fluid from the battery to the indicators. Two tubes of glass about one-fourth of an inch in diameter, and 3 inches high, are placed in front of the disk, with the alphabet engraved on a metallic plate placed between them, with the number of deflexions required to express each letter, stated in plain figures. On the top of each of these tubes, which contain spirits of wine, is a small but powerful cylindrical magnet about one-fourth of an inch in diameter, from the bottom of which are suspended by magnetic attraction, two needles with the points upwards.

On completing the galvanic circuit, these needles are deflected with equal rapidity with one on an axis; and on breaking connexion, the needle is instantly arrested in its fall to the perpendicular by the density of the fluid, with almost as dead a stop as the seconds hand of a watch, avoiding the vibration so annoying in the old system, which tends so much to puzzle and mislead.—*Lond. Mining Journ., Vol. XXI, p.* 183.

Bakewell's Electric Telegraph.—This is a modification of the instrument of Alex. Bain, Esq., noticed under the head of Electro-chemical Telegraphs, employing the same chemical agent, but instead of holes cut in paper, the message to be sent is written on a sheet of tin foil with sealing wax varnish; this is placed on the transmitting cylinder; all the lines of the non-conducting varnish serving to break the connexion. On the receiving cylinder, a sheet of paper moistened with acidulated ferro prussiate of potash is placed. When the connexion is completed, electro-chemical decomposition is effected; and where any interruption occurs, no change takes place.

Improvements in Electric Telegraphs, by John McGregor.—In No. 1409

of the *London Mechanics' Magazine*, for 1850, there is a notice of a patent for some improvements in Electric Telegraphs, and amongst the abstract of claims is the following:—

"8. An arrangement for sounding one out of a number of alarums."

It is impossible, of course, to infer from this brief notice what are the particulars of the invention, and I am not aware of the mode at present adopted. If there be none, by which one only out of a number of stations may be signalled, then I would propose for consideration a plan for effecting this desirable object which occurred to my mind some time ago.

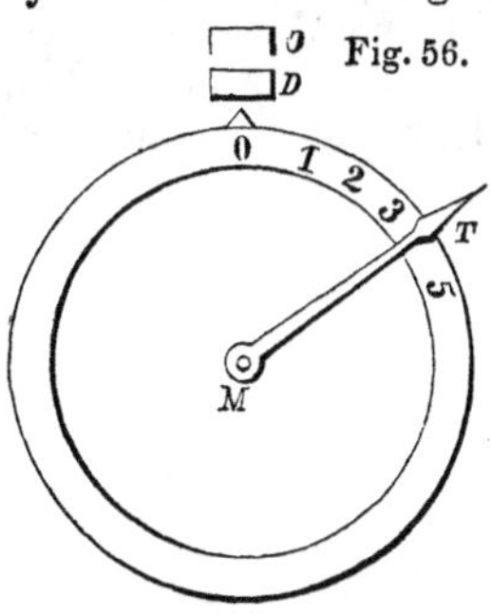

Fig. 56.

Let the accompanying figure represent a wheel, with marks 1, 2, 3, and 4, at equal distances on the circumference, and corresponding in number to the whole number of stations, say 60, connected by telegraph.

Let the axle of this wheel be made to turn once in a minute by clock-work, and the wheel be so placed on the axle that so long as a detent D rests on a projection P (opposite to the mark O), the wheel shall be at rest; but when D is lifted (by electricity), the wheel shall have sufficient friction-hold on the axle to cause it to turn round in the same time—that is, once in a minute. Now let R be a radial arm, capable of being placed at any of the marks 1, 2, 3, &c., and furnished with a projection T, which shall always pass free of D, but be caught by a catch C, provided that catch descends when T is within a certain distance on either side of the line C M. The catch C is supposed to be moved by electricity, and if it falls so as to strike T, the wheel will be stopped, a certain circuit completed, and a bell rung; but if C does not fall on T, it will be wholly inoperative on the machine.

A wheel similar to that described should be at every station, and in general the radial arm R, at each station, should be left opposite to the particular number denoting that station.

Thus the arm R, at No. 2 or No. 27, will be at angles at the line D M, particularly representing such stations respectively.

Supposing magnets, circuits, and bells to be so arranged that the bell of each station shall be set ringing only when a current is completed through C and T, we may describe the action of the instrument as follows:

If station No. 20 *requires to correspond with No.* 35, *then*—

1. Put the arm R opposite the mark 35 on the rim.
2. Send a current along the wire which will release the detents D *at all the stations*, and all the wheels will commence moving (at nearly the same rate.)
3. When the point T comes under C, (that is, in 35 seconds,) the similar point at station No. 35 will then be beneath its catch; therefore send another current along the line, which will affect only wheels No. 35 and No. 20, and will ring the bell of 35.
4. After the communication of the message, return the wheels 20 and 35 to their original position. All the other wheels will have gone round for *one minute*, and will *themselves* have come into the exact position they were in at first.

By this means, the average time (in the above supposed circumstances) required to signal one station would be half a minute; but if that should be thought too long(!) the wheels might move at double the proposed rate, and the convenience of this plan will depend on the time of revolution of the wheels, and the amount of margin which can be permitted on either side of a perfect agreement of their motions.

We shall see that a comparatively inaccurate adjustment would not impair the usefulness of this simple apparatus; for if the catch C were made of such a breadth as to operate on T, when it is at the distance from the line M C represented by *nearly* half an interval on either side of that line, an error of nearly half a second in a minute may be allowed without deranging the instrument.

ON THE

TELEGRAPHIC LINES OF THE WORLD.

UNITED STATES.

In giving an account of the number of telegraphic lines, it will be proper to place the United States as first on the list, from the number and extent of the lines, and from the extensive use made of them in every department, both for business and pleasure. Still, it will be but an approximation to the number, for they are like the spider's web, forming a complete network over the length and breadth of the land, from the extreme north-eastern point to the western boundary of Missouri, adjoining the Indian territory. A continuous line of telegraph now extends from the verge of civilization on the western frontier (east of the Rocky Mountains) to the north-eastern extremity of the United States; and the time is not far distant when we shall have a telegraph from the Mississippi river to San Francisco. This is no fancy sketch, as the route is already selected for the California line, and a most interesting Report was presented to the Senate of the United States in the session of 1851, by the Committee on Post Offices and Post Roads.

"The route selected by the Committee is, according to the survey of Captain W. W. Chapman, U. S. Army, one of the best that could be adopted, possessing as it does great local advantages. It will commence at the City of Natchez, in the State of Mississippi, running through a well settled portion of Northern Texas, to the town of El Paso, on the Rio Grande, in latitude 32°; thence to the junction of the Gila and Colorado rivers, crossing at the head of the Gulf of California, to San Diego, on the Pacific; thence along the Coast to Monterey and San Francisco. By this route, the whole line between the Mississippi River and Pacific Ocean will be south of latitude 33°; consequently, almost entirely free from the great difficulties to be encountered, owing to the snow and ice on the Northern route, by the way of the South Pass, crossing the Sierra Nevada Mountains in latitude 39°. The whole distance from the Mississippi to San Francisco will be about 2400 miles."

The great benefits to be derived, the Report fully and ably sets forth, whether in a military, commercial, or social point of view.

"In a commercial point of view, the line in question assumes a gigantic importance, and presents itself not only in the attitude of a means of communication between the opposite extremes of a single country, however great, but as a channel for imparting knowledge between distant parts of the earth. With the existing facilities, it requires months to convey information from the sunny climes of the East to the less favored, in point of climate, but not less important regions of the West, teeming as they do, with the products of art and enterprise. Let this line of wires be established, and the Pacific and Atlantic Oceans become as one, and intelligence will be conveyed from London to India in a shorter time than was required ten years since to transmit a letter from New York to Liverpool."

"Nor does the importance of the undertaking claim less interest, when regarded in a social point of view. California is being peopled daily and hourly by our friends, our kindred, and our political brethren. The little bands that a few centuries since landed on the Western shores of the Atlantic, have now become a mighty nation. The tide of population has been rolling onward, increasing as it approached the setting sun, until at length our people look abroad upon the Pacific, and have their homes almost within sight of the spice groves of Japan. Although separated from us by thousands of miles of distance, they will be again restored to us in feeling, and still present to our affections, through the help of this noiseless tenant of the wilderness."

In the Congressional *Globe* of April 6, 1852, Mr. Douglass presented the memorial of Henry O'Reilly, proposing a system of intercommunication by mail and telegraph, between the Atlantic and Pacific States. All he asks is permission to establish a telegraphic line from the Mississippi Valley, where the wires now terminate, to the Pacific Ocean, and to be protected by a line of military posts, so that he can keep up the communication for the benefit both of the Government and of the public. Mr. O'Reilly states in this memorial, that within two years from this time, with this line completed, he would be able to deliver the European news on the shores of the Pacific within one week from the time it left the European Continent. The motion was referred to the Committee on Territories.

These are but a part of the advantages set forth in the bill, with a strong recommendation from the Committee for its passage.

The authorities of Newfoundland have granted to Mr. H. B. Tibbatts and associates, of New York, the exclusive right to construct and use the magnetic telegraph across that island, for the period of thirty years. The grant is designed to facilitate Mr. Tibbatts in his scheme for the establishment of steam and telegraphic communication between New York and Liverpool or London, *in five days*. The telegraph is to extend from New York to St. Johns, from whence a line of steamers is to run to Galway, where another line of telegraph is to commence, extending to London. This latter line will, it is said, be completed during the current year. The distance from St. Johns to Galway is 1647 miles, or about five days' sail.

There are numerous lines in actual and successful operation under the title of Morse, House, and Bain, each giving every facility to the business man.

A recent letter from Charles T. Chester, Esq., Telegraphic Engineer, who is connected with the Morse Line, the first and most extensive one in the United States, gives the following statistics of the facilities for the transmission of intelligence along their lines in the chief cities of this country.

"Three Morse wires run to Boston, three to Buffalo, five to Philadelphia, four to Washington, and two on to New Orleans; on the Western and Canada routes there is generally but one."

New York and Boston Magnetic Telegraph Company, from N. York to Boston, about 250 miles; three wires, one passing through Providence, R. Island, the other through Springfield, Mass., using the Morse patent.

Merchant's Telegraph Company, from New York to Boston, about 250 miles; two wires passing through Providence, using Bain's patent.

Boston and Portland Telegraph Company, from Boston to Portland, 100 miles; one wire, using Morse's patent.

The Merchant's Telegraph Company have one wire from Boston to Portland, 100 miles; Bain's patent.

The New York and Boston Telegraph Company, and Merchant's Telegraph Company, between New York and Boston, have consolidated and formed one company under the title of N. York and N. England Union Telegraph Company; Boston and Portland are also included in the new Company, which extends from New York to Portland.

Maine Telegraph Company, from Portland to Calais, Maine, about 350 miles; one wire; Morse's patent.

St. Johns and Halifax line, from Calais to Halifax, about 400 miles; one wire; Morse's patent.

There is a line of Bain Telegraph from Boston through N. Hampshire to Burlington, Vt., thence to Ogdensburg, New York; about 350 miles; one wire.

New York, Albany, and Buffalo line, from N. York to Buffalo, through Albany and Troy; 513 miles long; three wires, using Morse's patent.

New York State Telegraph Company, from N. York to Buffalo, via Albany, two wires; 550 miles long; with a branch from Syracuse to Ogdensburgh, via Oswego; about 150 miles; one wire: also a branch from Troy to Saratoga, 36 miles; one wire; use Bain's patent. There is also a Morse line from Syracuse to Oswego, about 40 miles.

House Telegraph Company, from N. York to Buffalo, via Albany, 550 miles; two wires; use House's patent.

New York and Erie Telegraph, from New York to Dunkirk, via Newburgh, Binghamton, and Ithaca; 440 miles, one wire; Morse's patent.

New York and Erie Railroad Telegraph, for Railroad use, along the line of N. York and Erie Railroad, 460 miles; Morse's patent.

Magnetic Telegraph Company, from New York to Washington, via Philadelphia; seven wires, 260 miles; Morse's patent.

House Line from New York to Philadelphia, 100 miles, one wire; House's patent.

Troy and Canada Junction Telegraph Company, from Troy to Montreal, through Burlington, Vt., 260 miles; one wire; Morse's patent.

Erie and Michigan Telegraph Company, from Buffalo to Milwaukie, via Cleveland, Detroit, and Chicago; one wire all the way; second wire from Buffalo to Cleveland; 800 miles long; Morse's patent.

Cleveland and Cincinnati Telegraph Company, from Cleveland to Cincinnati; 250 miles long; two wires; Morse's patent.

Cincinnati to St. Louis, via Indianapolis, 400 miles long; one wire; Morse's patent.

Cleveland and Pittsburg Telegraph Company, from Cleveland to Pittsburg, 150 miles, one wire; Morse's patent.

Cleveland and Zanesville Line, from Cleveland to Zanesville, 150 miles; one wire; Morse's patent.

Lake Erie Telegrapn Company, from Buffalo to Detroit, via Cleveland, 400 miles; one wire; Morse's instrument, built under O'Reilly's contract with Morse, with branch from Cleveland to Pittsburg, 150 miles; one wire.

Cincinnati and Sandusky City Line, about 200 miles; one wire; Morse's patent.

Toledo to Terra Haute, via Forte Wayne, about 300 miles; one wire; Morse's patent.

Chicago to Dayton, one wire; Morse's line.

Chicago to St. Louis, via Peoria, about 400 miles; one wire; Morse's patent.

Milwaukie to Green Bay; 200 miles; one wire; Morse's patent.

Milwaukie to Galena, via Madison, about 250 miles; one wire; Morse's patent.

Chicago to Janesville; one wire; Morse's patent.

Buffalo and Canada Junction Telegraph Company, from Buffalo to Lewiston; one wire; connecting with a wire in Canada that runs to Toronto, about 200 miles.

There are three companies, if not four, owning the line from Boston to Halifax; from Portland to Calais, Maine, one company, using the Morse instrument; from Calais to Halifax, the Morse instrument is used; the line in each province is owned by separate companies, organized under charters from their respective legislatures.

No. 7. The New York and Boston Morse line extends from New York to Boston; to reach Halifax it connects at Boston with lines in No. 6.

The Northwestern Telegraph Company that extends in Wisconsin and Northern Illinois from Chicago to Waukegon, Ill., to Kenoska, Wis., Ravine, Milwaukie, Port Washington, Shebbygon, Shebbygon Falls, Greenbush, Fond du Lac, Oshkosh, Neenok, or Winnebago Rapids, to Appleton and Green Bay; whole distance by the line, 267 miles; hence, from Milwaukie west to Waukosha, Palmyra, Whitewater, Jefferson, Lake Mills, Madison, Dodgeville, Mineral Point, to Shullsburgh and Galena, Illinois; and from Madison, the Capital of Wisconsin, to Sank Prairie, Boraboo, and St. Winnebago; whole distance, 238 miles; from Chicago west to Naperville, Aurora, Oswego, Balaria, Geneva, St. Charles, Elgin, Dundee, Woodstock, Morengo, Belvidere, Rockford, Freeport, and Galena; from Rockford north up Rock River to Rockton, Beloit, Wis., Janesville, to Whitewater, and there intersects. Also, cross line from Rockford, Ill., down Rock River to Byron, Mount Morris, Oregon, Grand Detour, to Dixon; 310 miles; making in all in this Company, 815 miles.

The above list will give an approximation of the number of the Morse lines, obtained principally from E. Cornell, Esq., President N. York and Erie Telegraph Company, and S. W. Hotchkiss, Esq.

The first American telegraphic line was established in May, 1844, be tween Washington and Baltimore, over a length of 40 miles.

The line from Washington to Baltimore was then extended to Philadelphia and New York, over a distance of 250 miles. It reached Boston in 1845, and became the great line of the North, from which branched two others: one, the length of 1000 miles, from Philadelphia to Harrisburg, Lancaster, Pittsburg, Ohio, Columbus, Cincinnati, Louisville (Kentucky), and

St. Louis (Missouri); the other, the length of 1300 miles, from New York to Albany, Troy, Utica, Rochester, Buffalo, Erie, Cleveland (Ohio), Chicago (Illinois), and Milwaukie (Wisconsin).

A fourth line goes from Buffalo to Lockport, Queenstown, the Lakes Ontario and Erie, the Cataracts of Niagara, Toronto, Kingston, Montreal, Quebec, Halifax, and the Atlantic Ocean, over an extent of 1395 miles.

Two lines South; one from Cleveland to New Orleans, by Cincinnati; the other from Washington to New Orleans, by Fredericksburg, Charleston, Savannah, and Mobile. The first is 1200 miles long, the second 1700 miles. This line has been extended West to Independence, Missouri.

The entire length of the line from New York to New Orleans, via Charleston, Savannah, and Mobile, is 1966 miles; and this distance was not worked in one circuit, nor can it be with either of the existing systems with the best mode of insulating in use. The only instance of direct communication was secured by dividing the line into several circuits, probably five or six, and connecting those circuits through the agency of an instrument termed a connector, the effect of which is to cause one circuit to work the other through the entire series, thus producing a result similar to working through the entire line in one circuit. The connector is an instrument first invented and applied by E. Cornell, Esq., of N. York, on the N. York, Albany, and Buffalo line, at Auburn N. York, to work a branch line from Auburn to Ithaca, for the purpose of taking news reports at Ithaca; at the same time they were being transmitted from N. York to Buffalo on the main line; this was adopted in the year 1846; it was found to work admirably, and he afterwards modified it so as to make it applicable to working both ways in a main line, or in other words, to make it capable of working a number of series of circuits in a main line; the instrument was adopted for this purpose on the N. York and Erie, and Erie and Michigan lines, in the year 1848, and has been in constant use ever since; by it they having frequently worked direct from N. York to Milwaukie, 1300 miles. The instrument used on the New Orleans line, which was described in my Lectures on the Telegraph, was adopted by Mr. Chas. Bulkley, the then superintendant of the line, who claims it as his invention, made in 1850 or 1851.

The greatest distance that Mr. Cornell has known any lines to work in *one* circuit, was from Boston to Montreal, via N. York, Buffalo and Toronto, a distance of about 1500 miles; this, however, was done when the earth was frozen, and the lines thus insulated by the frost much better than man has yet contrived to insulate them without its aid. There are no lines working succesfully in *one* circuit more than 550 miles; lines may be so insulated as to work in one circuit under favorable states of the atmosphere from 8 to 1000 miles.

The House Printing Telegraph has only been in operation since 1846, but even in that short time has spread itself from N. York to St. Louis, N. York to Boston, and N. York to Philadelphia, working to the entire satisfaction of our business community, and wherever found, exciting the admiration of the curious, being able to print in Roman capitals communications in almost every language.

This line consists of the Boston and New York Telegraph Company, using the House Printing Telegraph; about 600 miles of wire, two wires;

with stations at Boston, Mass.; Providence, R. I.; Springfield, Mass.; Hartford, Conn.; New Haven, and New York.

A line is being constructed to connect with this Boston line, running from Springfield, Mass., to Albany, N. Y.; there to intersect the New York and Buffalo line, using the same instruments, extending from New York to Buffalo, a distance of 570 miles. One wire is now in operation, connecting with Poughkeepsie, Troy, Albany, Utica, Syracuse, Lyons, Rochester, Albion, Lockport, and Buffalo; and another wire, nearly completed the same distance. This line is to continue to St. Louis, Mo., connecting with Cleveland, Cincinnati, Louisville, and St. Louis, which will be completed the entire distance in 1852; the whole length being 1500 miles.

The New Jersey Magnetic Telegraph Company, using the House instruments, and the first line of this kind ever put in operation, extends from Philadelphia to New York; one wire, 132 miles; and another now being put up. For this information, I am indebted to the politeness of William J. Philips, Esq., Telegraphic Engineer on the House line at Philadelphia.

Making the whole number of miles 2202; rate, 25 cents for the first ten words from Philadelphia to New York.

The Bain Line, now a Morse Line, Mr. Henry J. Rodgers, General Superintendant from New York to Washington, has lately constructed, at an expense of $10,000, spars 310 feet high, at the Palisades and Fort Washington, ten miles above the City of New York, for the purpose of sustaining their wires over the river, instead of the method formerly employed, by passing the current through the water, by wires laid across the North River. He considers this method, by means of suspension on spars, as being more permanent and durable. The price of telegraphic despatches by this line is the same as the others. They have offices in Boston, Providence, New York, Philadelphia, Wilmington, Baltimore, and Washington

List of the Bain Telegraph Lines in the United States.

	Wires.	Miles.
1. New York to Boston, via. Providence, 250 miles each, .	2	500
2. Boston to Portland, ...	1	100
3. Boston through New Hampshire to Burlington, Vermont, thence to Ogdensburg, New York, ...	1	350
4. Troy to Saratoga, ...	1	36
5. New York to Buffalo, (513 miles each,)	2	1026
Total, .	7	2012

List of the Morse Telegraph Lines in the United States.

	Wires.	Miles.
1. Washington to New Orleans, by way of Richmond, Va., .	1	1716
2. Washington to New York, by way of Baltimore and Philadelphia, each 260 miles, ...	7	1820
3. Harper's Ferry to Winchester, Va., ...	1	32
4. Baltimore, by way of Pittsburg and Wheeling, to Cumberland,	1	324
5. Baltimore to Harrisburg, by way of York, Pa., . .	1	72
6. York to Lancaster, by way of Columbia, Pa., . . .	1	22
Carried up, ...	12	3986

	Wires.	Miles.
Brought up, ...	12	3986
7. Philadelphia to Lewistown, Del., ...	1	12
8. Philadelphia to Pittsburg, by way of Harrisburg, . .	1	309
9. Philadelphia to Pottsville, by way of Reading, . .	1	98
10. Reading to Harrisburg, ...	1	51
11. New York to Boston, about 250 miles, by way of Providence, Rhode Island, and Springfield, Massachusetss, . .	3	750
12. New York to Buffalo, by way of Troy and Albany, .	3	1539
13. Syracuse to Oswego, N. Y., ...	1	40
14. Boston to Portland, by way of Dover, . . .	2	200
15. Worcester to New Bedford, by way of Providence, .	1	97
16. Worcester to New London, by way of Norwich, . .	1	74
17. Portland to Calais, Me., ...	1	350
18. Calais to Halifax via. St. Johns, ...	1	400
19. Troy to Montreal, Canada, by way of Rutland and Burlington,	1	278
20. Buffalo to Queenston, Canada, by way of Lockport, . .	1	48
21. Buffalo to Milwaukie, Wis., by way of Cleveland, Detroit, and Chicago; second wire from Buffalo to Cleveland	2	800
22. Pittsburg to Cincinnati, O., by way of Columbus, . .	1	310
23. Columbia to New Orleans, by way of Tuscumbia and Natchez,	1	638
24. New Orleans to Balize, at the mouth of the Mississippi, .	1	90
25. Cincinnati to St. Louis, Mo., by way of Vincennes, .	1	410
26. Cincinnati, Ohio, to Maysville, Ky., by way of Ripley, .	1	60
27. St. Louis to Chicago, by way of Alton, Ill., . . .	1	330
28. Alton to Galena, by way of Quincy, ...	1	380
29. St Louis to Independence, Mo., ...	1	25
30. New York to New Orleans, by way of Charleston, Savannah, and Mobile, ...	1	1966
31. New York to Dunkirk, via. Newburgh, Bighamton, and Ithaca,	1	440
32. New York and Erie Railroad Telegraph, for Railroad use, .	1	460
33. Cleveland to Cincinnati, ...	2	250
34. Cincinnati to St. Louis, via. Indianapolis, ...	1	400
35. Cleveland to Pittsburg, . . .	1	150
36. Cleveland to Zanesville, ...	1	150
37. Buffalo to Detroit, via. Cleveland, ...	1	400
38. Cincinnati to Sandusky City, ...	1	218
39. Toledo to Terra Haute, via. Forte Wayne, . . .	1	300
40. Newark to Zanesville, Ohio, ...	1	40
41. Mansfield to Sandusky, ...	1	40
42. Columbus to Portsmouth, Ohio, ...	1	90
43. Columbus to Lancaster, Ohio, ...	1	25
44. Lancaster to Logansport, ...	1	15
45. Cincinnati to Dayton and Chicago, (wire in Ohio,) .	1	100
46. Milwaukie to Green Bay, ...	1	200
47. Milwaukie to Galena, via. Madison, ...	1	250
48. Chicago to Janesville, ...	1	—
49. Banesville to Marietta, ...	1	66
Total, . .	62	15,835

Whole number of Morse line received; 70 wires, length, .	15,835 miles.
Whole number of House line received; number of wires, 6,	2,200 "
Whole number of Bain line received; number of wires, 6, .	2,012 "
Total number of miles in the United States, . .	20,047

There are not over 2200 miles of House wire up.

There is an "Erie and Allegheny Telegraph Company," having a line from Dunkirk, N. York, via Warren, Pa., thence to New Castle, Pa., and thence to Pittsburg.

Consolidation of Telegraphs.—We learn from the Cincinnati papers, that all the leading Telegraph lines in the West, and South, and Northwest have been united in business interests. The N. Orleans and Ohio line, extending from N. Orleans to Pittsburg; the People's line from N. Orleans to Louisville; the two wires, Louisville, Cincinnati, and Pittsburg line, and the Western line from Wheeling and Pittsburg to Baltimore and Washington city, are all direct parties to the contract—securing these arrangements.

The union brings the Morse and O'Reilly offices in Cincinnati and all other cities on the lines named together. In Cincinnati the Morse lines are removed to the O'Reilly office, which will hereafter be known as the *National Telegraph Office.*

"From an anual Report of the "Magnetic Telegraph Company," extending from Washington to New York, just published, we glean the following table of the number of messages sent, and the amount of money received for tolls for each month of the year. The business, it will be seen, is steadily on the increase:—

		Messages.	Receipts.
July,	1851,	13,463	$4,991·62
August,	"	16,580	5,391·96
September,	"	16,744	4,979·35
October,	"	18,641	6,322·98
November,	"	15,969	5,798·50
December,	"	17,896	7,249·73
January,	1852,	23,962	11,352·97
February,	"	27,880	11,341·75
March,	"	27,934	11,918·63
April,	"	25,523	11,114·01
May,	"	24,933	10,949·75
June,	"	25,298	11,832·03
		$253,857	$103,232·37

The first six months was before the consolidation with the Bain line; the last six was after the consolidation, and includes the receipts of both lines. The business of the several months fluctuates a little, though, by comparing the first six months with the last six, it will be seen that the use of the line is increasing wonderfully. The number of messages sent in the first six months, is 99,313, producing $34,733·14; and in the last six the number was 154,514, producing $68,499·23. It is proper to state, however, that, in January last, the "Magnetic Telegraph Company" became possessed of the wires of the Bain line, extending from Washington to New York, by which the Company's facilities were increased, and its business augmented beyond what it probably would have been without such facilities. The increase of December over July, and of June over January, and the very large business of October and March, the most active business months in the year, show the general and growing use of this wonderful invention by the public generally, as well as by that enterprising class of persons, the merchants, brokers, and bankers. The following table exhibits the annual receipts of this Company, which was the first organized in the country, from its commencement to the present:—

From January 27, 1846, to July 1, 1846	$ 4,228·77
" July 1, 1840, to July 1, 1847,	32,810·28
" July 1, 1846, to July 1, 1848,	52,252·81
" July 1, 1848, to July 1, 1849,	63,367·62
" July 1, 1849, to July 1, 1850,	61,383·98
" July 1, 1850, to July 1, 1851,	67,737·12
" July 1, 1851, to July 1, 1852,	103,860·84
Total amount received up to July, 1852,	$385,641·42

The capital of the Company is $370,000. It has six wires from Washington to Philadelphia, and seven from Philadelphia to New York. It has offices at Washington, Baltimore, Havre de Grace, Port Deposit, Wilmington, Philadelphia, Trenton, New Hope, Princeton, New Brunswick, Newark, Jersey City, and New York, and employs in its service, including messengers, outside laborers engaged in keeping the line in order, clerks, operators, etc., about one hundred and twenty-five persons. The distance from Washington to New York, by the line of the wires, is about two hundred and seventy-five miles; requiring between nineteen hundred and two thousand miles of wire. The cost for chemicals is considerable, and the amount of stationery quite immense; the single item of envelopes for the year reaching in number nearly one quarter of a million. This is the pioneer line of magnetic telegraph in the world, and very large sums have been expended in various experiments, the object all the time being to make it as perfect as possible. It is now, perhaps, all things considered, for its length, the best appointed and most reliable in the country, and probably the most productive in the world. Within the last two or three years, it has undergone thorough renovation, and while under its present management, the public may rest assured it will not suffer deterioration."

The Law of Telegraph in the U. States.—An Act Relating to the Commencement of Actions, &c., Relative to Penalties on Telegraphic Operators, &c.

PENNSYLVANIA LOCAL STATE LAW.

SEC. 7. That from and after the passage of this act, it shall not be lawful for any person connected with any line of telegraph within this Commonwealth, whether as superintendent, operator, or in any other capacity whatever, to use, or cause to be used, or make known, or cause to be made known, the contents of any despatch of whatsoever nature, which may be sent or received over any line of telegraph in this Commonwealth, without the consent or direction of either the party sending or receiving the same—and all despatches which may be filed at any office in this Commonwealth, for transmission to any point, shall be so transmitted without being made public, or their purport in any manner divulged at any intermediate point, on any pretence whatever, and in all respects the same inviolable secresy, safe keeping, and conveyance, shall be maintained by the officers and agents employed upon the several telegraph lines of this Commonwealth, in relation to all despatches which may be sent or received, as is now enjoined by the laws of the United States in reference to the ordinary mail service: *Provided*, That nothing in this act contained, shall be so construed, as to prevent the publication at any point of any despatch of a public nature, which may be sent by any person or persons with a view to general publicity.

Sec. 8. That in case any person, superintendent, operator, or who may be in any other capacity connected with any telegraph line in this Commonwealth, shall use, or cause to be used, or make known, or cause to be made known, the contents of any despatch sent from or received at any office in this Commonwealth, or in anywise unlawfully expose another's business or secrets, or in anywise impair the value of any correspondence sent or received, such person being duly convicted thereof, shall, for every such offence, be subject to a fine of not less than one hundred dollars, or imprisonment not exceeding six months, or both, according to the circumstances and aggravation of the offence.

Approved April 14, 1851.

I received the following interesting account of the telegraph in Ohio, showing the rapid progress which it is making in the West, for which account I am indebted to the politeness of J. H. Wade, Esq., of the "Wade Telegraph Office," Columbus, Ohio.

	Miles.
Cleveland and Cincinnati Telegraph Company, with two lines on separate routes, with an arm from Newark to Zanesville, and another from Mansfield to Sandusky; length of line, . , ...	640
Cincinnati and Sandusky Telegraph Company, line from Cincinnati to Sandusky,	218
Scioto Valley Telegraph Company, line from Columbus to Portsmouth,	90
Columbus and Lancaster Telegraph Company, line from Columbus to Lancaster, 25 miles, and an arm to Logansport, 15 miles, ...	40
Pittsburg, Cincinnati, and Louisville Telegraph Company, from Pittsburg to Louisville, two wires on same poles, 280 each, (in Ohio,) .	560
Cincinnati and St. Louis Telegraph Company, from Cincinnati to St. Louis,	50
House Printing Telegraph line, from Buffalo to Cincinnati, . .	325
Erie and Michigan Telegraph Company, from Buffalo to Milwaukie, with two wires as far as Cleveland; length of wire in Ohio, . . .	260
Lake Erie Telegraph Company, from Buffalo to Detroit, with branch to Pittsburg; length of wire in Ohio, ...	286
Cleveland, Wheeling, and Zanesville Telegraph Company, . .	225
Cleveland and Pittsburg Telegraph Company; length of wire in Ohio, . .	90
New Orleans and Ohio Telegraph Company, from Pittsburg to New Orleans; length of wire in Ohio, ...	260
Ohio, Indiana, and Illinois Telegraph Company, from Cincinnati to Dayton and Chicago; length in Ohio, about	100
Line from Zanesville to Marietta, ...	66
Total length of wire in Ohio, .	3210

CANADA.

From O. S. Wood, Esq., Montreal Telegraph Company, I have received the list of the lines in Canada.

	Miles.
The Montreal Telegraph Company's Line extends from Quebec to the Suspension Bridge at Niagara Falls; distance, ...	155
British North American Electric Telegraph Association, from Quebec to New Brunswick frontier; distance, ...	220
The Montreal and Troy Telegraph Company, from Montreal to New York State line at Highgate; distance, ...	47
The Bytown and Montreal Telegraph Company, from Bytown to Montreal; distance, ...	115
The Western Telegraph Company, from Hamilton to Port Sarnia, at the foot of Lake Huron; not now working; distance, ...	143
Niagara and Chippewa Line, from Niagara to Chippewa; distance, .	14
All the above lines have single wires.	
In course of construction, a line from Brantford to Simcoe and Dover; distance,	33
Also, a line from Kingston to Hamilton, via. Prince Edwards Co.; distance,	256
Total length in Canada, ...	983

ENGLAND.

The English telegraphs come next in extent to those of the U. States; they were first established in 1845, and may be divided into two classes, the railway and the commercial. The railway telegraphs are used for the purpose of sending communications relative to railway matters, while the commercial are employed for the transmission of public and private messages at fixed rates of charges. They are mostly built on the railroads, and in some instances a railroad company will construct a line, and give the use of it to a company, and as an equivalent, the telegraph lends its aid to expedite the business of the railroad. The telegraph company between London and Liverpool receives one thousand pounds a year for doing the business of the railroad company, and the railroad people afford them all the facilities for repairing the line, even so far as sending an extra engine, without charge, when there is not a regular train going out soon; and every man employed on the railroad is under instructions to report immediately to the nearest telegraph office, anything he may find to be out of order on the line. In fact, a line of telegraph is almost considered an indispensable part of the equipage of all well regulated roads in England. The instruments principally in use are those of Messrs. Cook and Wheatsone, Jacob Brett, and Brett and Little. There is a line of Bain's Electro-Chemical Telegraph from London to Manchester, and from Manchester to Liverpool. Also, a line of Bain's Electric Telegraph, connecting Edinburgh and Glasgow, a distance of 46 miles: the whole extent of telegraphic lines is estimated at 2225 miles. The principal ones are as follows:

ENGLAND, SCOTLAND, AND IRELAND.

I extract from the Manual of Mr. Walker, telegraphic engineer, a list of the lines of the Electric Telegraphs of England, for 1852.

	Miles.	Wires.	Apparatus.
Edinburgh and Glasgow, ...	47½	5	8
Line of the Tunnel, ...	1	2	2
Carried over, . . .	48½	7	10

	Miles.	Wires.	Apparatus.
Brought over,	48½	7	10
Edinburgh and the North Branch to Dundee,	26	3	6
" " " Perth,	6	3	0
Edinburgh and Granton,	3	3	3
Line to Leith,	1½	3	3
Line of Tunnel,	1	2	2
North British,	58	5	8
Branch to Dalkeith,	1¼	2	2
" Haddington,	5	2	2
Line of the Tunnel,	1¾	2	2
York, New Castle, and Berwick.			
New Castle to Berwick,	65½	5	7
York to Darlington,	45	7	15
Darlington to New Castle,	38½	8	14
Branch to Shields,	11	3	2
" Sunderland,	2¼	3	2
" Durham,	2¼	2	1
" Richmond,	9	2	1
Fatfield and South Shields,	19	1	4
Branch to Stockton,	½	1	2
York and North Midland.			
Normanton to York,	24½	0	5
York to Scarborough,	42½	3	5
Branch to Harrowgate,	18	3	2
Hull and Selby,	36	5	5
Hull and Bridlington,	33	3	4
Normanton to the junction at Milford,	10	2	2
Manchester and Leeds,	51	7	24
Preston and Wyre,	20	3	4
Liverpool and Southport,	13¼	3	3
East Lancashire,	12½	3	0
Midland Railway.			
Birmingham and Gloucester,	53	7	9
" " Derby,	6½	7	6
" " Derby,	34¾	5	0
Derby and Lincoln,	48¾	3	4
" Rugby,	24½	7	7
" Rugby,	24¾	5	0
Leicester and Peterborough,	4¾	3	0
" Peterborough,	23	5	11
" Peterborough,	25¼	7	0
Derby and Leeds,	73	7	25
Branch to Sheffield,	5	3	2
Leeds and Bradford,	11	6	5
" Bradford,	2¾	3	0
" Bradford line of Tunnel,	1½	2	2
Branch to Skipton,	15¼	3	5
London and North Western.			
London to Birmingham,	5	9	0
" Birmingham,	107½	7	10
" Birmingham line of Tunnel,	1	3	2
" Birmingham Inclined Plane,	1¼	6	6
East Junction to London,	½	2	4
Birmingham and Manchester,	80	7	7
Do. do. do.	5	8	0
Junction to Ardwick,	3¼	8	0
Manchester and Liverpool,	31½	6	5
Do. do. line of Tunnel,	1½	2	3
South Devon.			
Branch to Torquay,	4	3	2
Newmarket Railway,	17	5	4
Carried up,	1177	235	259

	Miles.	Wires.	Apparatus.
Brought up,	1177	235	259
Eastern Union,	16¾	5	7
Line of the Tunnel,	2¾	2	3
London to Southampton,	74	4	4
Do. do.	6	6	2
Branch to Portsmouth,	21	4	4
" Gosport,	5	4	1
Southampton and Dorchester,	61	3	7
Branch to Poole,	2	3	2
Eastern Counties.			
London to Brandon,	88¼	7	40
" Stratford,	33¾	2	4
Line to Brick Lane,	½	2	3
Branch to Enfield,	3¼	2	2
" Hertford,	7	3	3
Cambridge and St. Ives,	14¾	3	5
Ely and Peterborough,	30	5	7
March and Wisbeach,	9	3	2
London and Colchester,	51¼	5	13
Forestgate and Stratford,	1¼	1	2
Maldon and Braintree,	12	3	3
Stratford and Junction of the Thames,	2¾	3	2
North Woolwich,	2¾	3	2
Norfolk Railway.			
Brandon to Norwich,	37¾	7	19
Do. do.	10¼	1	7
Norwich and Yarmouth,	20	9	0
Branch to Lowestoft,	12	5	0
" Dereham,	12	3	2
Dereham and Fakenham,	12¼	2	2
North Staffordshire.			
Stoke to Norton Bridge,	10¾	3	3
Branch to Colwich,	18¾	2	2
Stoke to Burton,	29½	3	5
" " depot,	⅔	2	2
North Staffordshire.			
Stoke to Crewe,	14½	3	4
Harecastle Line of the Tunnel,	1	2	2
Branch to Macclesfield,	19½	3	4
Valley of Churnet,	27	2	0
South Staffordshire,	9¼	2	3
Do. do,	2	3	1
Northampton and Peterborough,	47	3	10
Northampton prolongated to Wolverton,	10½	4	2
London and Croydon,	8	3	4
Great Western,	19	4	2
Line of the Streets of London,	variable,		10
Manchester and Sheffield,	2	3	3
Manchester Line of the Tunnel of Woodhead,	3¼	3	2
Ambergate, Matlock, and Buxton,	11½	2	3
London and Blackwall,	3½	0	0
Line of Caldon Low Quarry,	3¼	1	4
Mines of the coal of Moira,	½	2	2
Maryport and Whitehaven	½	4	4
Line of the Company of Iron Mines of Butterley,	2½	1	2
South Eastern.			
London to Dover,	88	0	29
" Rochester,	31	4	18
" Bricklayer's Arms,	4	2	2
Carried over,	2093¾	396	530

	Miles.	Wires.	Apparatus.
Brought over,	2093⅔	396	530
Tunbridge to Tunbridge Wells,	5	3	6
" Hastings Road,	1	2	2
" Laboratory,	0	1	2
Paddock Wood to Maidstone,	10	3	5
Ashford to Ramsgate,	30	3	5
Minster to Deal,	9	3	6
Ramsgate to Margate,	4	3	2
Total,	2152⅔	414	558

Their mode of construction in England is very expensive, amounting in some cases to $600 per mile. Posts of fir are ranged at convenient distances along the side of the principal railways; each post is furnished with an insulator of earthenware, and also capped with a wooden roof having dripping eaves to throw the water from the wires. The latter are made of galvanized iron, two of which are needed on a line working with Cook and Wheatstone's instruments.

The press of England use the telegraph but little, and pay heavily for what they get by it. The *London Times* pays one thousand pounds per annum for a certain amount daily, and in addition, they pay for all extra communications of importance. The charge for transmission of communications by the Electric Telegraph Company's telegraphs in England, is at the rate of one penny per mile for the first fifty miles, and one farthing per mile for any distance beyond one hundred miles. The South Eastern Railway Company's charges for telegraphic communications are even much higher than those of the former. Thus, twenty words transmitted eighty-eight miles is charged the large sum of $2·42. These facts show that telegraph companies, as well as the public at large, would derive much greater advantages from their construction on a more economical plan, like that of the American system. In many parts of the United States where railways do not exist, the wires are stretched across the prairies without any protection whatever, except the general good will of the people at large. The cheap construction of these lines renders them liable to frequent disorder, and consequently needing continual repair, so that perhaps it might have been more economical to have expended more in the commencement. Its advantages are, however, abundantly proved, as the poorest person in the U. States or Canada, is enabled by the low rate of charges to use any of the telegraphs for domestic purposes. A message of twenty words can be sent a distance of 500 miles in the United States for $1, while in England the same would cost from $7 to $8.

Sub-Marine Telegraph, 1852.—A London letter under date of June 4th, says: The chief event of the week has been the laying down of the submarine telegraph between the coasts of England and Ireland, a distance of 64 miles. On the 2d instant, at 4 o'clock in the morning, the operation commenced by the departure of a steamer from Holyhead, and at half past eight in the evening a gun was fired at Dublin by means of the electric wire. The process has been an inexpensive one, and will probably prove remunerative, and lead to the establishment of many other lines. Among these, one of the first will be from the port of Harwich, on the east coast of England, to Holland, a concession for that purpose having lately been granted by the Dutch Government.

A similar communication with Belgium, between Dover and Ostend, is also contemplated. These enterprises will all be carried out by separate interests. The company that first established the practicability of such a method of ocean communication, by laying down the wire between England and France, might have secured all the advantages of the extension of the principle, but their Board of Directors have been incessantly quarrelling among themselves, and have consequently brought their own shares to a discount. In June, 1852, the telegraph between Dover and Ostend was completed; it is seventy English miles long.

Telegraph Extensions, June 27.—Private letters received per Atlantic state that F. N. Gisborne, Esq., the agent of the Newfoundland Electric Telegraph Company, has contracted in England for the land wire, through Newfoundland, upon very favorable terms. Mr. Gisborne has also entered into contracts for the sub-marine line, connecting Newfoundland with Nova Scotia, upon terms much less than estimated. Messrs. Newall & Co. of London, the contractors for the submarine, have also entered into contract to lay down a line from the Hague to Harwich, a distance of 135 miles, and are now negotiating with the French Government for a line from France to Algiers; a stretch of 400.

IRELAND.

An Irish Sub-marine Line Telegraph, between Fort Patrick and Donoughadee, was to be opened on the 10th of June.

A line of telegraph has been opened between Dublin and Galway, and was in operation in June, 1852.

PRUSSIA.

The Prussian Telegraph system is characterized as simple, substantial, effective and economical. A Royal Commission was appointed in 1844, to ascertain the best method of constructing lines; they, after experiment, determined on that of copper wire enclosed in gutta percha, and buried two feet beneath the surface; they are generally made to follow the track of railways, and in passing over bridges or aqueducts, are enclosed in iron piping, or when through rivers in chain pipes. They use but one wire, which terminates in an earth battery, consisting of a zinc plate 6 feet long, $2\frac{1}{2}$ feet wide, and $\frac{1}{8}$-th of an inch in thickness. The instruments used are those of Morse, Siemens, Halske, and Kramer, together with Daniel's battery. In the principal offices, a printing and a colloquial instrument are employed, but each in turn is worked by the one wire only, notice being given that one or the other is to be used, according to circumstances. Morse's is the printing telegraph used, and differs but very little from that used in the U. States. Those of Siemens and Kramer are both colloquial telegraphs, but Siemens' is chiefly used. The whole cost, as determined from detailed estimates, is less than $200 per English mile. Besides the government lines of telegraph, most of the railway companies in Prussia have also their own telegraphs, which are constructed according to the system in this country by one wire suspended on poles along the railways. The average cost of this form of telegraph is about $100 per mile; their whole length is estimated at 1493 miles, having their central point at Berlin, from whence they radiate as follows:

Instruments used.	Stations and points passed through.	Distance in miles.
Siemens and Halske's Patent,	From Berlin to Frankfort on the Main, established in February, 1849, ...	350
Kramer's Bell Telegraph,	From Berlin through Cologne to Achen, established in June, 1849, ...	362
	Stations are Potsdam, Magdeburgh, Ochsertleben, Brunswick, Hanover, Minder, Haurm, Dusseldorf, Deutz, Cologne.	
Seimens and Halske's Patent,	From Dusseldorf to Elberfeld, ...	16
Morse's Apparatus,	From Berlin through Minder to Rolu, . .	81
Siemens and Halske's,	" " to Hamburgh, ...	142
" "	" " Stettin, ...	62
" "	" " through to Oderburgh to Breslau, .	280
" "	" Halle to Leipzic, ...	17
" "	" Leipzic to Berlin, ...	115
" "	" Leipzic to Frankfort on the Main, . .	204
Siemens' Telegraph,	" Berlin to Gross Bercen	
" "	A contemplated one from Berlin to Konigsberg to Dantzic.	
Morse Instrument,	From Hamburgh to Cuxhaven, ...	80

The Prussian method of burying the wires beneath the surface, protects them from destruction by malice, and makes them less liable to injury by lightning.

AUSTRIA.

The Austrian Telegraphs diverge from Vienna, in the following manner:

1, From Vienna through Olmutz to Prague, 237 miles.
2, " " " Bumn " 211 "
3, " " to Pressburgh, 35 "
4, " " through Prevau to Oberberg, 140 "
5, " " " Bruck, Cilli, Layback to Trinte, 284 "
6, " " " Lintz to Salzburg, 156 "
7, " Prague to the boundary of Saxony, to connect with the line from Dresden, is nearly complete as far as the boundary of Bohemia, on which Storer's apparatus will be used; on the other a modification of Morse's by Robinson, printing about 600 words per hour; also, a modification of Bain's needle telegraph, by Ekling, of Vienna, containing an arrangement of 45 needles, averaging about 190 words of six letters each per hour. The Austrians have adopted this system of correspondence, mostly since 1847; their network of telegraphs extends over a space of more than 1053 miles, having 106 stations, which will be increased to 200 stations, if the present projected lines are constructed. The line from Lintz to Salzburg, has a connexion with the Bavarian one from Munich to the latter place, and makes use of Stochriss' instrument. A line between Venice and Milan with its branches is already commenced.

SAXONY AND BAVARIA.

Saxony and Bavaria have government lines which connect with the Prussian and Austrian lines, and establish a communication with Berlin, Dresden, Munich, and Vienna. Nearly all the railroad companies have private lines for their own use, and preparations are now making, which in no distant future will include every town of importance throughout Germany in this network of communication.

Those of Saxony extend over 265 miles, the principal of which are annexed: From Leipzig to Hoff, 94 miles; from Leipzig to Dresden, 62 miles; Dresden to Konigstien, 15 miles; Dresden to the boundary of Bohemia; Dresden to Hoff, 94 miles. Stochriss' needle instrument is principally used in this country; likewise, in Bavaria his bell apparatus. The extent of lines in the latter country is about 455 miles. From Munich to Salzburg, 74 miles, connecting with the Austrian lines of Ling and Vienna; from Munich through Augsburgh to Hoff, 226 miles, connecting with the line to Dresden in Saxony; from Munich to Augsburg, 31 miles; one under construction from Augsburg, through Nuremburgh and Bamburgh to Hoff; from Bamburgh to Wurzburg, Aschappenburg, and Frankfort, 125 miles under construction.

TUSCANY.

The lines in Tuscany number 120 Italian miles, commenced in 1847, under the direction of Matteucci; they also follow the railroad. From Florence to Livourne; from Empoli to Sienne; from Pisa to Lucca, and from Florence to Patro; which makes in all, 120 Italian miles, or nearly 60 leagues. The total length of the wires is 121 leagues, weighing 70,000 pounds; 2488 posts.

The expense of placing the wire, which cost at first 400 pounds per mile, is reduced to 30 or 40 francs at present, that the wires are placed by the guardians of the telegraph. The telegraphic apparatus is furnished in part by M. Brequet, and part by the constructor of the University, M. Piercci; a complete apparatus costs 600 livres.

The following is a table of necessary expense for the establishment of the Tuscan lines:—

	Livres.	Sous.	
Iron Wire,	23,348	8	
Posts of fir tree,	21,426	13	4
Tenders,	3,347		
Porcelain shield,	2,627	13	
Wooden box,	1,772	13	4
Furniture, and supplies of the office,	8,183	18	8
Laying of copper wire, varnish,	5,314	13	4
Machines and piles,	26,043	17	
Timber, cost of posts, administration, studies, and superintendance of the work,	3,443	3	4
Total,	95,507	10	

GERMANY.

The telegraph lines of Germany have chiefly been established within the last three years. Gauss and Weber at Gottingen, and Steinhiel at Munich, had short lines of telegraph, in 1834 and 1837; but the railroad companies were the first to make a proper appreciation of them, and establish lines for their own benefit. The first great line along the railway from Mentz to Frankfort, was erected by Fardly, a mechanician of Manheim, with Wheatstone's index apparatus. It was this line that aroused the attention of the Prussian Government, and caused the appointment of a committee to experiment on the matter.

No. 781 of the London *Mining Journal* for 1850, states that 2000 miles of telegraph are already open in Germany, and that 1000 more will be added in 1851; it works now from Cracow to Trieste, a distance of 700 miles, and a general union of the Austrian, Prussian, Saxon, and Bavarian lines was soon expected, with a tariff of charges nearly as low as that of the United States.

FRANCE.

The French are inferior in telegraphic enterprise to most of the other European countries. In that country the telegraph is under the control of government officers, and all the government business is done by signals, understood by those only who are in the pay of the government; the tariff is too high, and but little use is made of it, as the existing government does not wish it brought into general use: this is much unlike the republicanism of the U. States. The principal instruments in use are those of Br`quet and Foy, which prints from 10 to 12 signs per minute; this is used along the railroad from Paris to Rouen. Wheatstone's needle telegraph and also the instruments of Dujardin and Gardiner are made use of That of Brett is employed on the connecting line of England and France, between Dover and Calais, and Bain's Chemical Telegraph has more lately been introduced. The lines mostly originate in Paris, from which they stretch northward to Amiens, Arras, Valenciennes, Donae, Lille, Dunkirk, Calais, and Boulogne. South, they extend to Orleans, Louis, Chevres, Angiers, Blois, Bourges, and Chateauroux; East, to Chalons, on the main; West, to Versailles, Rouen, Havre, and Dieppe: the whole extent being from 400 to 600 miles. Another line is about to be, or is opened from Paris to Lyons. In last April, the government published the establishment of several offices on each line which could be used for private correspondence; there were six of these points on the northern line, the same number on the southern, two on the western, and one on the eastern. The committee appointed for the purpose, recommended a general distribution of them on all the lines. The government have adopted the following tariff of charges, for a despatch of twenty words, including the names of the sender:—

		f.	c.			f.	c.
From Paris to	Arras,	4 f.	80 c.	From Paris to	Angers,	5 f.	88 c.
"	Valenciennes,	5	64	"	Bourges,	7	60
"	Lille,	6	36	"	Nevers,	5	88
"	Calais,	6	36	"	Chateauroux,	6	72
"	Dunkirk,	7	56	"	Chalons,	6	24
"	Orleans,	7	32	"	Rouen,	5	70
"	Tours,	4	56	"	Havre,	5	76

To estimate the expense between each of these places, it is only necessary to find the difference of that between them and Paris respectively. For despatches of more than twenty words, a fourth is to be added for every ten words, so that this tariff will be double for sixty words.

I have translated the following list of the lines of France, from the "Traité de Telegraphic Electrique," by Moigno, second edition, 1852.

1st, Line of the North, from Paris to Valenciennes, by Amiens, Arras, Douae, Lille, with a branch to Dunkirk, Calais, and Boulogne, 90 leagues.

2d, Line of the South, from Paris to Chateauroux, by Orleans, Blois, Tours, Bourges, with a continuation to Bordeaux one way, and another to Nantes.

3d, The line of the East, from Paris to Chalons sur Marne, prolonged to Strasburg, by Vetoy, Nancy, &c.

4th, The line from Paris to Havre, by Rouen and Dieppe.

5th, The line of Montereau to Troyes.

6th, The line of Metz to Nancy, &c.

The entire length of the finished lines form three hundred leagues, (about 750 English miles,) and according to Moigno, they have committed the irreparable fault of suppressing the old telegraphs.

HOLLAND.

The instrument used in Holland is a modification of Morse's by Mr. Wm. Robinson; this gentleman is an American; he has obtained the privilege of erecting and managing lines of magnetic telegraph, in the United Kingdoms of Norway and Sweden for fifty years. A company of heavy capitalists of this city and Stockholm, have commenced in the work, which is to begin immediately. A similar privilege is expected from the Government of Denmark. Most of the Belgian and Holland Railroad Companies have constructed telegraphs; there is one now in operation from Amsterdam to Rotterdam, and the Holland Government has authorized the construction of one from Amsterdam to the Helder, and one from Rotterdam to Vleissingin.

ITALY.

Considerable progress has been made in the construction of lines throughout the Italian States. By virtue of an ordinance of the Minister of Public Works, the telegraphs which are to connect Rome on one side with Cevita Vecchia and the sea, and on the other side with the Austrian boundary at Ferrara, will be established at an early day.

SPAIN.

In Spain, the line from Aranjuez to Madrid is complete, and others are being laid down to Seville, Cadiz, Valenten, Barcelona, and the frontier of France. Before long there will be a general telegraphic communication from one extremity of Europe to the other, and when the connexion between Dover and Calais shall have been completed, the people of London will be able to communicate with those of nearly every capital on the continent, extending over a space of nearly 6000 miles.

RUSSIA.

A Prussian engineer has gone to St. Petersburg, in order to establish electro-magnetic telegraphs throughout the whole Russian monarchy.

MEXICO.

A contract has been entered into by the Mexican Government, with Wm. George Stewart, Esq., the Mexican Consul at New York, and Senor Juan de la Grariga, of Mexico, to construct a line from Vera Cruz to the City of Mexico, a distance of three hundred miles; one hundred and twenty of which, as far as El Oge de Argua, was to have been completed on the 1st of May, 1851. Another line will soon be built between Acapulco and the City of Mexico. When both are completed, there will be a magnetic communication between the Atlantic and Pacific.

A letter from Mexico informs us of the progress of the magnetic telegraph in that country. It appears that the party who went from the U. States to that country for the purpose of putting up a line of telegraph from the City of Mexico to Vera Cruz, have finished it from the former city to Napolucan, a distance of about 150 miles, and half way to Vera Cruz. The other half will be finished in two and a half months. The line already up is doing a very fair business; the receipts averaging $35 per day, and the expenses about $15. These receipts will be largely increased when the line is finished to Vera Cruz, as the largest portion of the business transactions of the country is between that City and the City of Mexico, including Puebla and Orizaba. Another line is in contemplation from the City of Mexico to Acapulco, on the Pacific, 300 miles further, which will connect the Atlantic and Pacific. This will be a highly important connexion, considering our California possessions on the Pacific.

CUBA.

The Governor General has ordered the publication of the concessions made to companies for the establishment of electric telegraphs through all points, and to the principal cities of Cuba. The lines will be established from Villanueva to Union, crossing several small towns in their way; from Union to Matanzas; from Buerba to Macagua; from Tinguaro to Jucaro; from Navagas to Isabel; from San Felipe to Batabano, and from Rincon to Guanajay, by San Antonio. The companies will be obliged to commence the works six months after the date of the concession, and to establish them with the greatest possible activity.

The Cubaneras have discovered the benefits the magnetic telegraph confers by facilitating business and transmitting communications from one point to another. They are, therefore, setting about establishing telegraph lines throughout the Island. Two companies have been formed for this purpose. One of these companies, with a capital of $20,000, propose a line from Havana to Cienfuegos, passing through Isabel, Trinidad, and Manzanillo, to Cuba. From this point it will be extended to Bayams, and thence to Guanagos and Pinar del Rio, ending at San Juan and Martenez. The second line, which also starts from Havana, will communicate with Cardenas, Matanzas, Siena, Morena, Sagua la Grand, San Juan de los Remedios, Neuvitas, Moron, and Halguin, and will end at Cuba, having three branches to Puerto Principe, Sancto Spiritus, and Villa Clara. The same company propose a line from Havana to Hariel, Cubanas, and Bahia Honda; the capital of this company is $300,000. These lines, when completed, will connect the capital with every considerable town on the Island.

VALPARAISO.

The telegraph between Valparaiso and Santiago, is progressing rapidly. Messages have already been sent over one-third of the line, (from Casa Blanca to this city.) From present appearances, the line will be through in less than forty days, as the poles are already up more than three-quarters of the distance.

INDIA.

This all infusing enterprise has aroused the lethargic inhabitants of the tropical climate. An electric telegraph has been erected in India, and is now in successful operation: the telegraph will soon belt both continents.

INDEX.

ERRATA.

Page 1, first line, for Τελε, read Τηλε.

" 32, first line, for "but without contact," read "but without *actual* contact."

www.ingramcontent.com/pod-product-compliance
Lightning Source LLC
LaVergne TN
LVHW021401110826
845150LV00007B/1738